JOY
OPERATIONS™

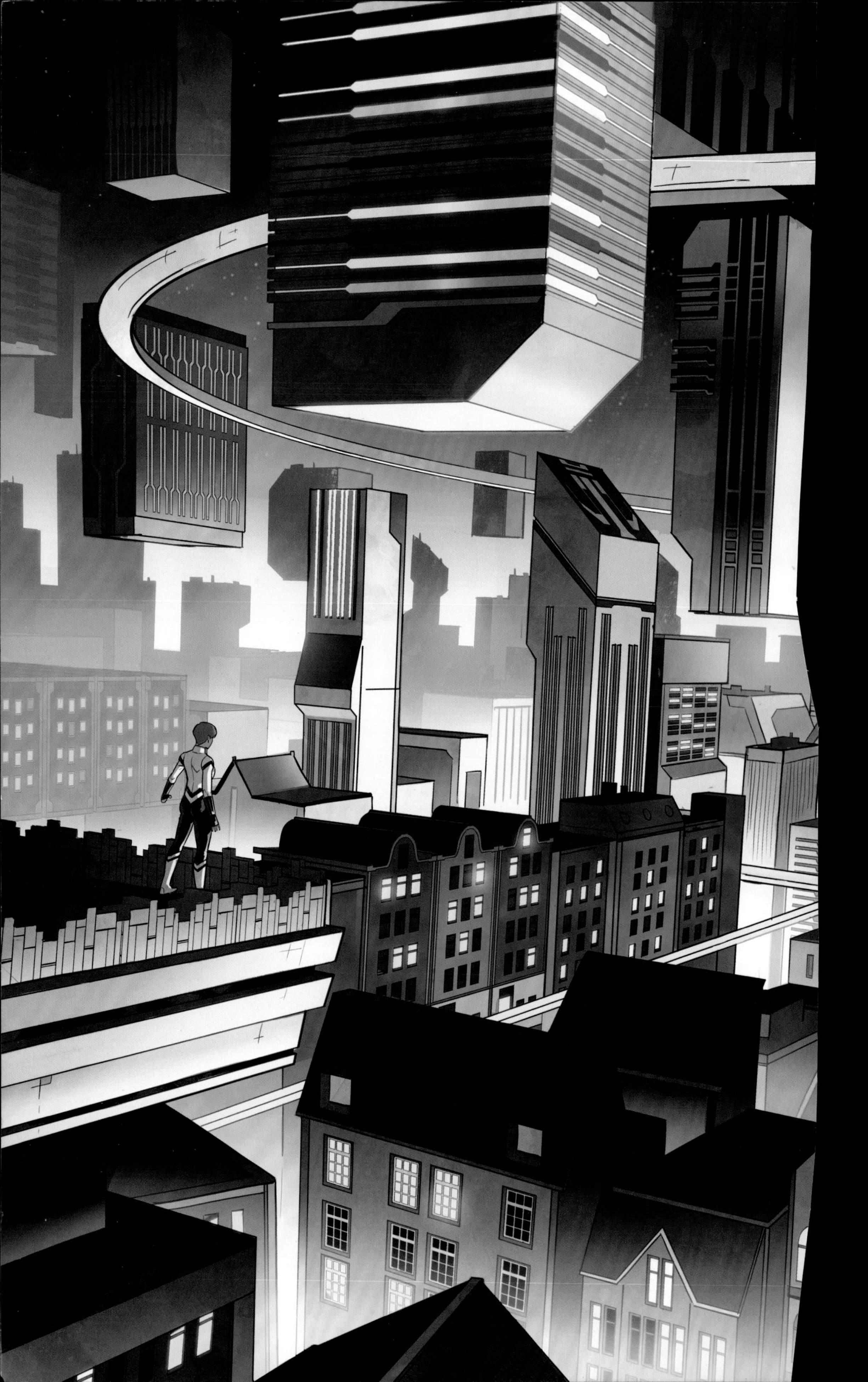

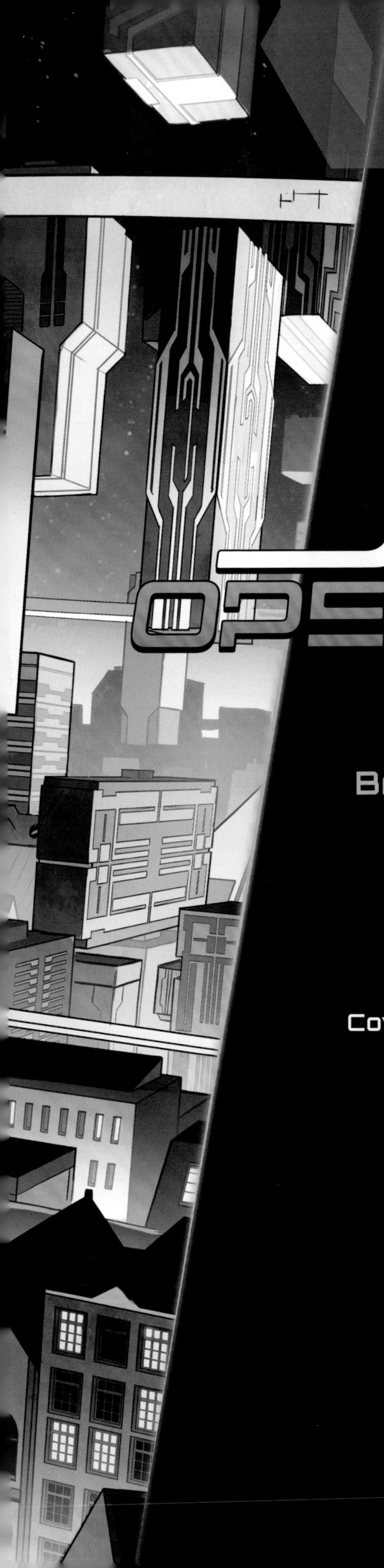

JOY OPERATIONS™

Created by
Brian Michael Bendis
and
Stephen Byrne

Lettering
Joshua Reed

Cover and Chapter Breaks by
Stephen Byrne

JINXWORLD

DARK HORSE BOOKS

President and Publisher
Mike Richardson

Editor
Daniel Chabon

Designer
Rick DeLucco

Assistant Editors
Chuck Howitt and Misha Gehr

Digital Art Technician
Betsy Howitt

To find a comics shop in your area, visit comicshoplocator.com.

This volume collects all issues of *Joy Operations* as well as all covers and extra content.

Published by
Dark Horse Books
A division of
Dark Horse Comics LLC
10956 SE Main Street
Milwaukie, OR 97222

DarkHorse.com

First edition: August 2022
Ebook ISBN 978-1-50672-947-3
Trade paperback ISBN 978-1-50672-946-6

10 9 8 7 6 5 4 3 2 1
Printed in China

FSC
www.fsc.org
MIX
Paper from responsible sources
FSC® C169962

Library of Congress Cataloging-in-Publication Data

Names: Bendis, Brian Michael, author. | Byrne, Stephen (Comic book artist), illustrator. | Reed, Josh, letterer.
Title: Joy operations / created by Brian Michael Bendis and Stephen Byrne ; letters by Joshua Reed.
Description: First edition. | Milwaukie, OR : Dark Horse Books, 2022. | "This volume collects all issues of Joy Operations as well as all covers and extra content." | Summary: "Fifty-five years from now. Joy is an En·Voi. A special agent of one of the Jonando Trust. Trusts are corporate-owned cities that are the centerpiece of modern society. She rights wrongs for the trust. She is excellent. Perfection. Hard on herself. Driven. Almost legendary in some parts. Until one day a voice pops in her head trying to get her to betray everything she has ever believed. This meticulously-designed Akira meets Inception journey shows us a new future like only comics can. All this and also an exclusive look behind-the-scenes and a look forward to other Jinxworld projects coming exclusively to Dark Horse."-- Provided by publisher.
Identifiers: LCCN 2022003460 (print) | LCCN 2022003461 (ebook) | ISBN 9781506729466 (trade paperback) | ISBN 9781506729473 (ebook)
Subjects: LCGFT: Science fiction comics. | Dystopian comics.
Classification: LCC PN6728.J69 B46 2022 (print) | LCC PN6728.J69 (ebook) | DDC 741.5/973--dc23/eng/20220224
LC record available at https://lccn.loc.gov/2022003460
LC ebook record available at https://lccn.loc.gov/2022003461

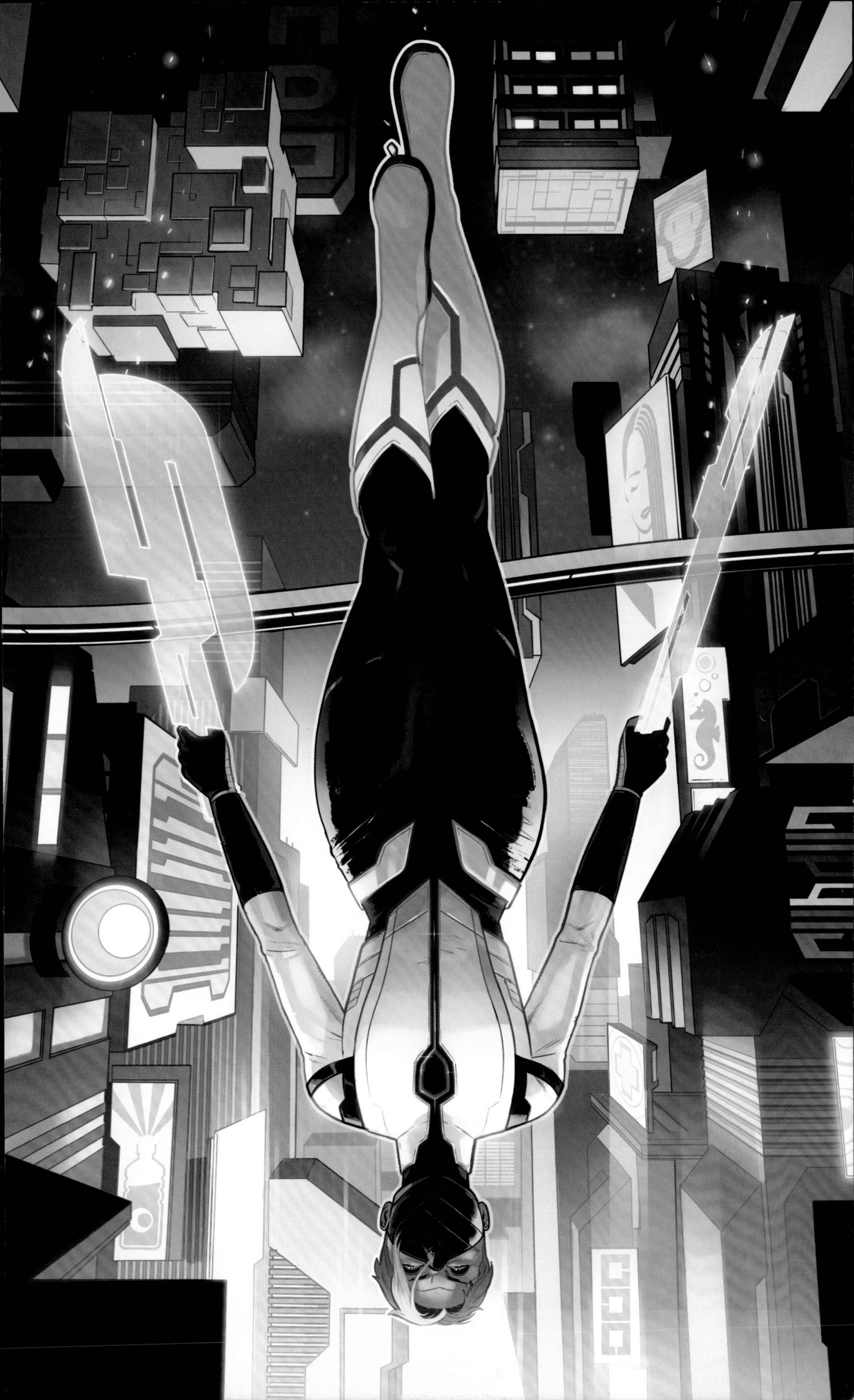

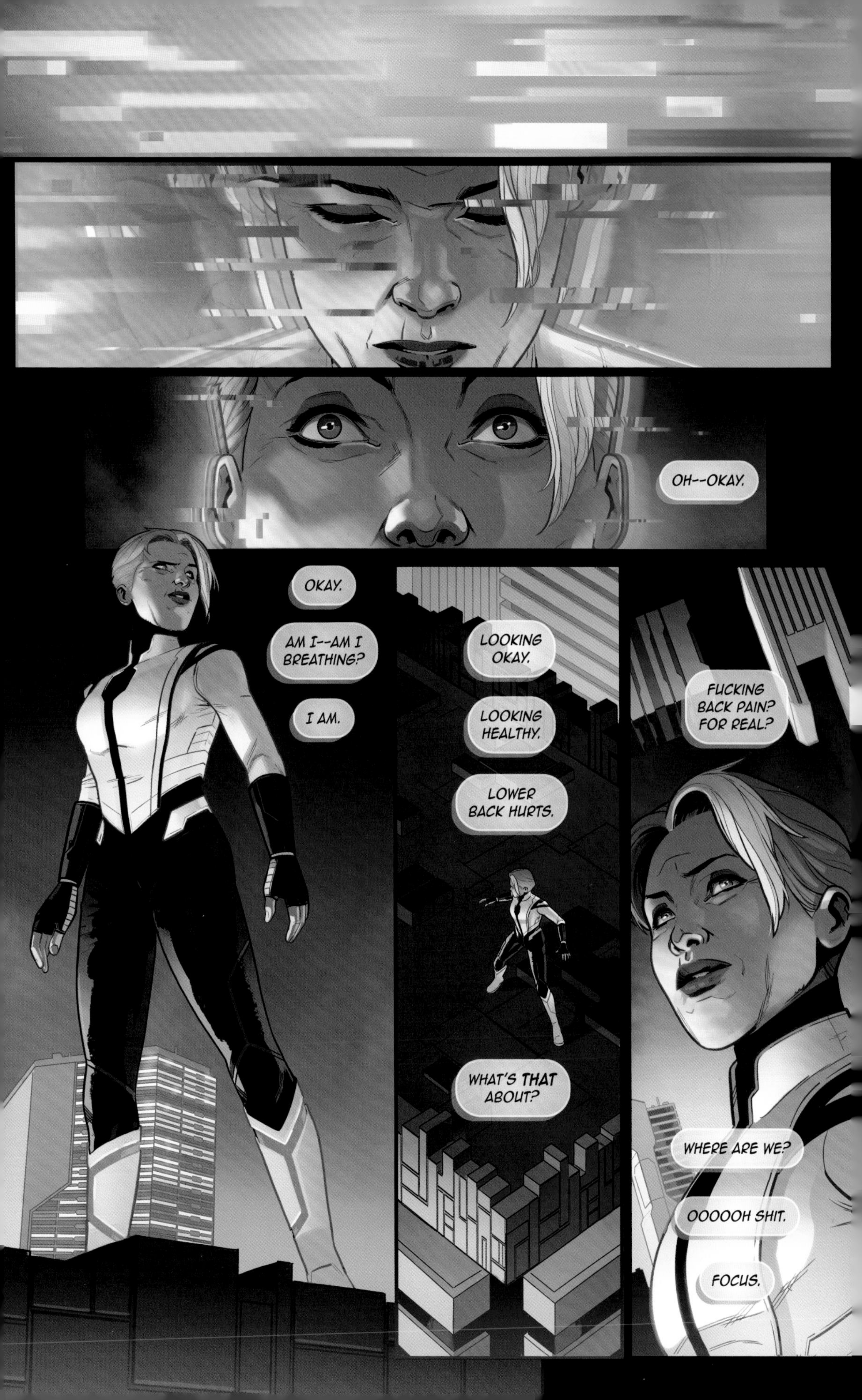
OH--OKAY.
OKAY.
AM I--AM I BREATHING?
I AM.
LOOKING OKAY.
LOOKING HEALTHY.
LOWER BACK HURTS.
WHAT'S THAT ABOUT?
FUCKING BACK PAIN? FOR REAL?
WHERE ARE WE?
OOOOOH SHIT.
FOCUS.

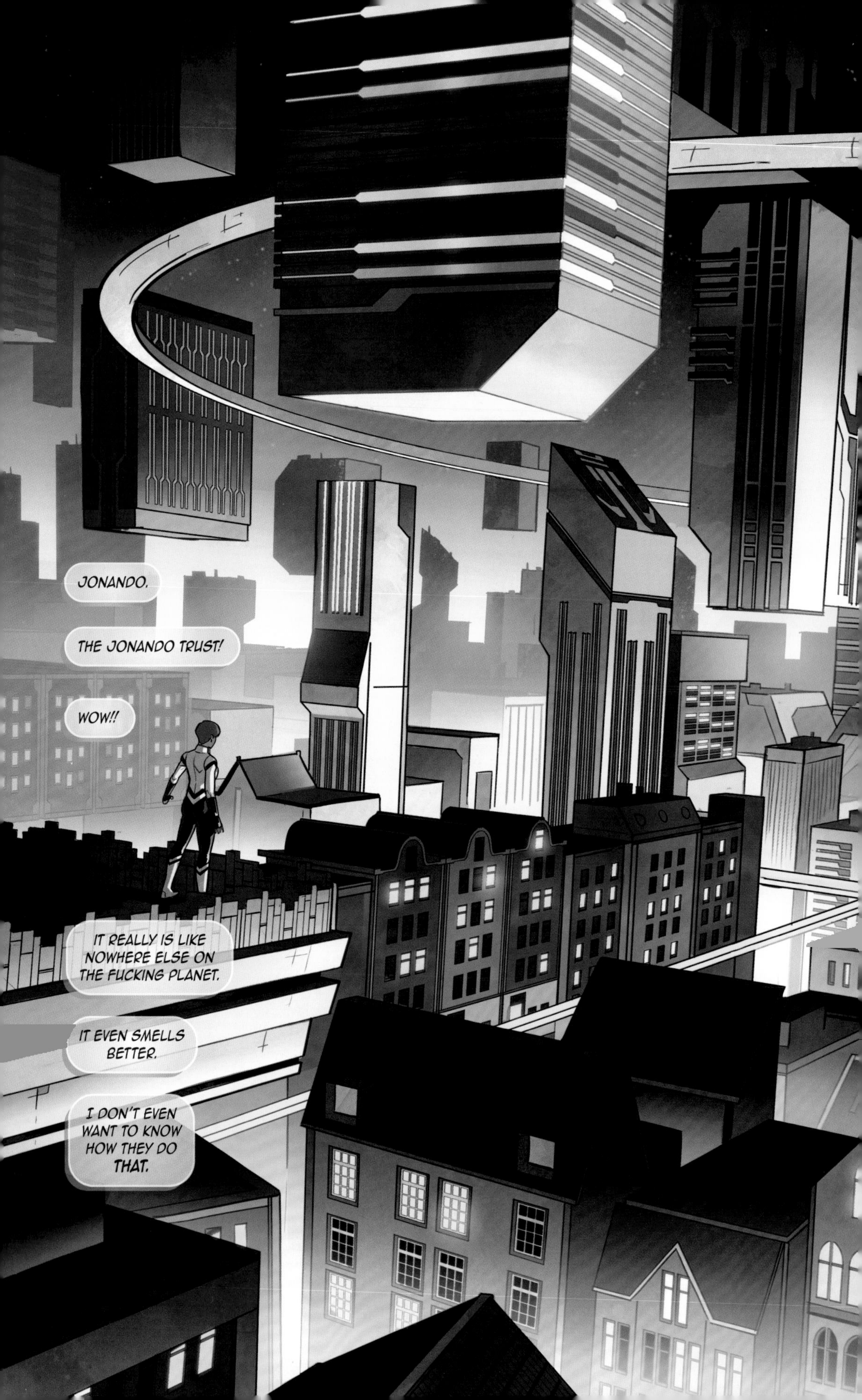
JONANDO.
THE JONANDO TRUST!
WOW!!
IT REALLY IS LIKE NOWHERE ELSE ON THE FUCKING PLANET.
IT EVEN SMELLS BETTER.
I DON'T EVEN WANT TO KNOW HOW THEY DO THAT.

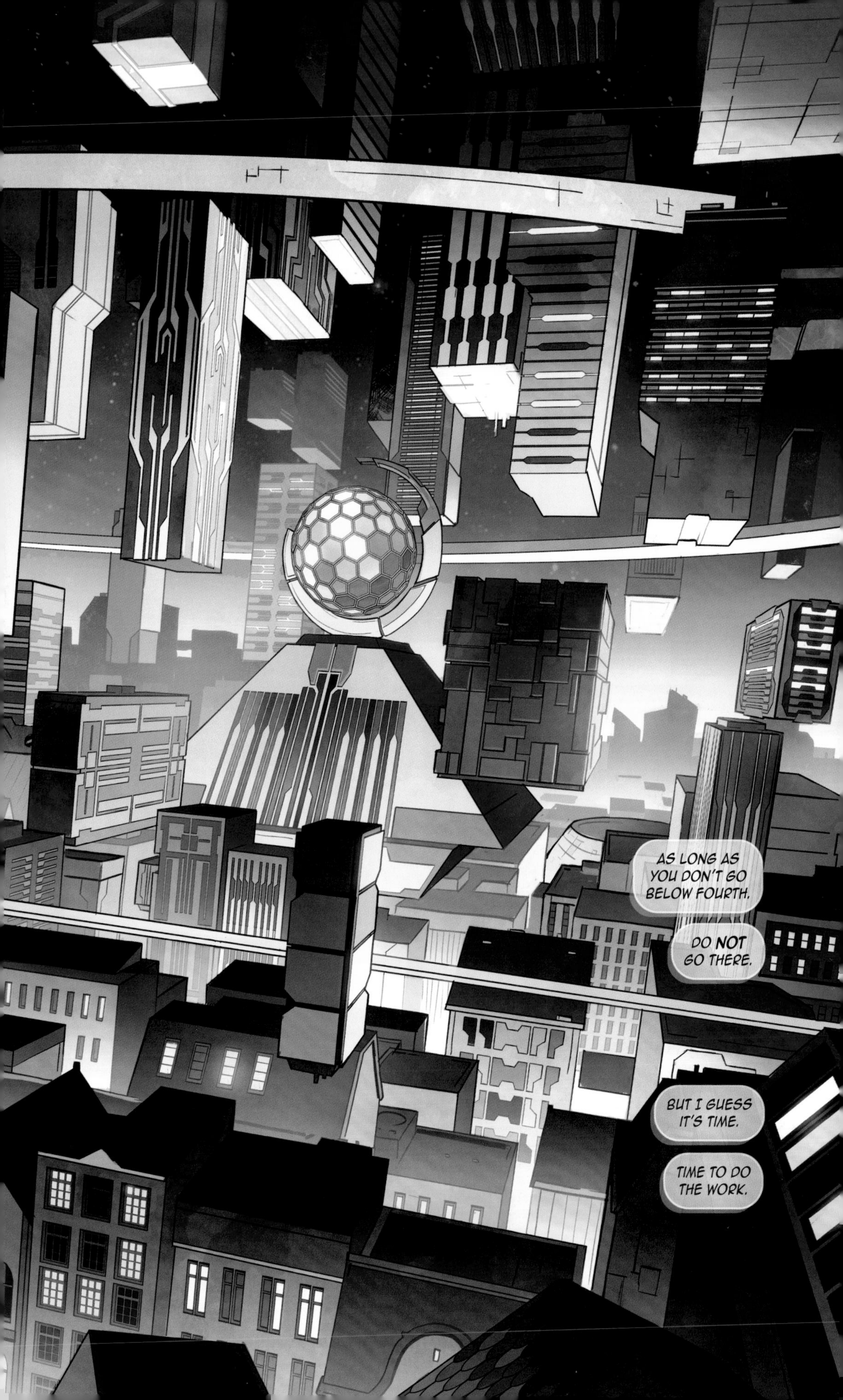
AS LONG AS YOU DON'T GO BELOW FOURTH.
DO **NOT** GO THERE.
BUT I GUESS IT'S TIME.
TIME TO DO THE WORK.

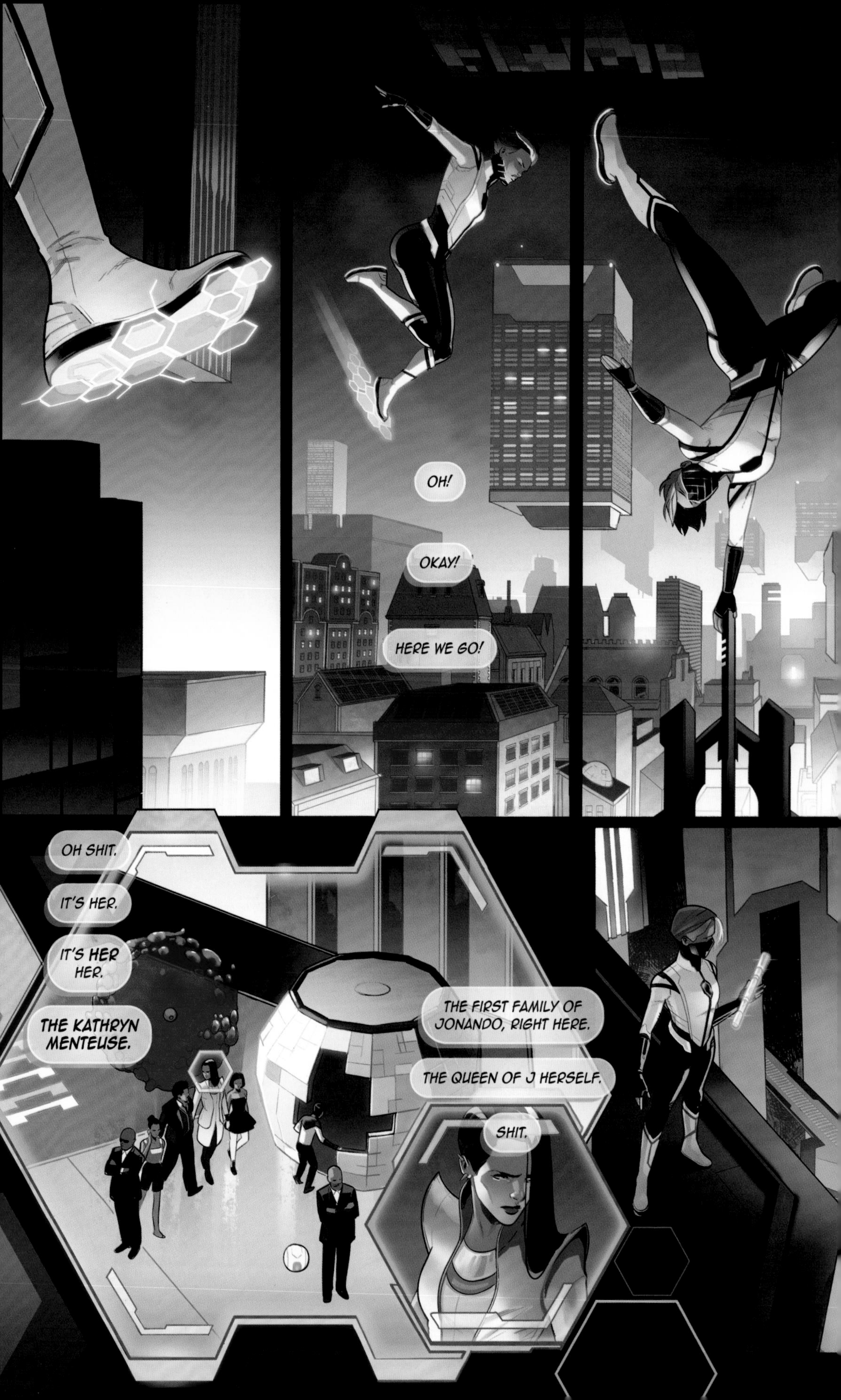
OH!
OKAY!
HERE WE GO!
OH SHIT.
IT'S HER.
IT'S HER HER.
THE KATHRYN MENTEUSE.
THE FIRST FAMILY OF JONANDO, RIGHT HERE.
THE QUEEN OF J HERSELF.
SHIT.

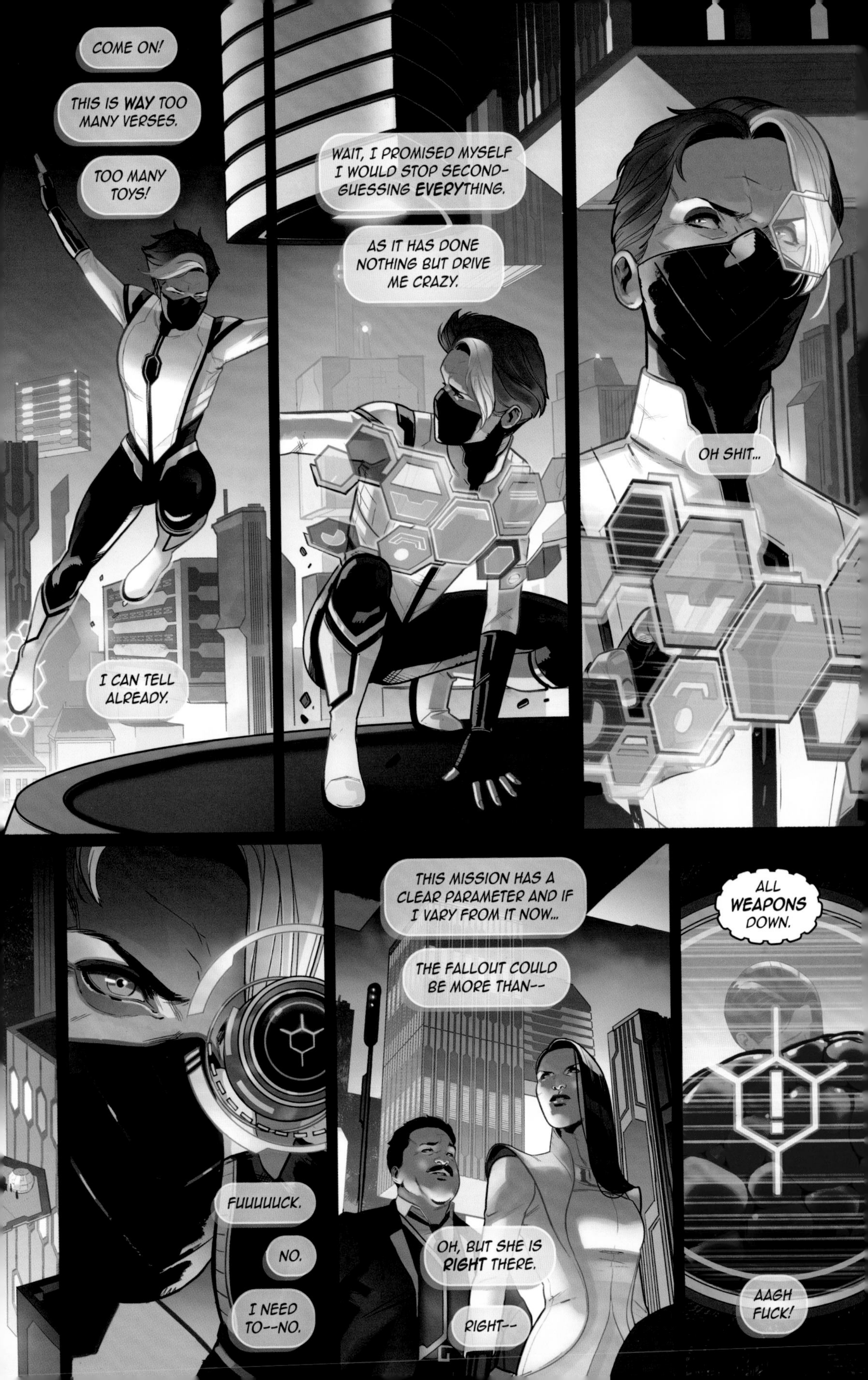
COME ON!
THIS IS WAY TOO MANY VERSES.
TOO MANY TOYS!
I CAN TELL ALREADY.
WAIT, I PROMISED MYSELF I WOULD STOP SECOND-GUESSING EVERYTHING.
AS IT HAS DONE NOTHING BUT DRIVE ME CRAZY.
OH SHIT...
FUUUUUCK.
NO.
I NEED TO--NO.
THIS MISSION HAS A CLEAR PARAMETER AND IF I VARY FROM IT NOW...
THE FALLOUT COULD BE MORE THAN--
OH, BUT SHE IS RIGHT THERE.
RIGHT--
ALL WEAPONS DOWN.
AAGH FUCK!

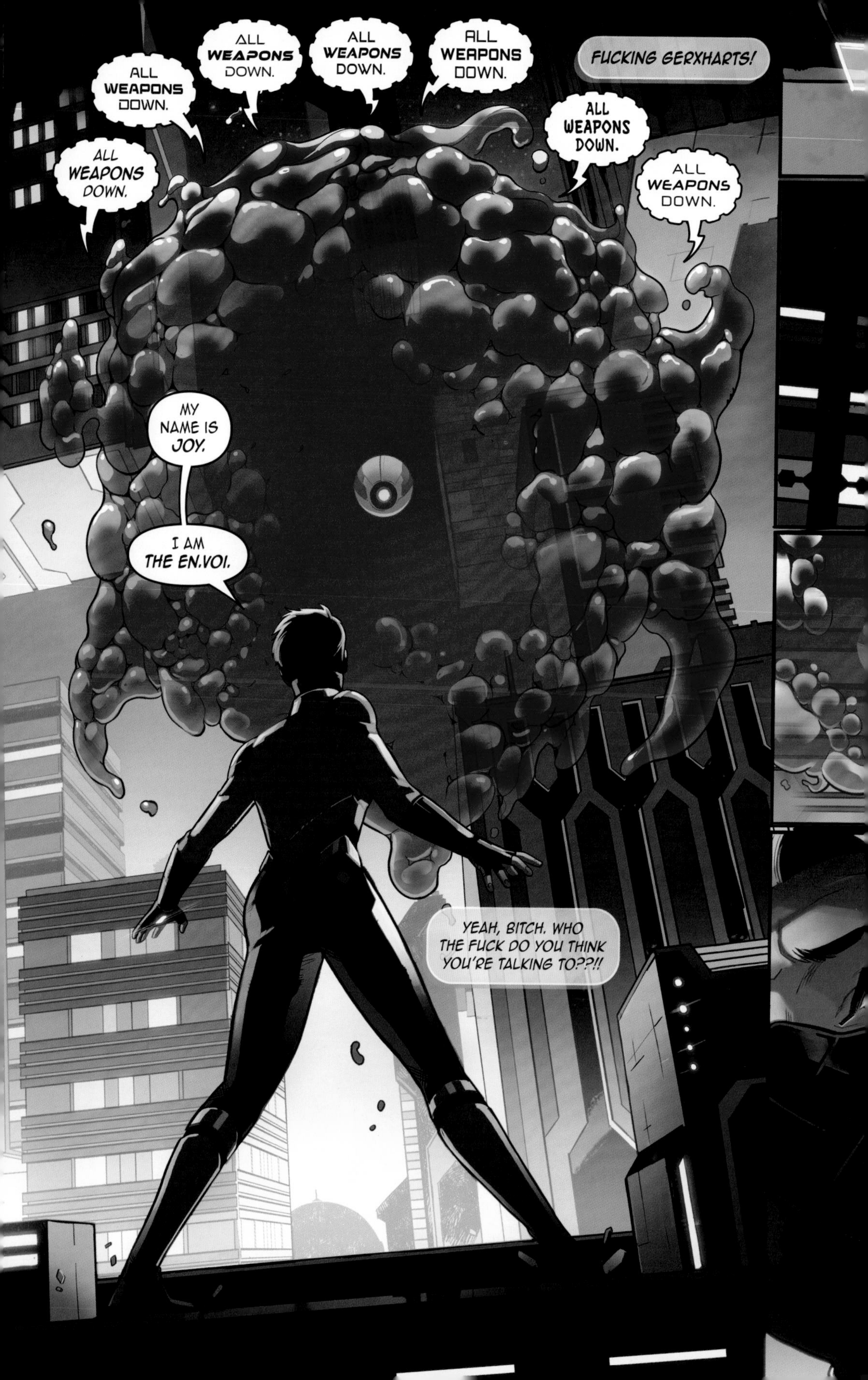

ALL WEAPONS DOWN.
ALL WEAPONS DOWN.
ALL WEAPONS DOWN.
ALL WEAPONS DOWN.
ALL WEAPONS DOWN.
FUCKING GERXHARTS!
ALL WEAPONS DOWN.
ALL WEAPONS DOWN.
MY NAME IS JOY.
I AM THE EN.VOI.
YEAH, BITCH. WHO THE FUCK DO YOU THINK YOU'RE TALKING TO??!!

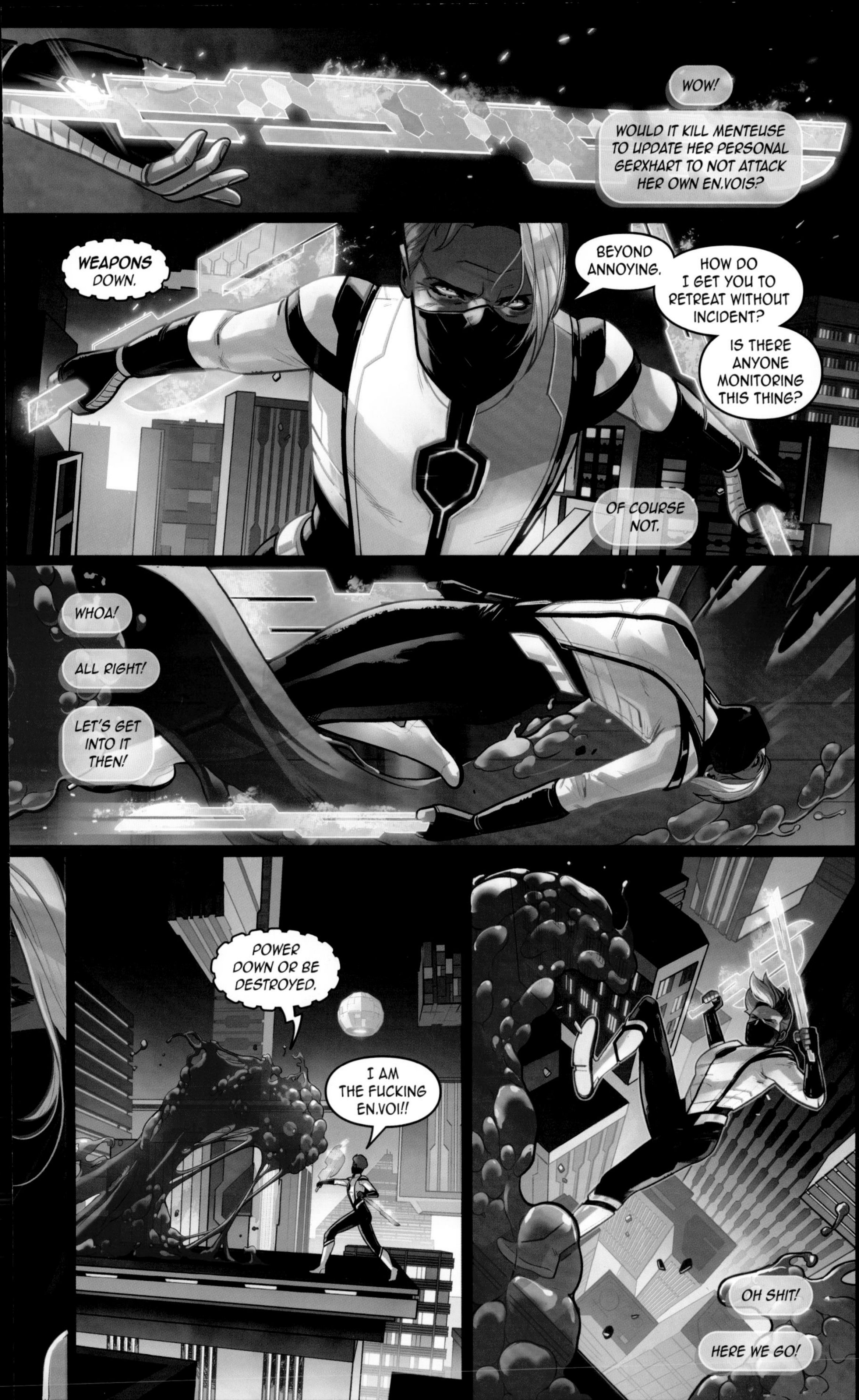
WOW!
WOULD IT KILL MENTEUSE TO UPDATE HER PERSONAL GERXHART TO NOT ATTACK HER OWN EN.VOIS?
WEAPONS DOWN.
BEYOND ANNOYING.
HOW DO I GET YOU TO RETREAT WITHOUT INCIDENT?
IS THERE ANYONE MONITORING THIS THING?
OF COURSE NOT.
WHOA!
ALL RIGHT!
LET'S GET INTO IT THEN!
POWER DOWN OR BE DESTROYED.
I AM THE FUCKING EN.VOI!!
OH SHIT!
HERE WE GO!

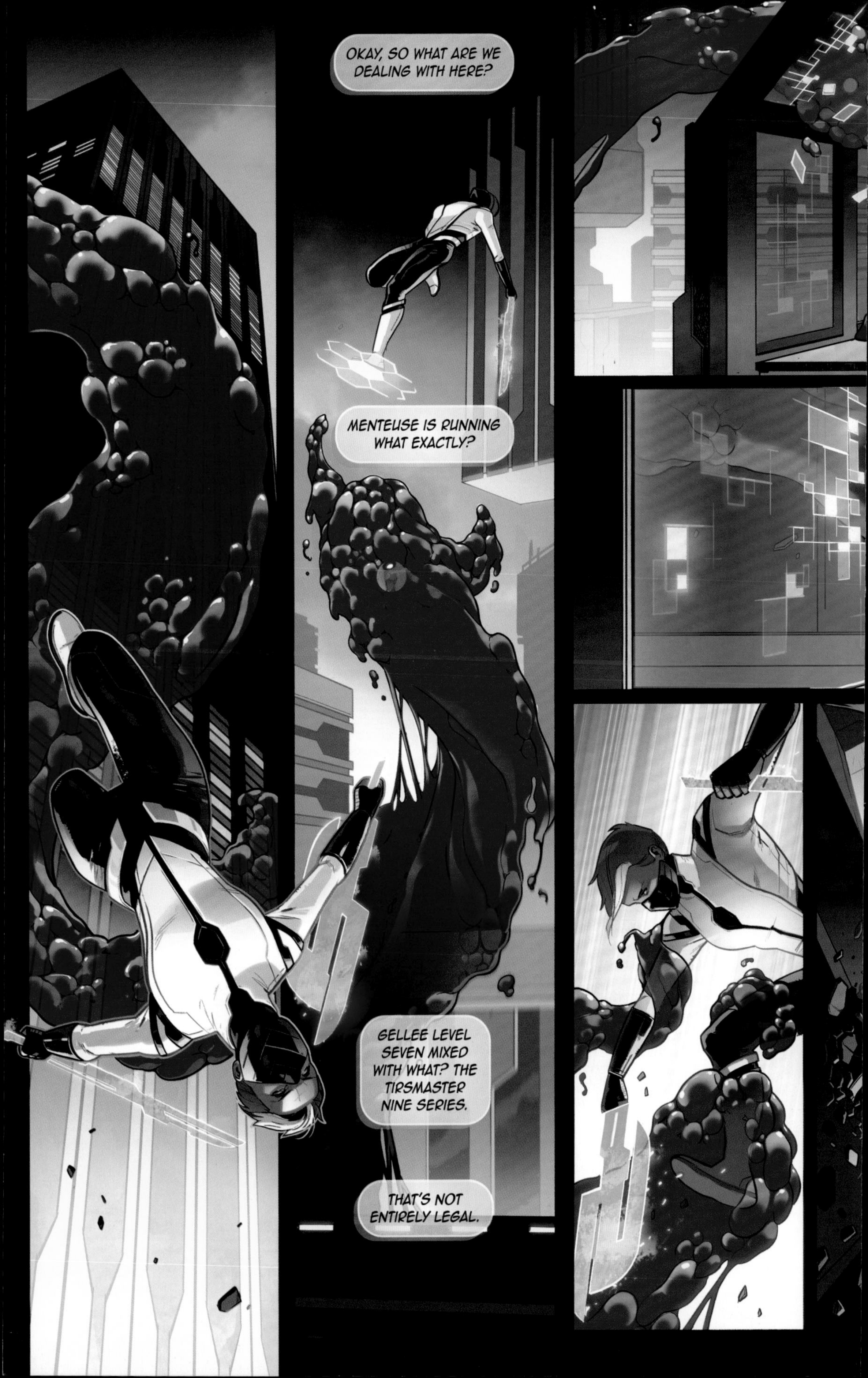
OKAY, SO WHAT ARE WE DEALING WITH HERE?
MENTEUSE IS RUNNING WHAT EXACTLY?
GELLEE LEVEL SEVEN MIXED WITH WHAT? THE TIRSMASTER NINE SERIES.
THAT'S NOT ENTIRELY LEGAL.

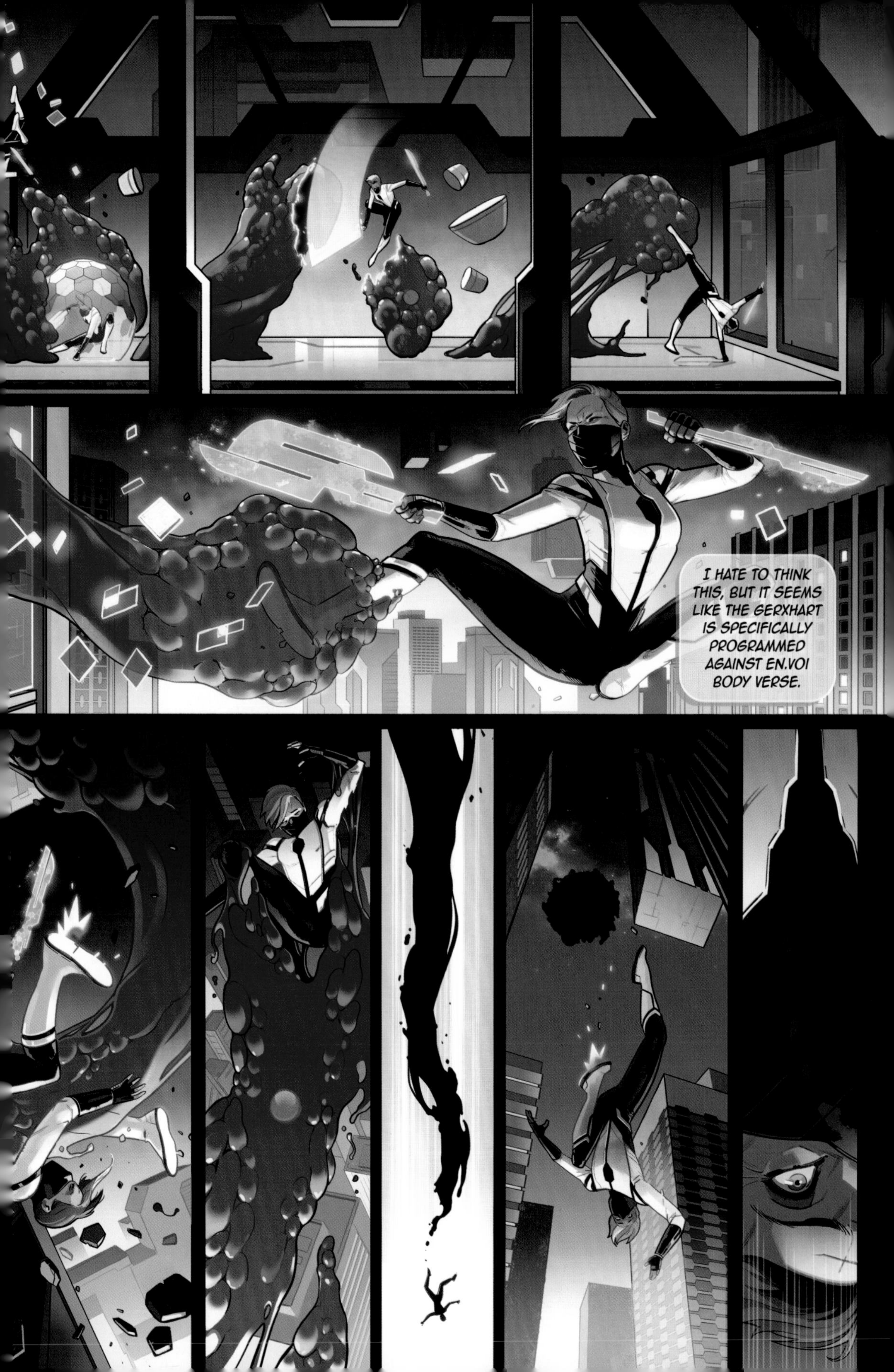
I HATE TO THINK THIS, BUT IT SEEMS LIKE THE GERXHART IS SPECIFICALLY PROGRAMMED AGAINST EN.VOI BODY VERSE.

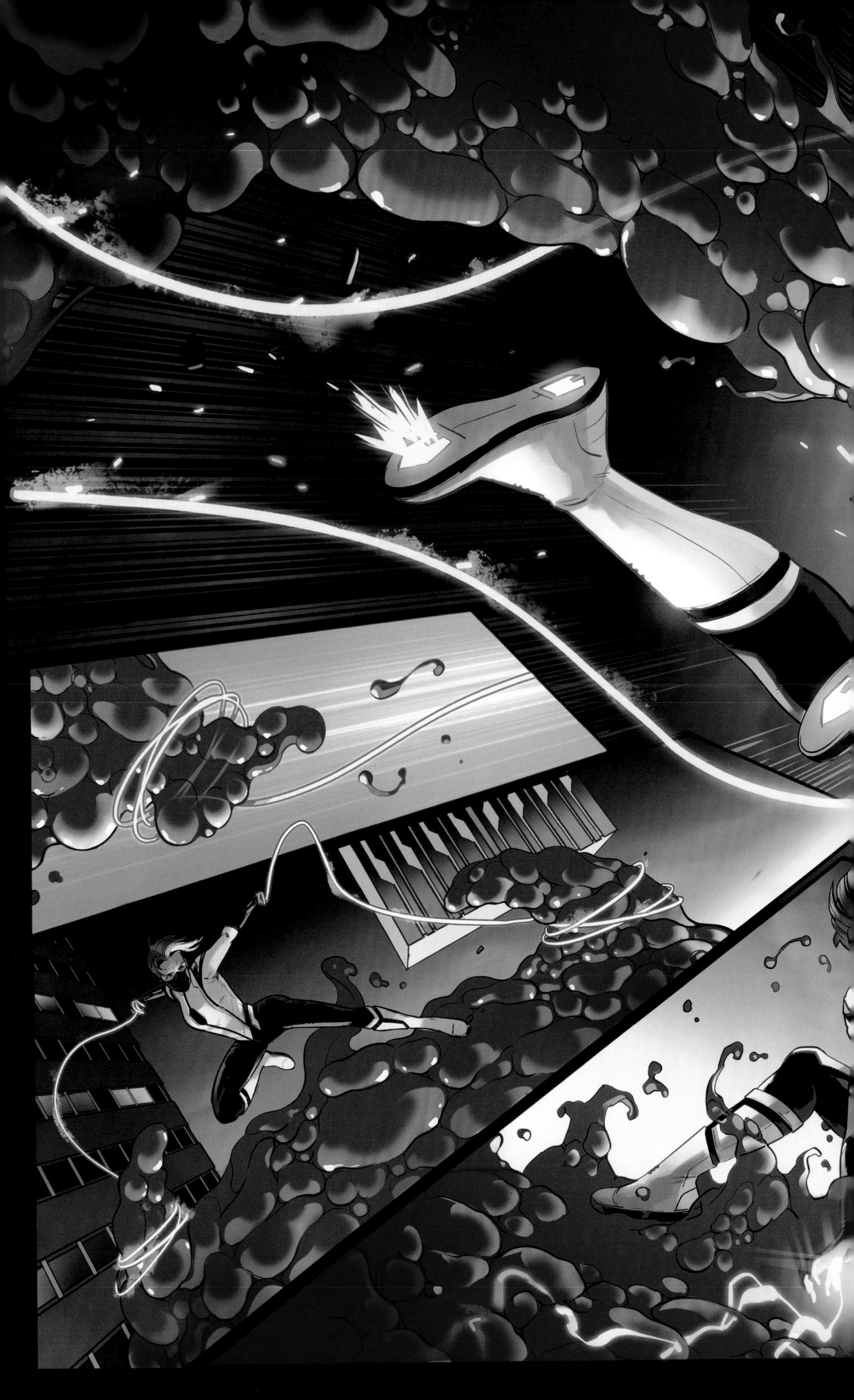

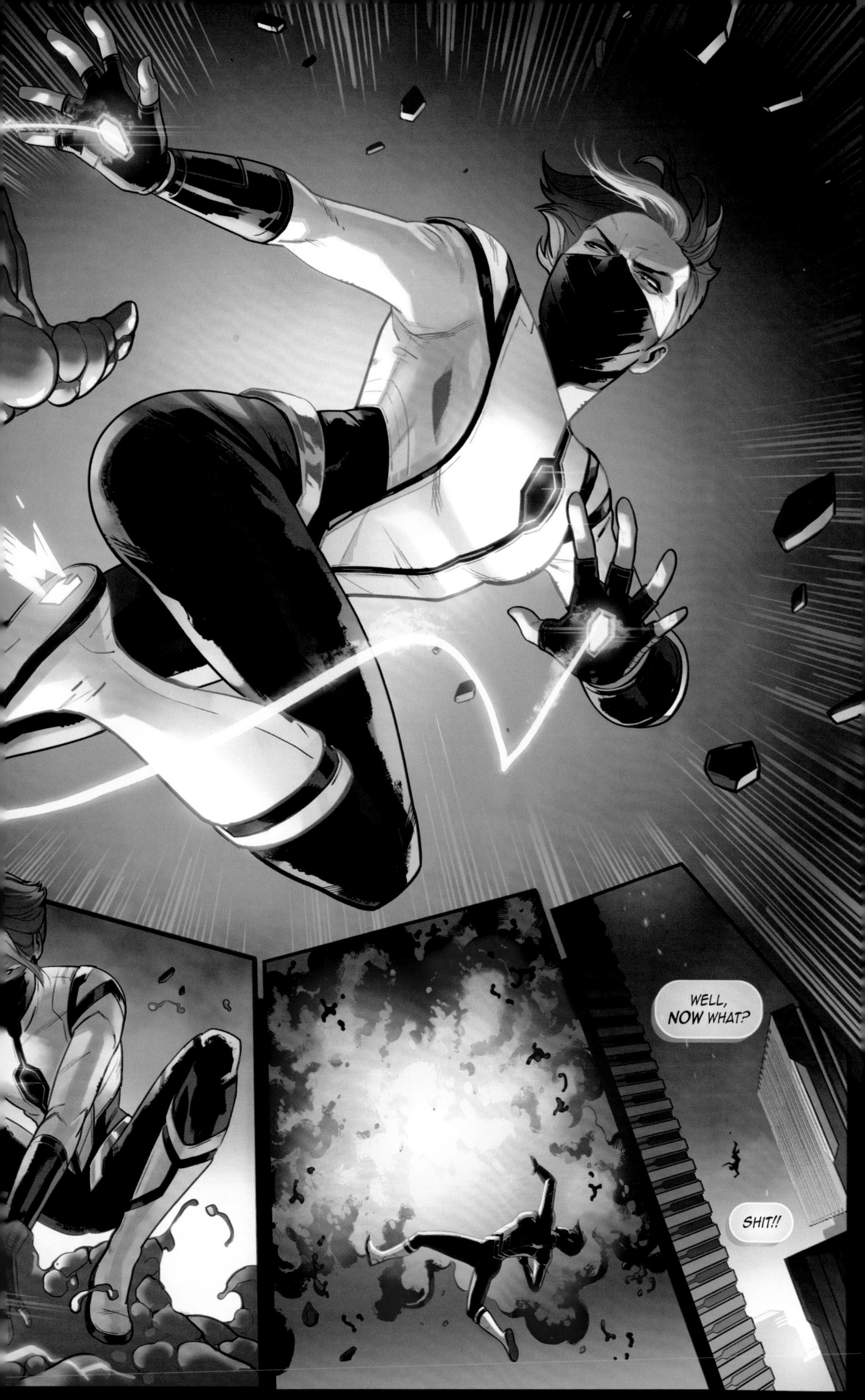
WELL, NOW WHAT?
SHIT!!

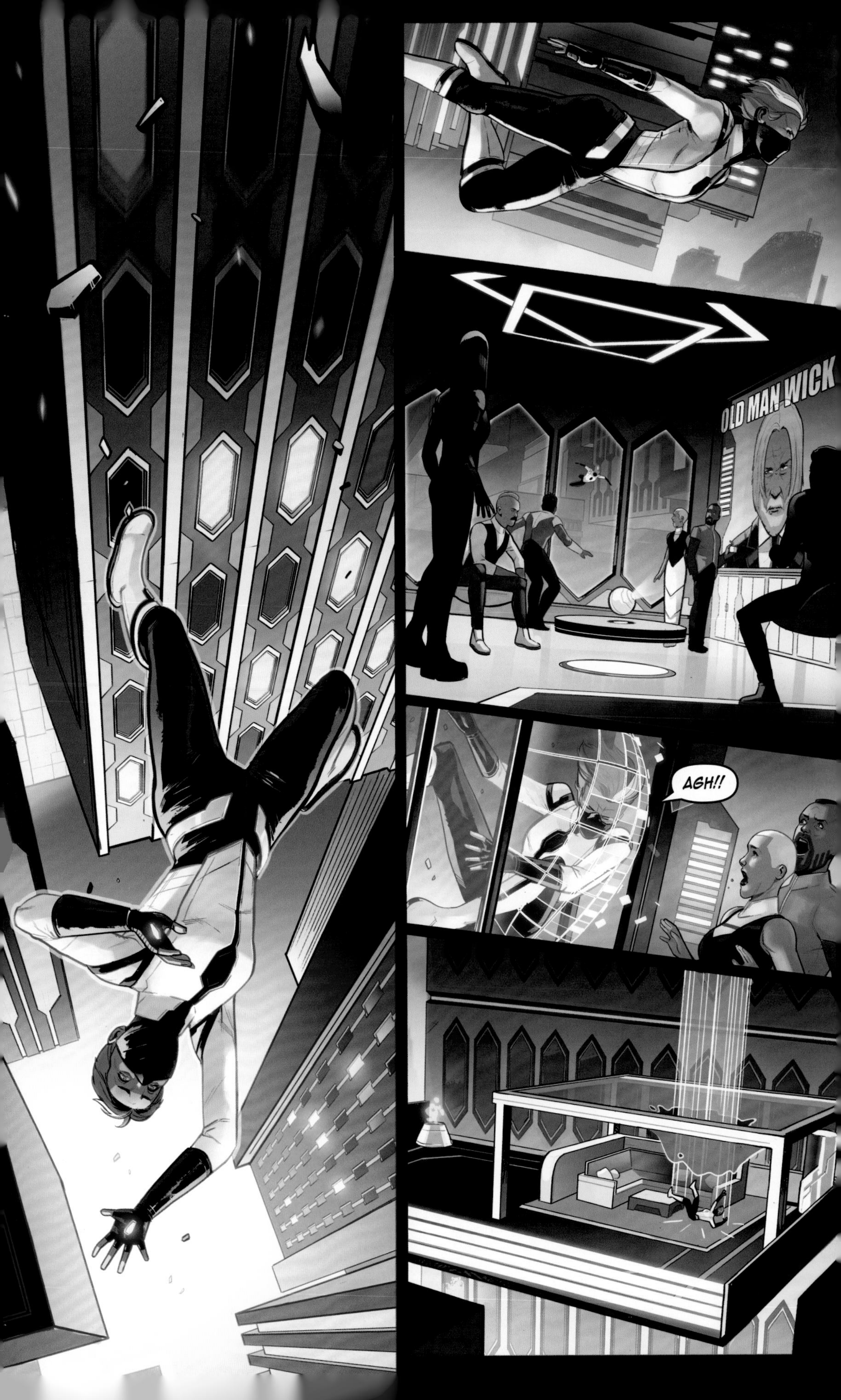
OLD MAN WICK
AGH!!

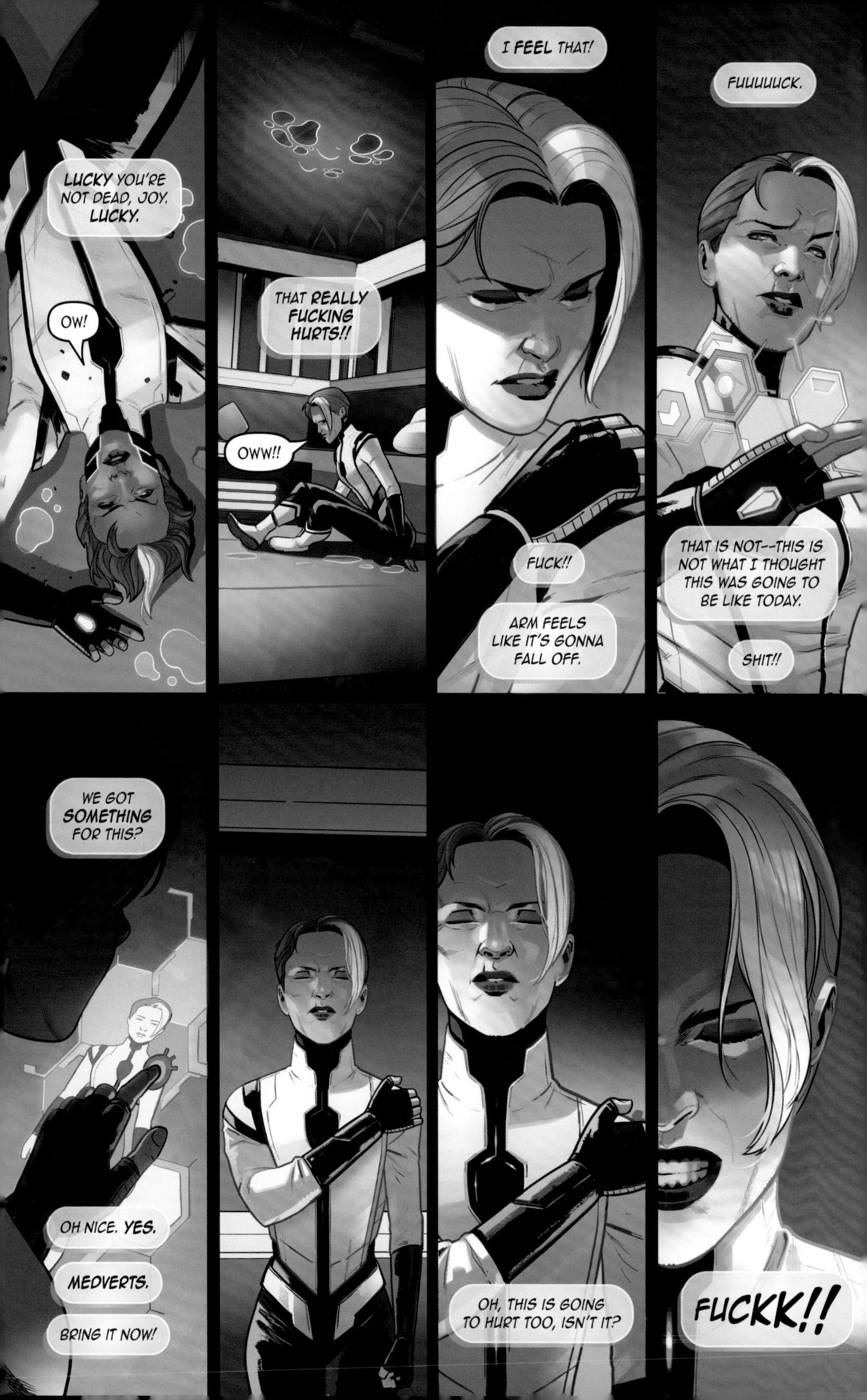
LUCKY YOU'RE NOT DEAD, JOY. LUCKY.
OW!
THAT REALLY FUCKING HURTS!!
OWW!!
I FEEL THAT!
FUCK!!
ARM FEELS LIKE IT'S GONNA FALL OFF.
FUUUUUCK.
THAT IS NOT--THIS IS NOT WHAT I THOUGHT THIS WAS GOING TO BE LIKE TODAY.
SHIT!!
WE GOT SOMETHING FOR THIS?
OH NICE. YES.
MEDVERTS.
BRING IT NOW!
OH, THIS IS GOING TO HURT TOO, ISN'T IT?
FUCKK!!

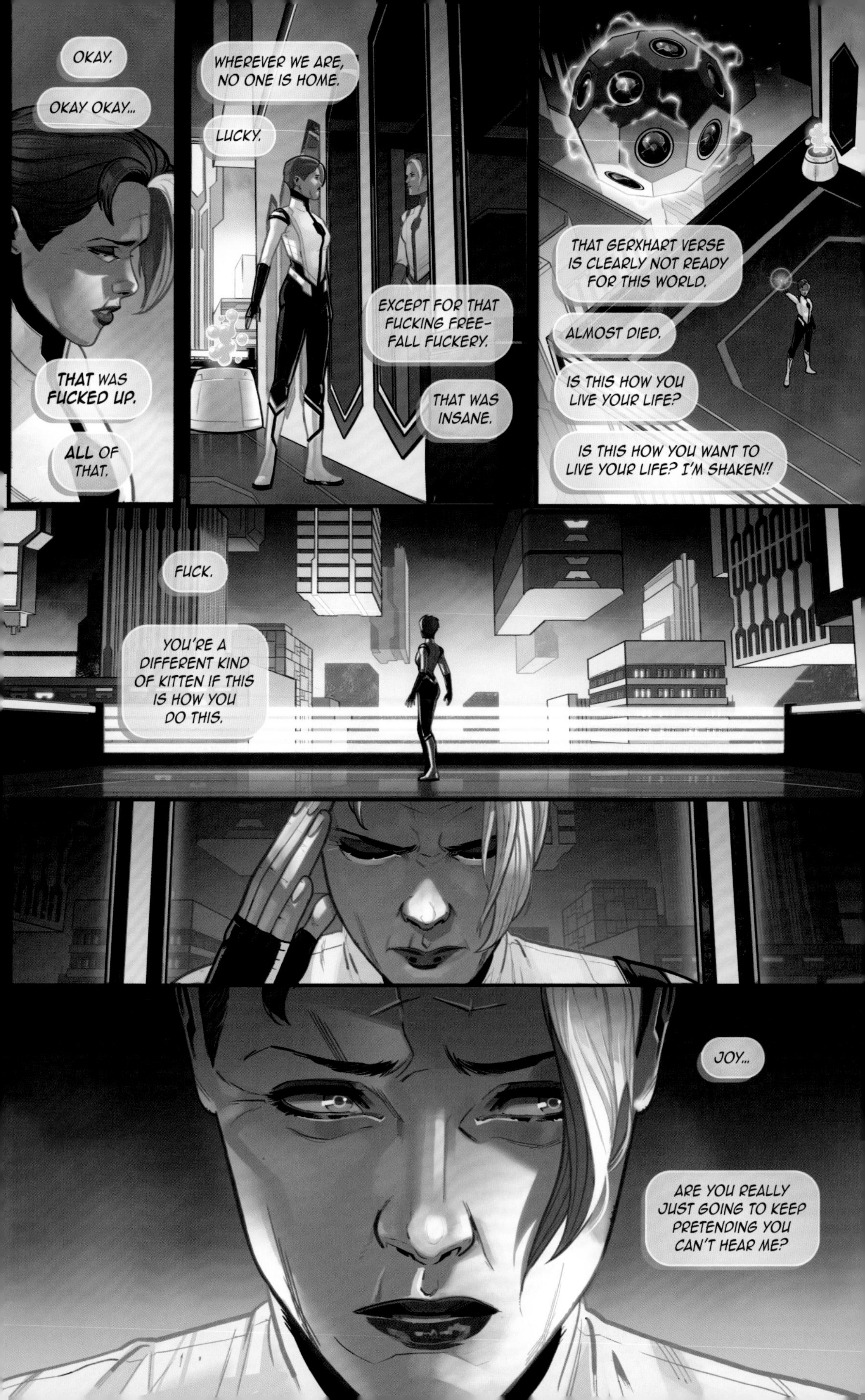
OKAY.
OKAY OKAY...
THAT WAS FUCKED UP.
ALL OF THAT.
WHEREVER WE ARE, NO ONE IS HOME.
LUCKY.
EXCEPT FOR THAT FUCKING FREE-FALL FUCKERY.
THAT WAS INSANE.
THAT GERXHART VERSE IS CLEARLY NOT READY FOR THIS WORLD.
ALMOST DIED.
IS THIS HOW YOU LIVE YOUR LIFE?
IS THIS HOW YOU WANT TO LIVE YOUR LIFE? I'M SHAKEN!!
FUCK.
YOU'RE A DIFFERENT KIND OF KITTEN IF THIS IS HOW YOU DO THIS.
JOY...
ARE YOU REALLY JUST GOING TO KEEP PRETENDING YOU CAN'T HEAR ME?

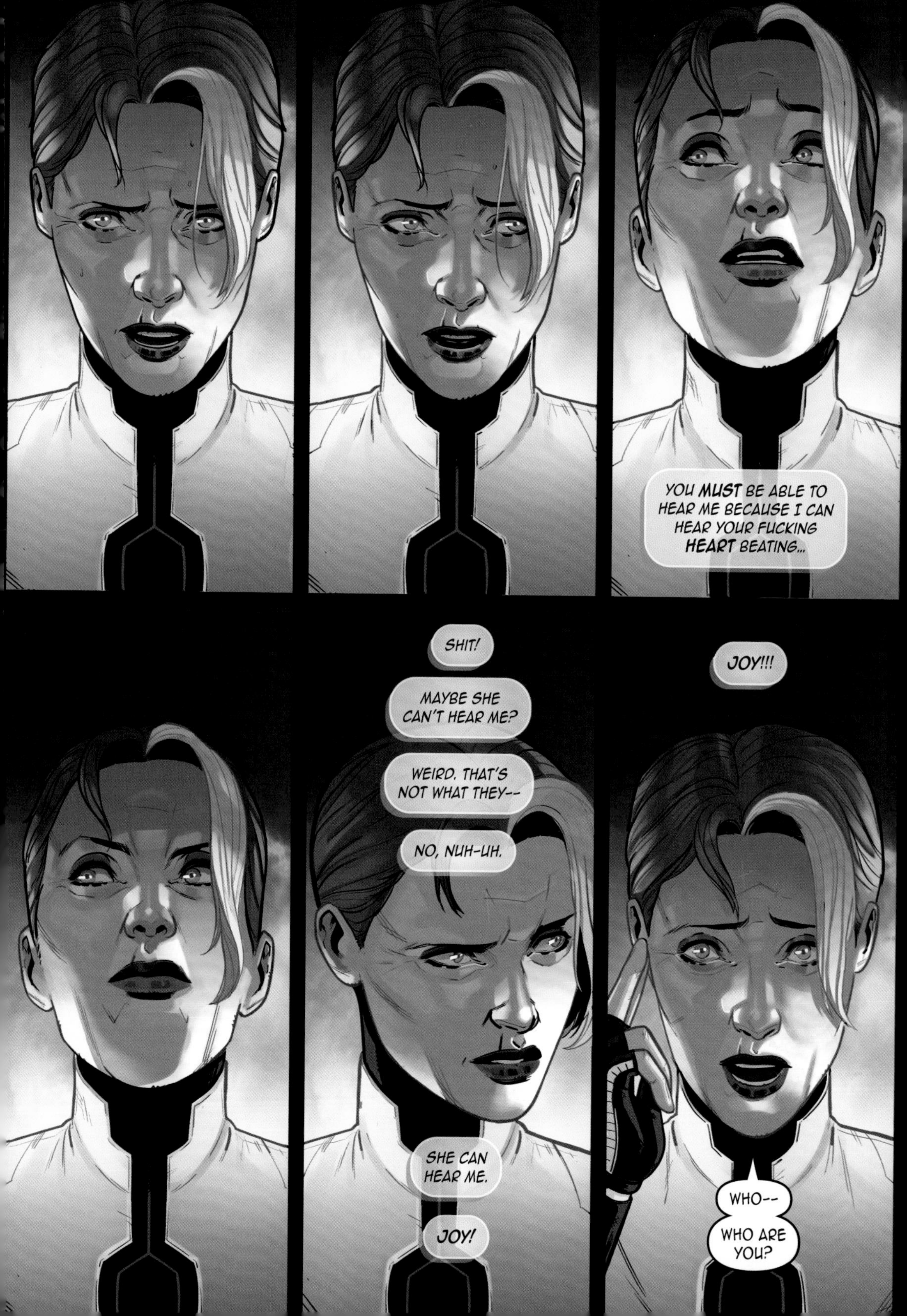
YOU **MUST** BE ABLE TO HEAR ME BECAUSE I CAN HEAR YOUR FUCKING **HEART** BEATING...
SHIT!
MAYBE SHE CAN'T HEAR ME?
WEIRD. THAT'S NOT WHAT THEY--
NO, NUH-UH.
SHE CAN HEAR ME.
JOY!
JOY!!!
WHO--
WHO ARE YOU?

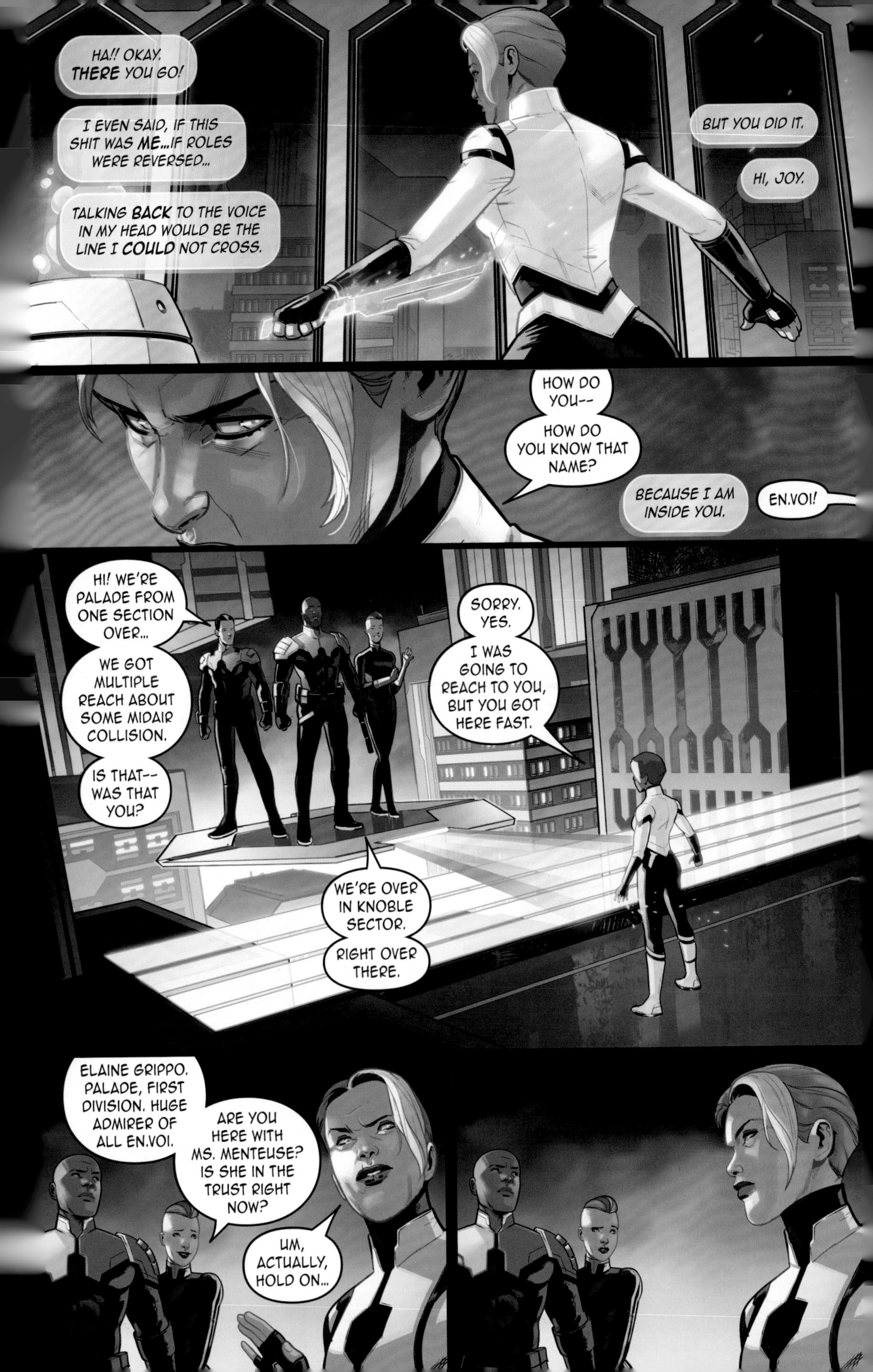
HA!! OKAY. THERE YOU GO!
I EVEN SAID, IF THIS SHIT WAS ME...IF ROLES WERE REVERSED...
TALKING BACK TO THE VOICE IN MY HEAD WOULD BE THE LINE I COULD NOT CROSS.
BUT YOU DID IT.
HI, JOY.
HOW DO YOU--
HOW DO YOU KNOW THAT NAME?
BECAUSE I AM INSIDE YOU.
EN.VOI!
HI! WE'RE PALADE FROM ONE SECTION OVER...
WE GOT MULTIPLE REACH ABOUT SOME MIDAIR COLLISION.
IS THAT--WAS THAT YOU?
SORRY. YES.
I WAS GOING TO REACH TO YOU, BUT YOU GOT HERE FAST.
WE'RE OVER IN KNOBLE SECTOR.
RIGHT OVER THERE.
ELAINE GRIPPO. PALADE, FIRST DIVISION. HUGE ADMIRER OF ALL EN.VOI.
ARE YOU HERE WITH MS. MENTEUSE? IS SHE IN THE TRUST RIGHT NOW?
UM, ACTUALLY, HOLD ON...

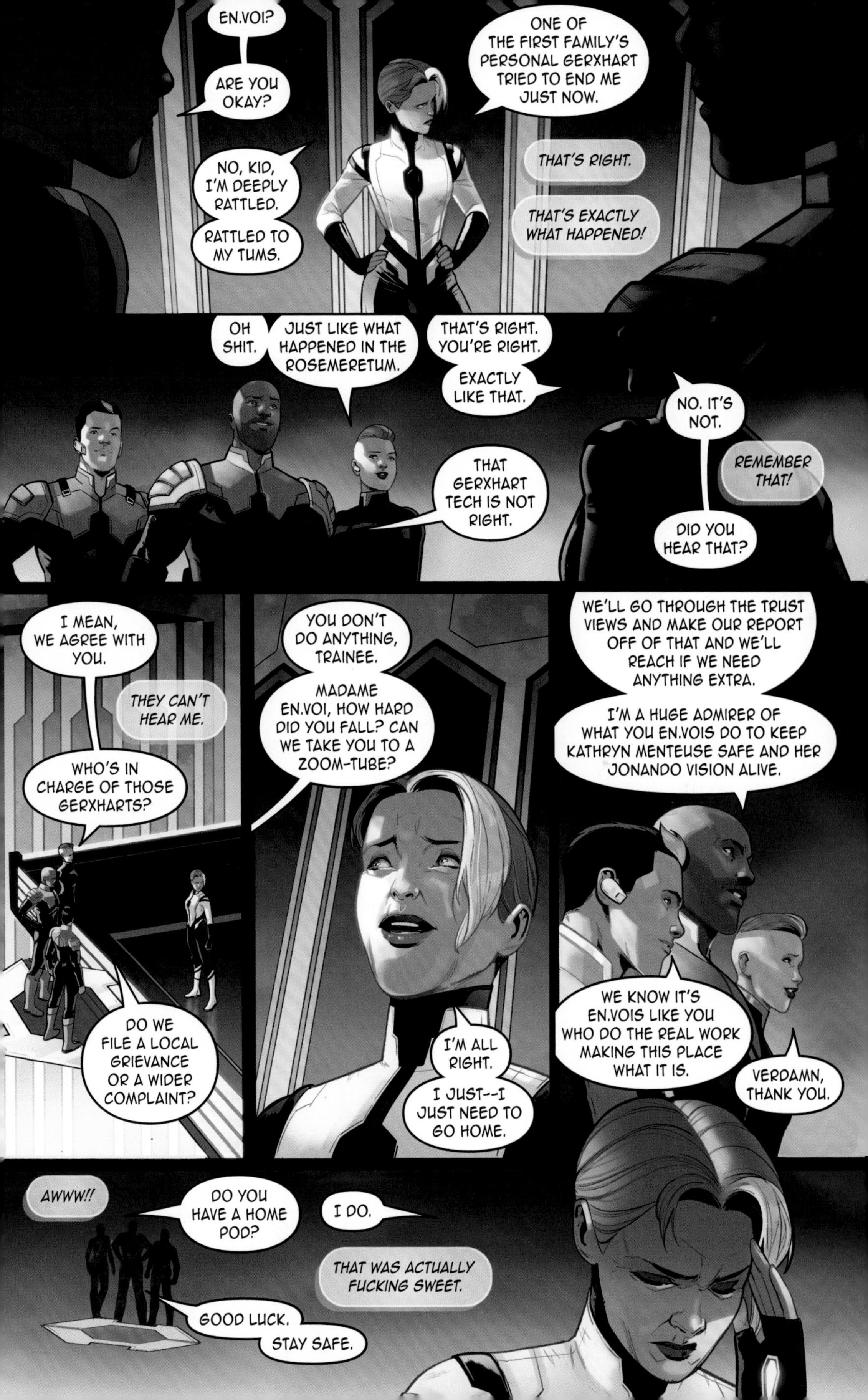
EN.VOI?
ARE YOU OKAY?
ONE OF THE FIRST FAMILY'S PERSONAL GERXHART TRIED TO END ME JUST NOW.
NO, KID, I'M DEEPLY RATTLED.
RATTLED TO MY TUMS.
THAT'S RIGHT.
THAT'S EXACTLY WHAT HAPPENED!
OH SHIT.
JUST LIKE WHAT HAPPENED IN THE ROSEMERETUM.
THAT'S RIGHT. YOU'RE RIGHT.
EXACTLY LIKE THAT.
NO. IT'S NOT.
REMEMBER THAT!
THAT GERXHART TECH IS NOT RIGHT.
DID YOU HEAR THAT?
I MEAN, WE AGREE WITH YOU.
THEY CAN'T HEAR ME.
WHO'S IN CHARGE OF THOSE GERXHARTS?
DO WE FILE A LOCAL GRIEVANCE OR A WIDER COMPLAINT?
YOU DON'T DO ANYTHING, TRAINEE.
MADAME EN.VOI, HOW HARD DID YOU FALL? CAN WE TAKE YOU TO A ZOOM-TUBE?
I'M ALL RIGHT.
I JUST--I JUST NEED TO GO HOME.
WE'LL GO THROUGH THE TRUST VIEWS AND MAKE OUR REPORT OFF OF THAT AND WE'LL REACH IF WE NEED ANYTHING EXTRA.
I'M A HUGE ADMIRER OF WHAT YOU EN.VOIS DO TO KEEP KATHRYN MENTEUSE SAFE AND HER JONANDO VISION ALIVE.
WE KNOW IT'S EN.VOIS LIKE YOU WHO DO THE REAL WORK MAKING THIS PLACE WHAT IT IS.
VERDAMN, THANK YOU.
AWWW!!
DO YOU HAVE A HOME POD?
I DO.
THAT WAS ACTUALLY FUCKING SWEET.
GOOD LUCK.
STAY SAFE.

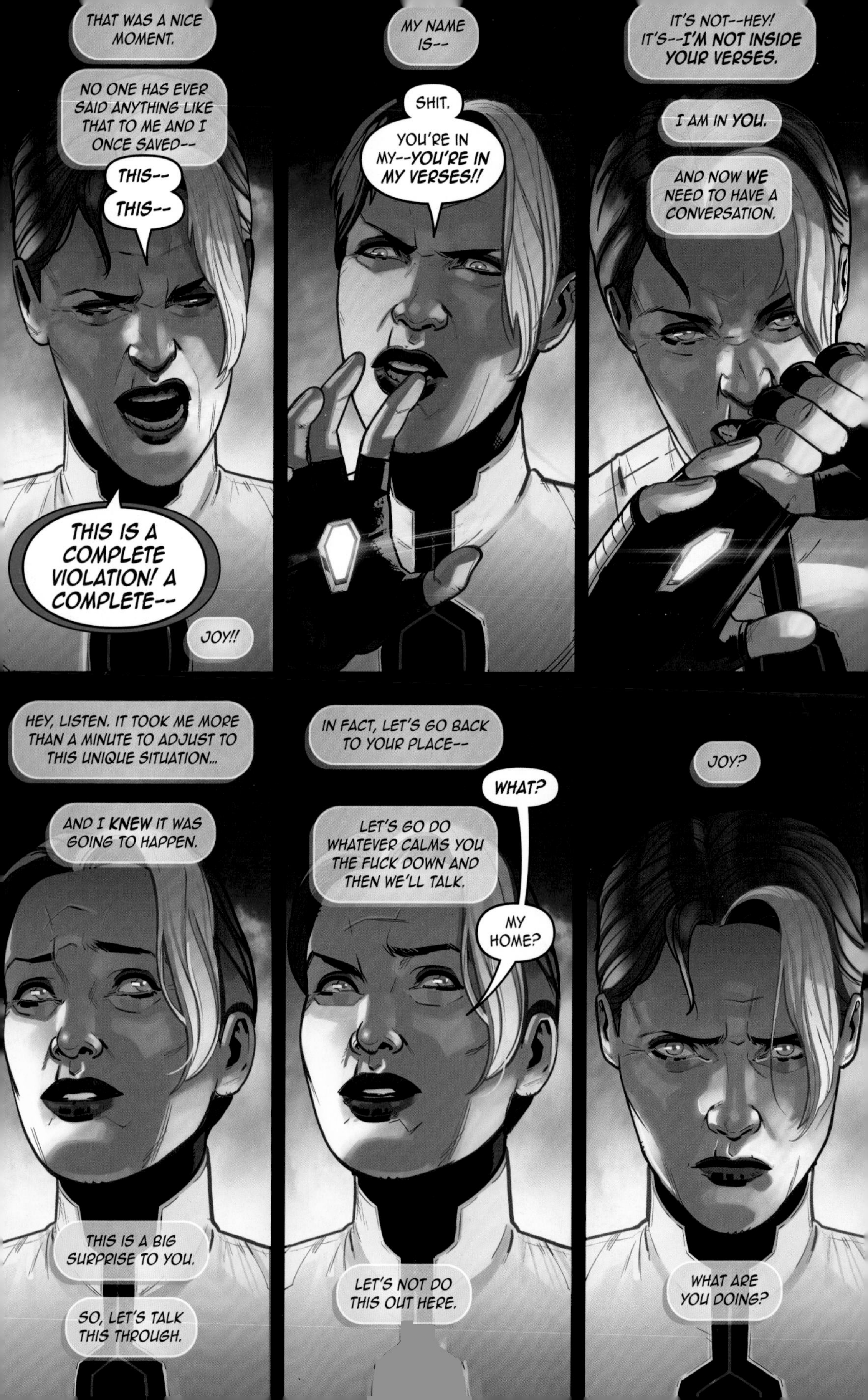
THAT WAS A NICE MOMENT.
NO ONE HAS EVER SAID ANYTHING LIKE THAT TO ME AND I ONCE SAVED--
THIS--
THIS--
THIS IS A COMPLETE VIOLATION! A COMPLETE--
JOY!!
MY NAME IS--
SHIT.
YOU'RE IN MY--YOU'RE IN MY VERSES!!
IT'S NOT--HEY! IT'S--I'M NOT INSIDE YOUR VERSES.
I AM IN YOU.
AND NOW WE NEED TO HAVE A CONVERSATION.
HEY, LISTEN. IT TOOK ME MORE THAN A MINUTE TO ADJUST TO THIS UNIQUE SITUATION...
AND I KNEW IT WAS GOING TO HAPPEN.
THIS IS A BIG SURPRISE TO YOU.
SO, LET'S TALK THIS THROUGH.
IN FACT, LET'S GO BACK TO YOUR PLACE--
WHAT?
LET'S GO DO WHATEVER CALMS YOU THE FUCK DOWN AND THEN WE'LL TALK.
MY HOME?
LET'S NOT DO THIS OUT HERE.
JOY?
WHAT ARE YOU DOING?

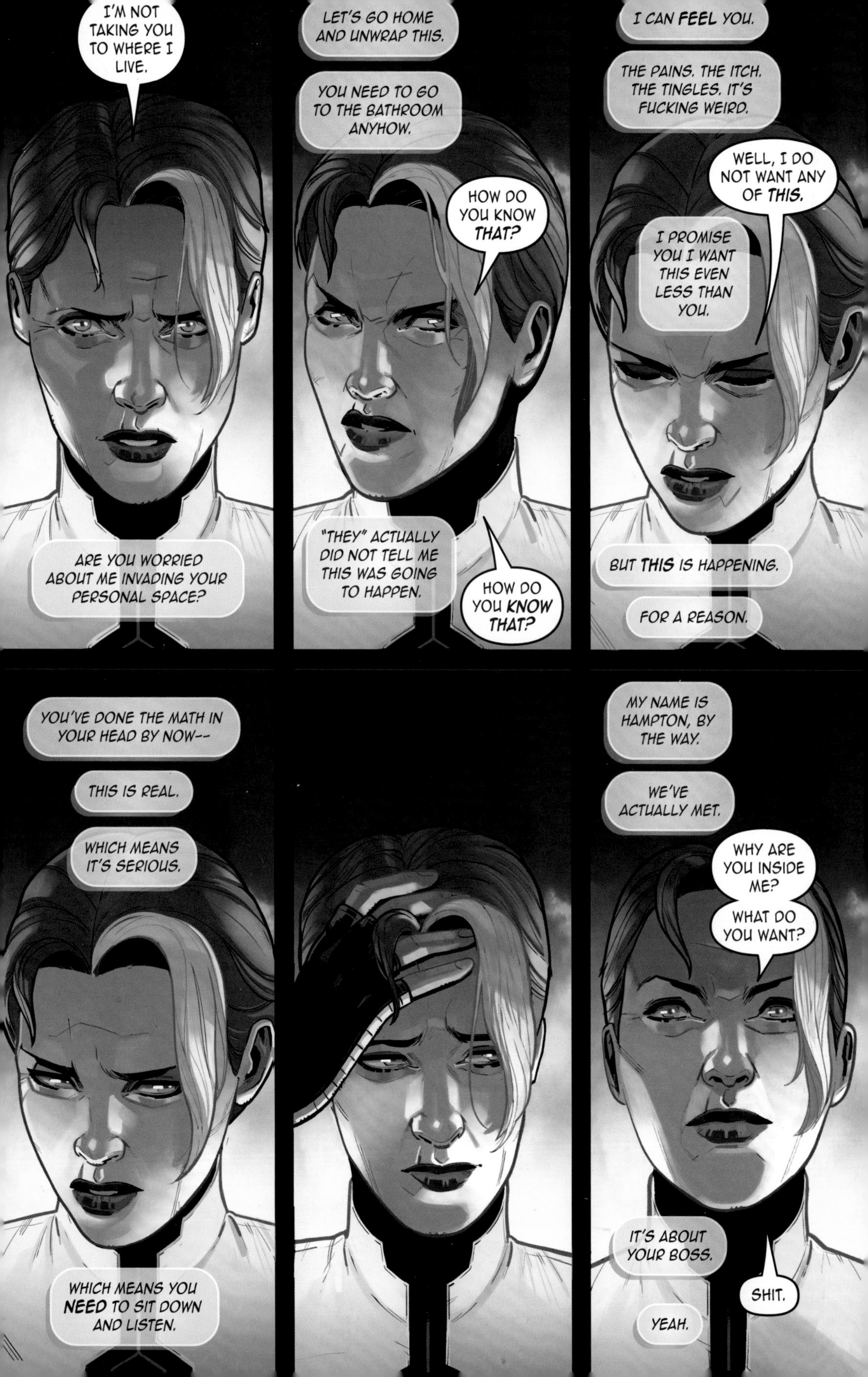
I'M NOT TAKING YOU TO WHERE I LIVE.
ARE YOU WORRIED ABOUT ME INVADING YOUR PERSONAL SPACE?
LET'S GO HOME AND UNWRAP THIS.
YOU NEED TO GO TO THE BATHROOM ANYHOW.
HOW DO YOU KNOW THAT?
"THEY" ACTUALLY DID NOT TELL ME THIS WAS GOING TO HAPPEN.
HOW DO YOU KNOW THAT?
I CAN FEEL YOU.
THE PAINS. THE ITCH. THE TINGLES. IT'S FUCKING WEIRD.
WELL, I DO NOT WANT ANY OF THIS.
I PROMISE YOU I WANT THIS EVEN LESS THAN YOU.
BUT THIS IS HAPPENING.
FOR A REASON.
YOU'VE DONE THE MATH IN YOUR HEAD BY NOW--
THIS IS REAL.
WHICH MEANS IT'S SERIOUS.
WHICH MEANS YOU NEED TO SIT DOWN AND LISTEN.
MY NAME IS HAMPTON, BY THE WAY.
WE'VE ACTUALLY MET.
WHY ARE YOU INSIDE ME?
WHAT DO YOU WANT?
IT'S ABOUT YOUR BOSS.
SHIT.
YEAH.

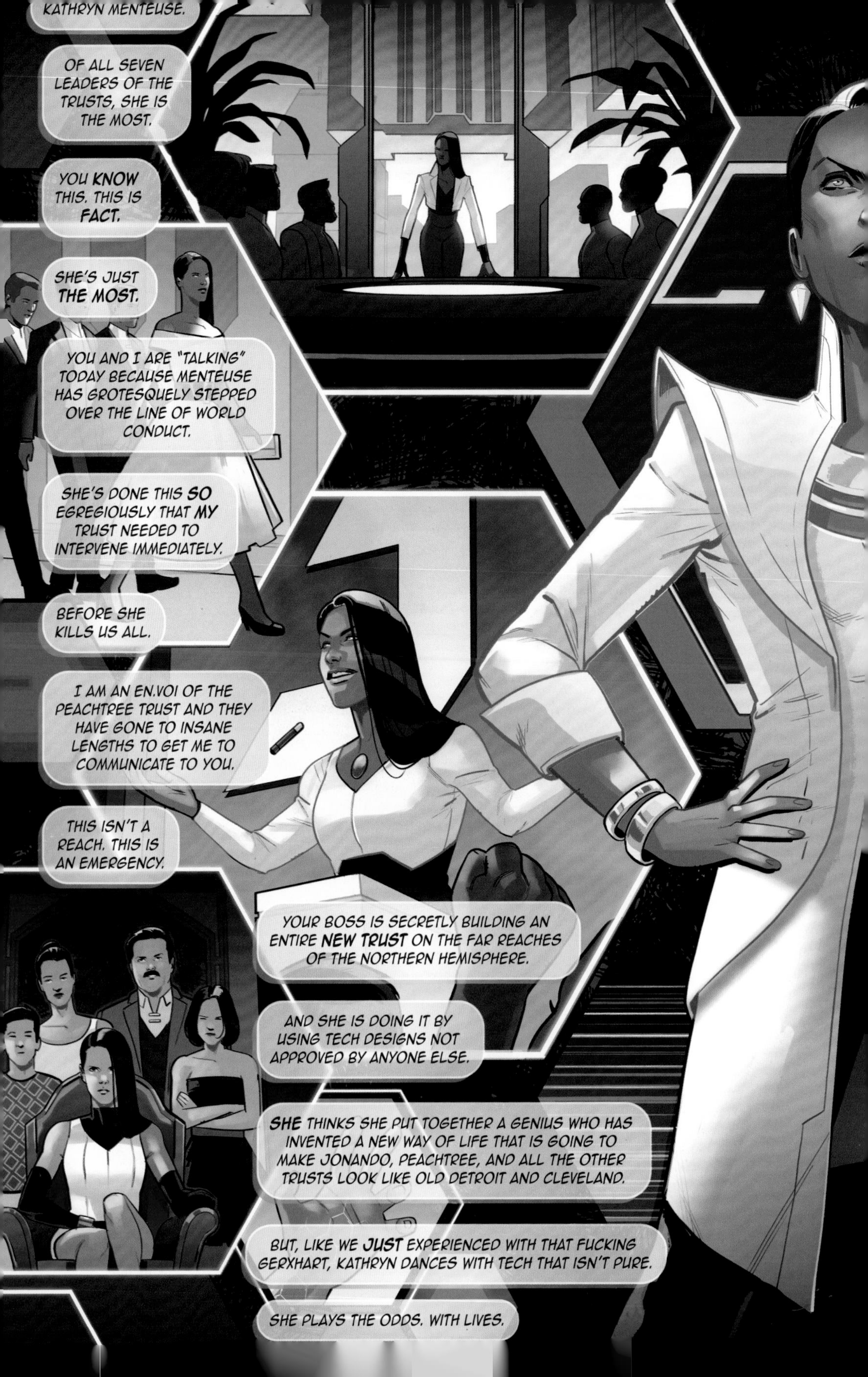
KATHRYN MENTEUSE.
OF ALL SEVEN LEADERS OF THE TRUSTS, SHE IS THE MOST.
YOU KNOW THIS. THIS IS FACT.
SHE'S JUST THE MOST.
YOU AND I ARE "TALKING" TODAY BECAUSE MENTEUSE HAS GROTESQUELY STEPPED OVER THE LINE OF WORLD CONDUCT.
SHE'S DONE THIS SO EGREGIOUSLY THAT MY TRUST NEEDED TO INTERVENE IMMEDIATELY.
BEFORE SHE KILLS US ALL.
I AM AN EN.VOI OF THE PEACHTREE TRUST AND THEY HAVE GONE TO INSANE LENGTHS TO GET ME TO COMMUNICATE TO YOU.
THIS ISN'T A REACH. THIS IS AN EMERGENCY.
YOUR BOSS IS SECRETLY BUILDING AN ENTIRE NEW TRUST ON THE FAR REACHES OF THE NORTHERN HEMISPHERE.
AND SHE IS DOING IT BY USING TECH DESIGNS NOT APPROVED BY ANYONE ELSE.
SHE THINKS SHE PUT TOGETHER A GENIUS WHO HAS INVENTED A NEW WAY OF LIFE THAT IS GOING TO MAKE JONANDO, PEACHTREE, AND ALL THE OTHER TRUSTS LOOK LIKE OLD DETROIT AND CLEVELAND.
BUT, LIKE WE JUST EXPERIENCED WITH THAT FUCKING GERXHART, KATHRYN DANCES WITH TECH THAT ISN'T PURE.
SHE PLAYS THE ODDS. WITH LIVES.

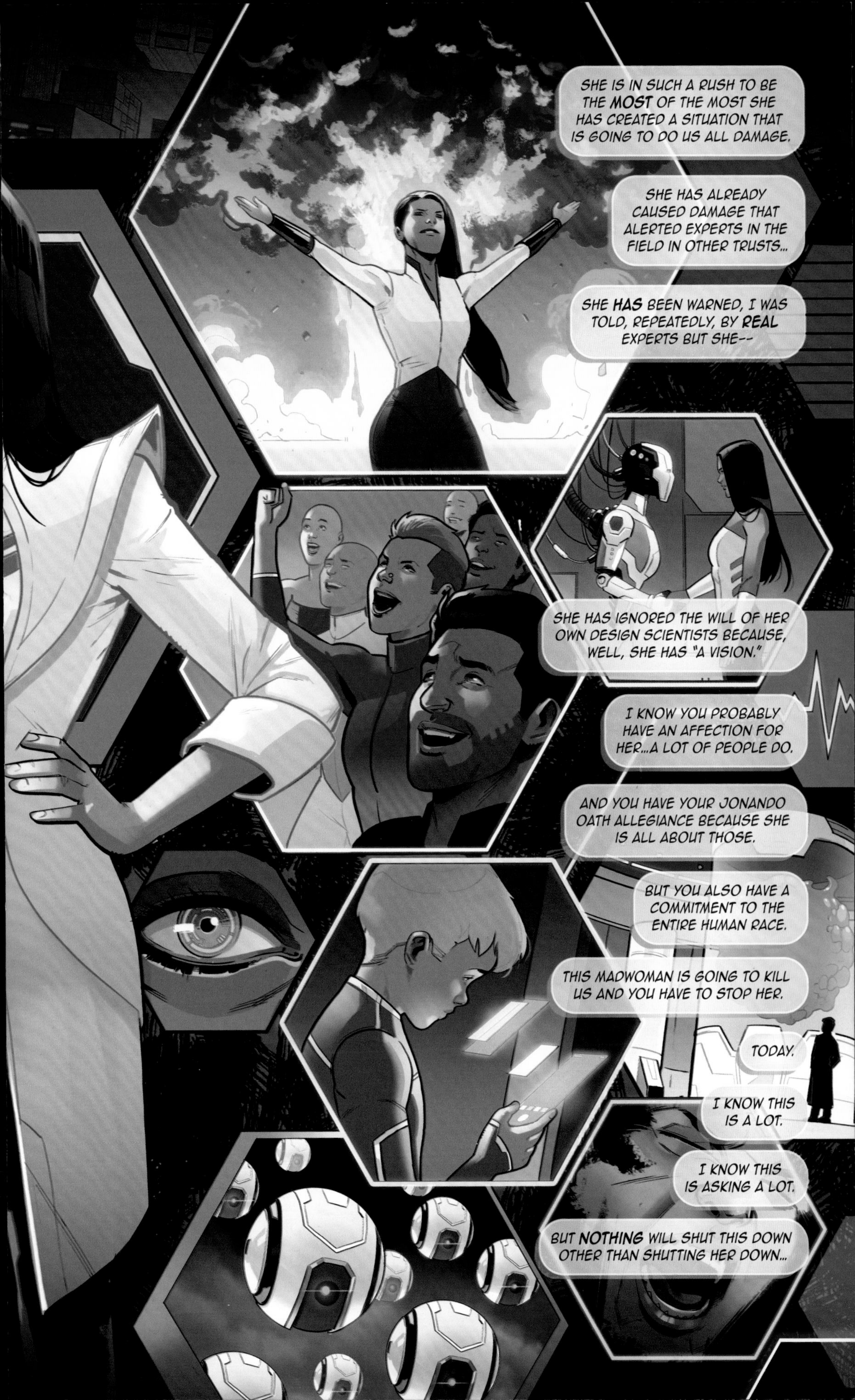
SHE IS IN SUCH A RUSH TO BE THE MOST OF THE MOST SHE HAS CREATED A SITUATION THAT IS GOING TO DO US ALL DAMAGE.
SHE HAS ALREADY CAUSED DAMAGE THAT ALERTED EXPERTS IN THE FIELD IN OTHER TRUSTS...
SHE HAS BEEN WARNED, I WAS TOLD, REPEATEDLY, BY REAL EXPERTS BUT SHE--
SHE HAS IGNORED THE WILL OF HER OWN DESIGN SCIENTISTS BECAUSE, WELL, SHE HAS "A VISION."
I KNOW YOU PROBABLY HAVE AN AFFECTION FOR HER...A LOT OF PEOPLE DO.
AND YOU HAVE YOUR JONANDO OATH ALLEGIANCE BECAUSE SHE IS ALL ABOUT THOSE.
BUT YOU ALSO HAVE A COMMITMENT TO THE ENTIRE HUMAN RACE.
THIS MADWOMAN IS GOING TO KILL US AND YOU HAVE TO STOP HER.
TODAY.
I KNOW THIS IS A LOT.
I KNOW THIS IS ASKING A LOT.
BUT NOTHING WILL SHUT THIS DOWN OTHER THAN SHUTTING HER DOWN...

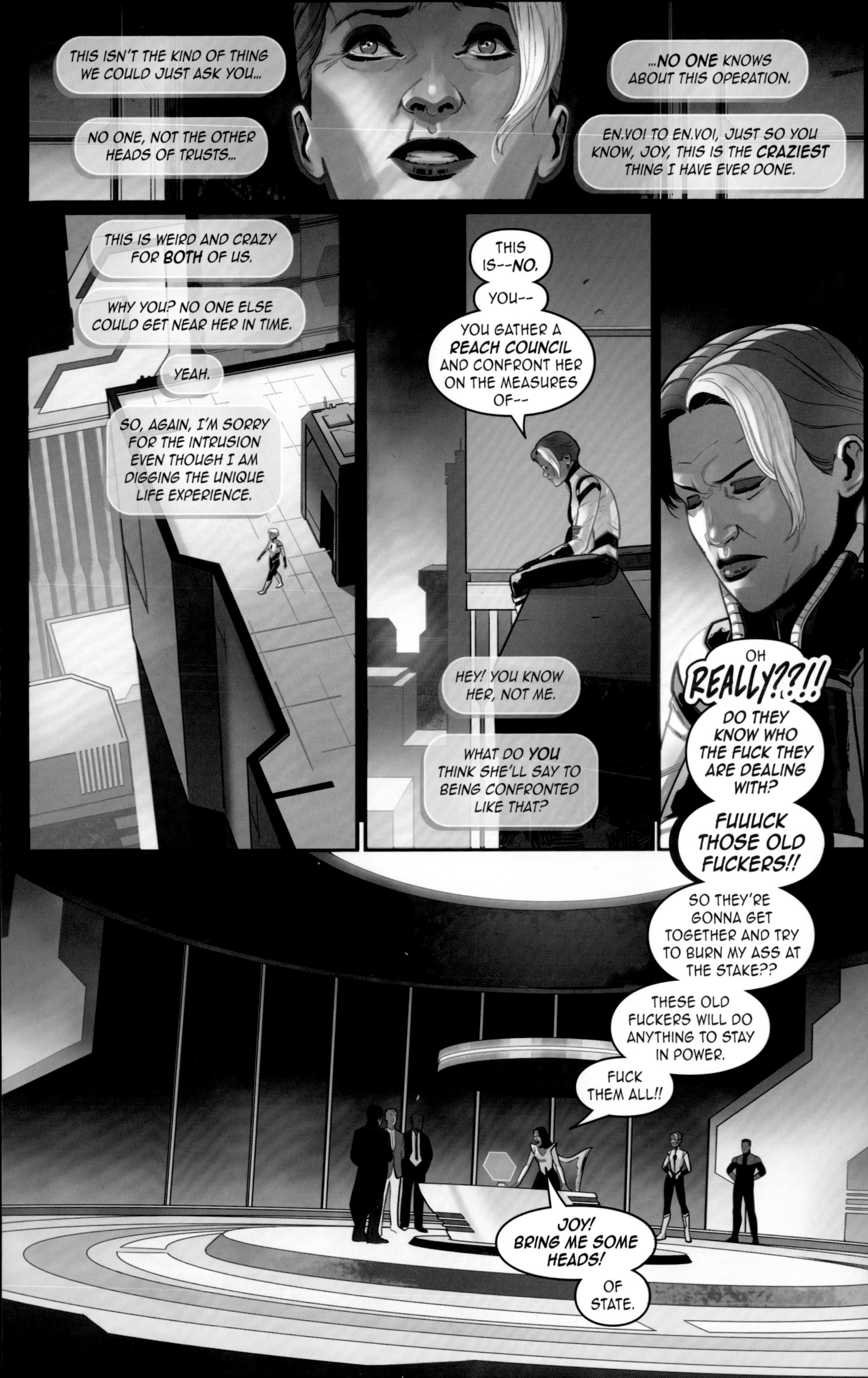
THIS ISN'T THE KIND OF THING WE COULD JUST ASK YOU...
NO ONE, NOT THE OTHER HEADS OF TRUSTS...
...NO ONE KNOWS ABOUT THIS OPERATION.
EN.VOI TO EN.VOI, JUST SO YOU KNOW, JOY, THIS IS THE CRAZIEST THING I HAVE EVER DONE.
THIS IS WEIRD AND CRAZY FOR BOTH OF US.
WHY YOU? NO ONE ELSE COULD GET NEAR HER IN TIME.
YEAH.
SO, AGAIN, I'M SORRY FOR THE INTRUSION EVEN THOUGH I AM DIGGING THE UNIQUE LIFE EXPERIENCE.
THIS IS--NO.
YOU--
YOU GATHER A REACH COUNCIL AND CONFRONT HER ON THE MEASURES OF--
HEY! YOU KNOW HER, NOT ME.
WHAT DO YOU THINK SHE'LL SAY TO BEING CONFRONTED LIKE THAT?
OH REALLY??!!
DO THEY KNOW WHO THE FUCK THEY ARE DEALING WITH?
FUUUCK THOSE OLD FUCKERS!!
SO THEY'RE GONNA GET TOGETHER AND TRY TO BURN MY ASS AT THE STAKE??
THESE OLD FUCKERS WILL DO ANYTHING TO STAY IN POWER.
FUCK THEM ALL!!
JOY! BRING ME SOME HEADS!
OF STATE.

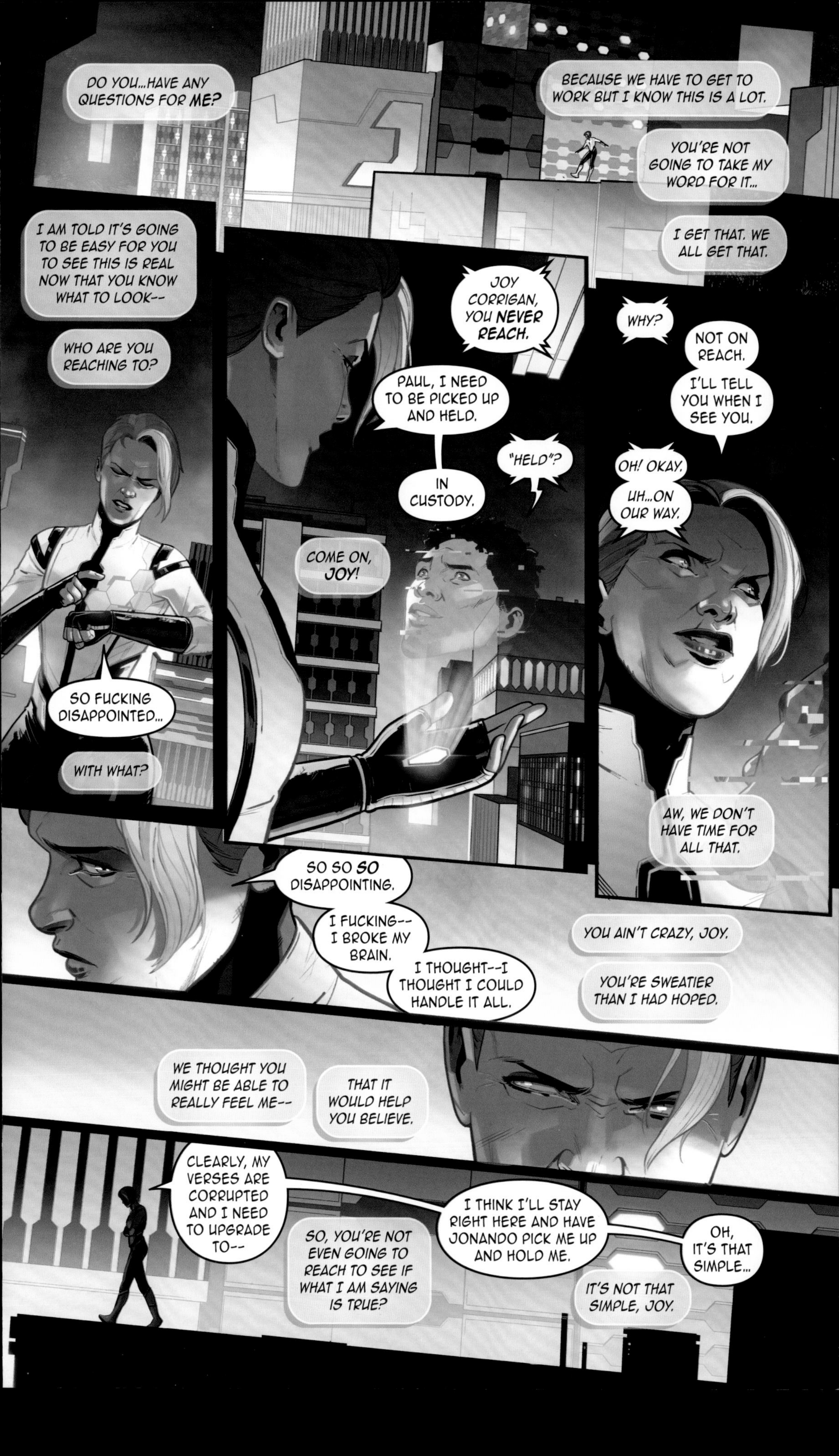
DO YOU...HAVE ANY QUESTIONS FOR ME?
BECAUSE WE HAVE TO GET TO WORK BUT I KNOW THIS IS A LOT.
YOU'RE NOT GOING TO TAKE MY WORD FOR IT...
I GET THAT. WE ALL GET THAT.
I AM TOLD IT'S GOING TO BE EASY FOR YOU TO SEE THIS IS REAL NOW THAT YOU KNOW WHAT TO LOOK--
WHO ARE YOU REACHING TO?
JOY CORRIGAN, YOU NEVER REACH.
PAUL, I NEED TO BE PICKED UP AND HELD.
"HELD"?
IN CUSTODY.
COME ON, JOY!
WHY?
NOT ON REACH.
I'LL TELL YOU WHEN I SEE YOU.
OH! OKAY.
UH...ON OUR WAY.
SO FUCKING DISAPPOINTED...
WITH WHAT?
AW, WE DON'T HAVE TIME FOR ALL THAT.
SO SO SO DISAPPOINTING.
I FUCKING-- I BROKE MY BRAIN.
I THOUGHT--I THOUGHT I COULD HANDLE IT ALL.
YOU AIN'T CRAZY, JOY.
YOU'RE SWEATIER THAN I HAD HOPED.
WE THOUGHT YOU MIGHT BE ABLE TO REALLY FEEL ME--
THAT IT WOULD HELP YOU BELIEVE.
CLEARLY, MY VERSES ARE CORRUPTED AND I NEED TO UPGRADE TO--
SO, YOU'RE NOT EVEN GOING TO REACH TO SEE IF WHAT I AM SAYING IS TRUE?
I THINK I'LL STAY RIGHT HERE AND HAVE JONANDO PICK ME UP AND HOLD ME.
OH, IT'S THAT SIMPLE...
IT'S NOT THAT SIMPLE, JOY.

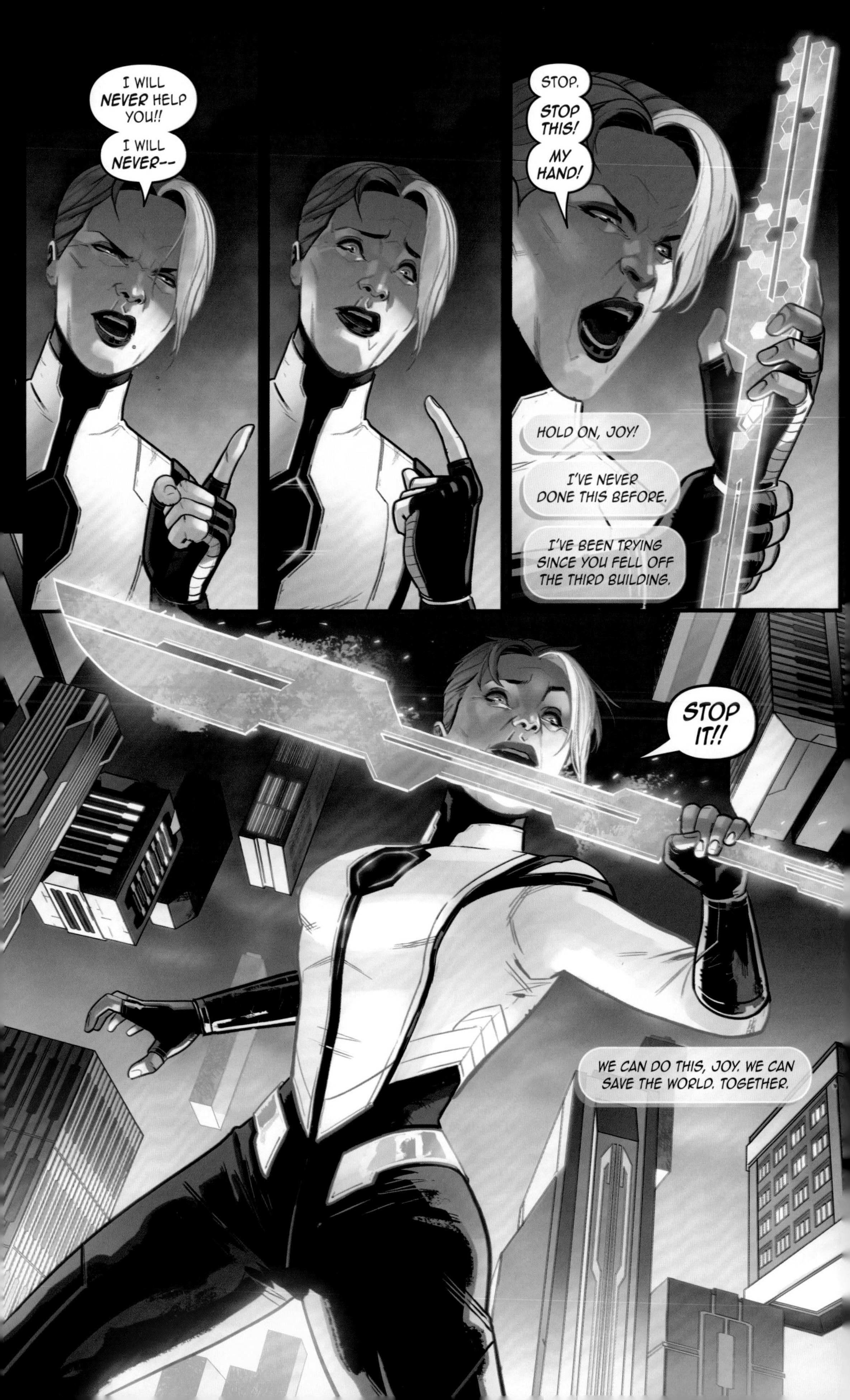
I WILL NEVER HELP YOU!!
I WILL NEVER--
STOP.
STOP THIS!
MY HAND!
HOLD ON, JOY!
I'VE NEVER DONE THIS BEFORE.
I'VE BEEN TRYING SINCE YOU FELL OFF THE THIRD BUILDING.
STOP IT!!
WE CAN DO THIS, JOY. WE CAN SAVE THE WORLD. TOGETHER.

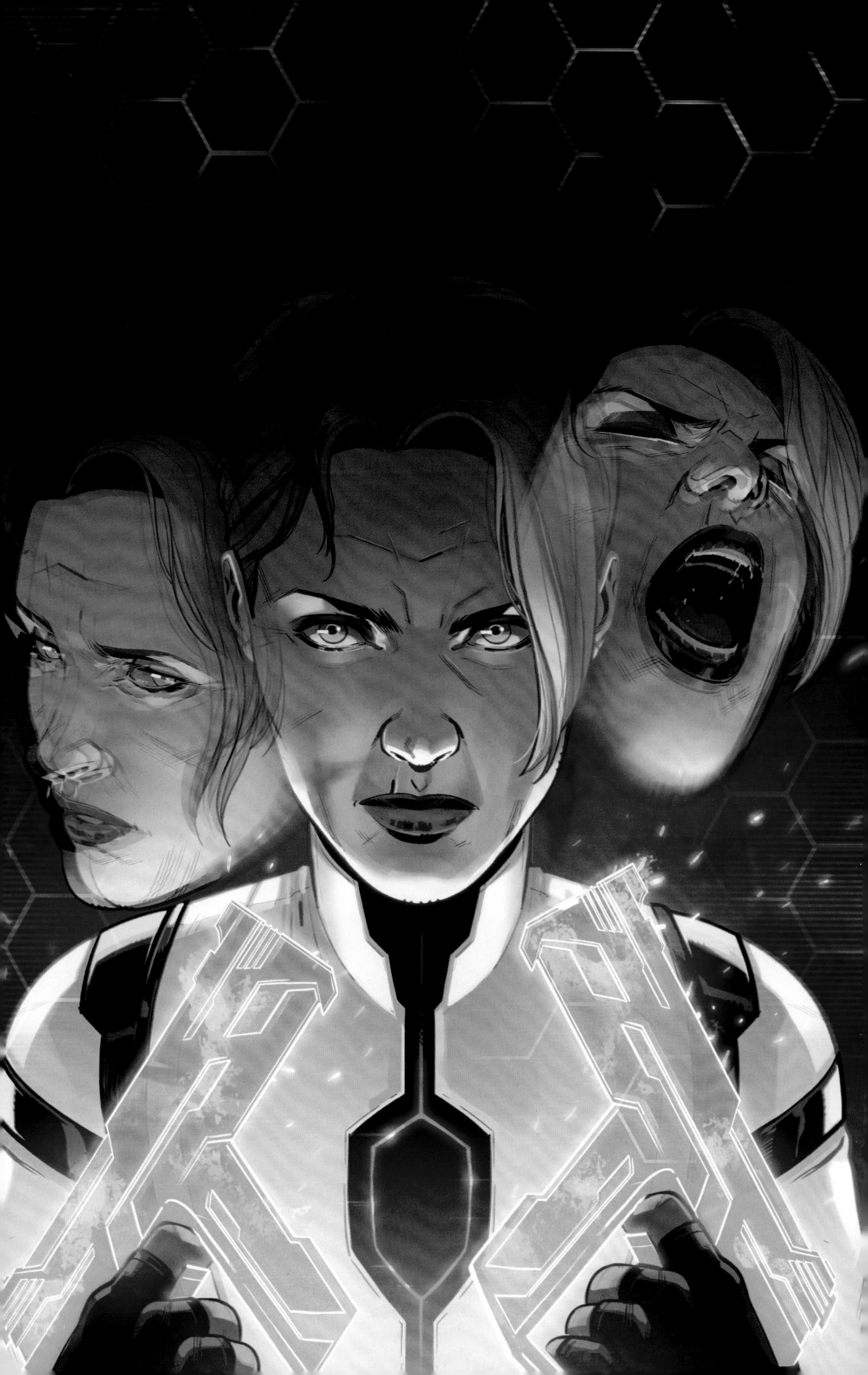

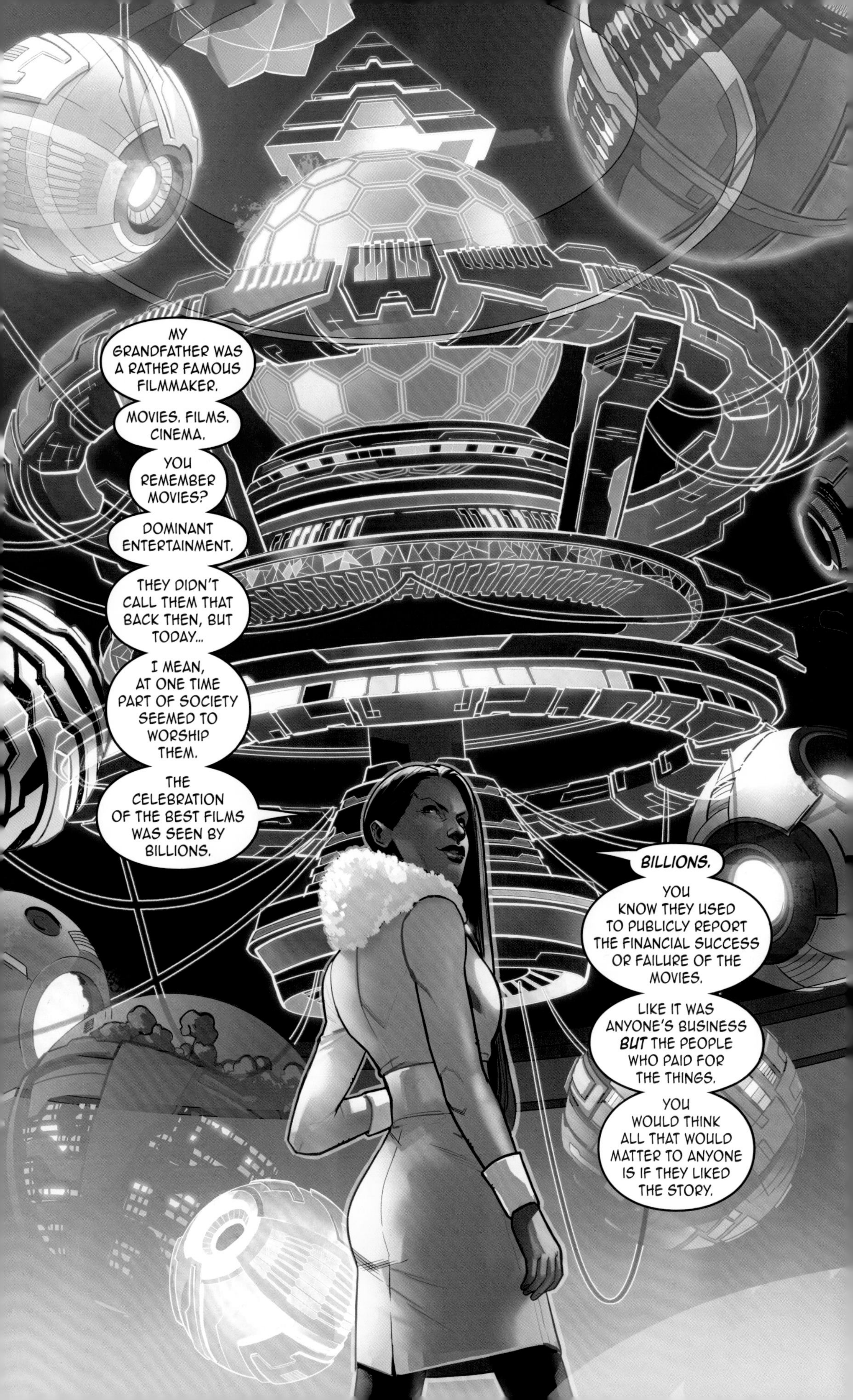
MY GRANDFATHER WAS A RATHER FAMOUS FILMMAKER.
MOVIES. FILMS. CINEMA.
YOU REMEMBER MOVIES?
DOMINANT ENTERTAINMENT.
THEY DIDN'T CALL THEM THAT BACK THEN, BUT TODAY...
I MEAN, AT ONE TIME PART OF SOCIETY SEEMED TO WORSHIP THEM.
THE CELEBRATION OF THE BEST FILMS WAS SEEN BY BILLIONS.
BILLIONS.
YOU KNOW THEY USED TO PUBLICLY REPORT THE FINANCIAL SUCCESS OR FAILURE OF THE MOVIES.
LIKE IT WAS ANYONE'S BUSINESS *BUT* THE PEOPLE WHO PAID FOR THE THINGS.
YOU WOULD THINK ALL THAT WOULD MATTER TO ANYONE IS IF THEY LIKED THE STORY.

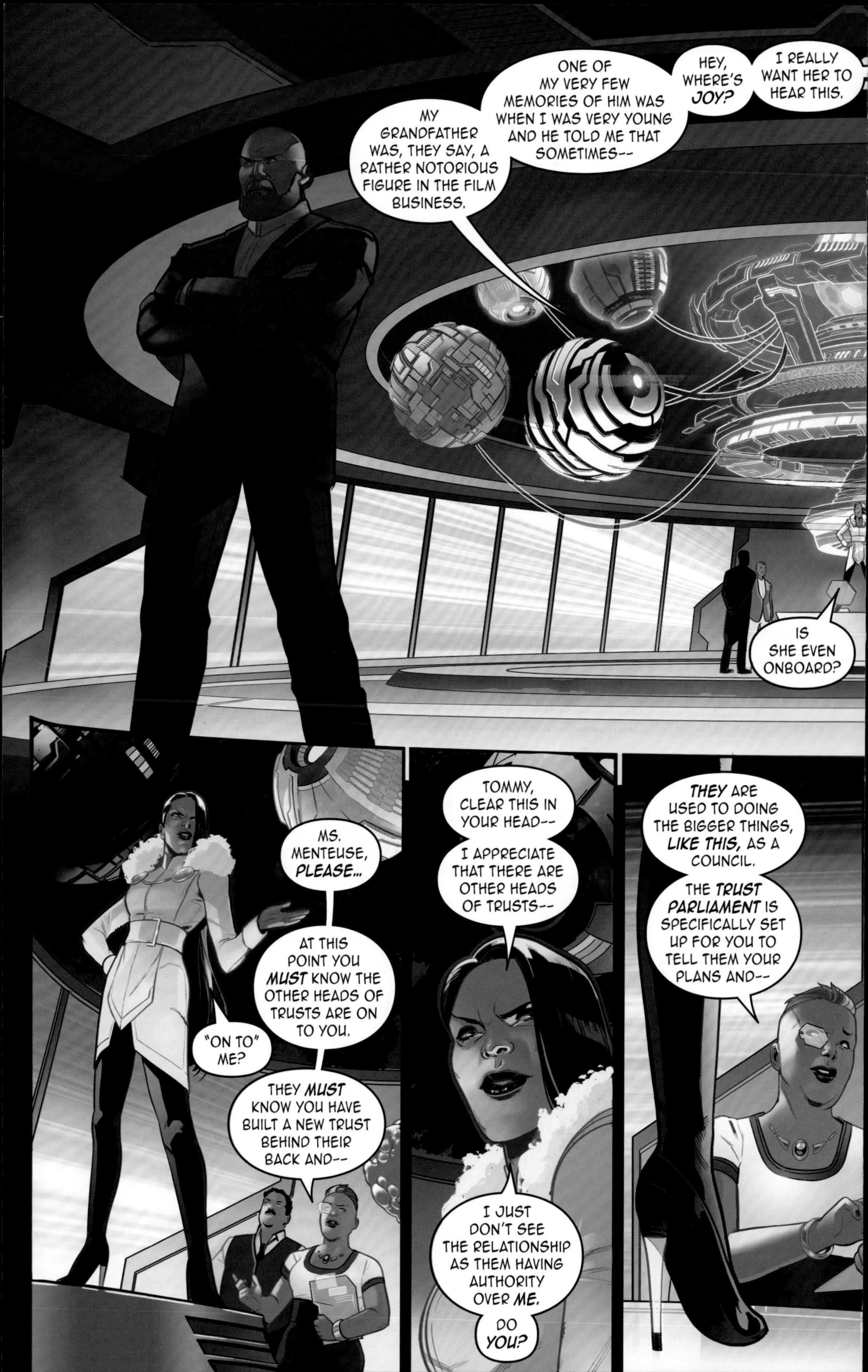
MY GRANDFATHER WAS, THEY SAY, A RATHER NOTORIOUS FIGURE IN THE FILM BUSINESS.
ONE OF MY VERY FEW MEMORIES OF HIM WAS WHEN I WAS VERY YOUNG AND HE TOLD ME THAT SOMETIMES--
HEY, WHERE'S JOY?
I REALLY WANT HER TO HEAR THIS.
IS SHE EVEN ONBOARD?
MS. MENTEUSE, PLEASE...
AT THIS POINT YOU MUST KNOW THE OTHER HEADS OF TRUSTS ARE ON TO YOU.
"ON TO" ME?
THEY MUST KNOW YOU HAVE BUILT A NEW TRUST BEHIND THEIR BACK AND--
TOMMY, CLEAR THIS IN YOUR HEAD--
I APPRECIATE THAT THERE ARE OTHER HEADS OF TRUSTS--
I JUST DON'T SEE THE RELATIONSHIP AS THEM HAVING AUTHORITY OVER ME.
DO YOU?
THEY ARE USED TO DOING THE BIGGER THINGS, LIKE THIS, AS A COUNCIL.
THE TRUST PARLIAMENT IS SPECIFICALLY SET UP FOR YOU TO TELL THEM YOUR PLANS AND--

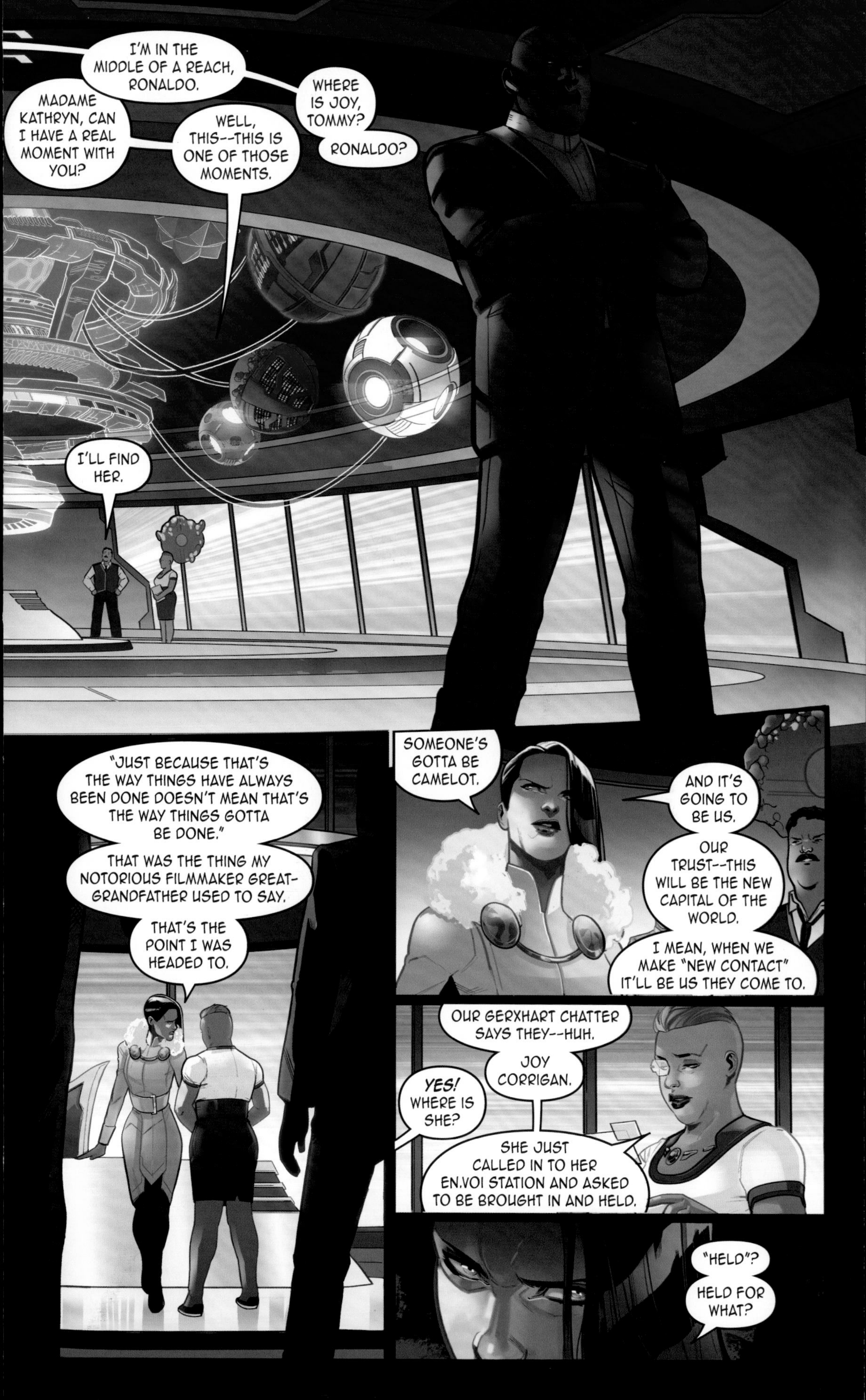
MADAME KATHRYN, CAN I HAVE A REAL MOMENT WITH YOU?
I'M IN THE MIDDLE OF A REACH, RONALDO.
WELL, THIS--THIS IS ONE OF THOSE MOMENTS.
WHERE IS JOY, TOMMY?
RONALDO?
I'LL FIND HER.
"JUST BECAUSE THAT'S THE WAY THINGS HAVE ALWAYS BEEN DONE DOESN'T MEAN THAT'S THE WAY THINGS GOTTA BE DONE."
THAT WAS THE THING MY NOTORIOUS FILMMAKER GREAT-GRANDFATHER USED TO SAY.
THAT'S THE POINT I WAS HEADED TO.
SOMEONE'S GOTTA BE CAMELOT.
AND IT'S GOING TO BE US.
OUR TRUST--THIS WILL BE THE NEW CAPITAL OF THE WORLD.
I MEAN, WHEN WE MAKE "NEW CONTACT" IT'LL BE US THEY COME TO.
OUR GERXHART CHATTER SAYS THEY--HUH.
JOY CORRIGAN.
YES! WHERE IS SHE?
SHE JUST CALLED IN TO HER EN.VOI STATION AND ASKED TO BE BROUGHT IN AND HELD.
"HELD"?
HELD FOR WHAT?

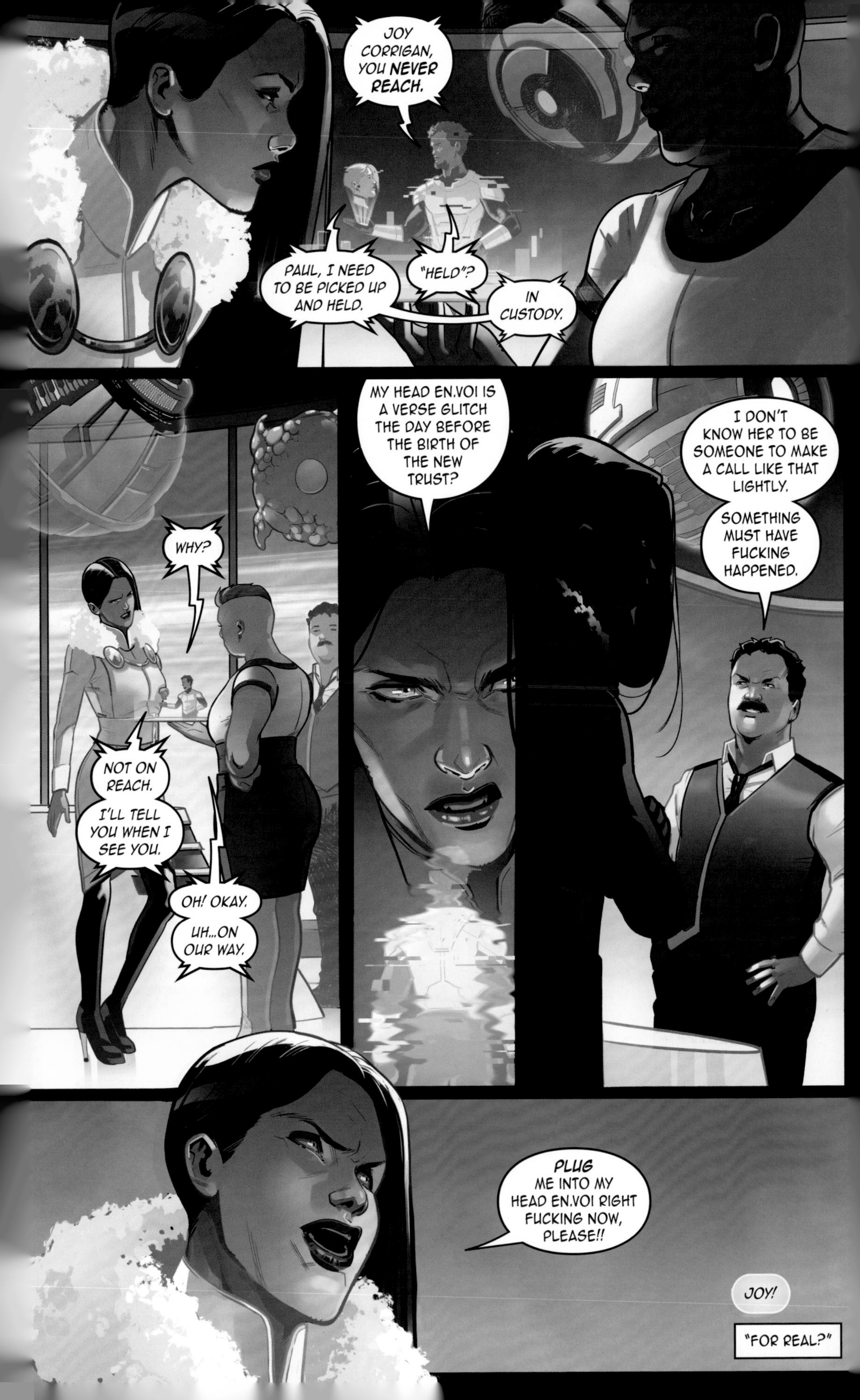
JOY CORRIGAN, YOU NEVER REACH.
PAUL, I NEED TO BE PICKED UP AND HELD.
"HELD"?
IN CUSTODY.
WHY?
NOT ON REACH.
I'LL TELL YOU WHEN I SEE YOU.
OH! OKAY.
UH...ON OUR WAY.
MY HEAD EN.VOI IS A VERSE GLITCH THE DAY BEFORE THE BIRTH OF THE NEW TRUST?
I DON'T KNOW HER TO BE SOMEONE TO MAKE A CALL LIKE THAT LIGHTLY.
SOMETHING MUST HAVE FUCKING HAPPENED.
PLUG ME INTO MY HEAD EN.VOI RIGHT FUCKING NOW, PLEASE!!
JOY!
"FOR REAL?"

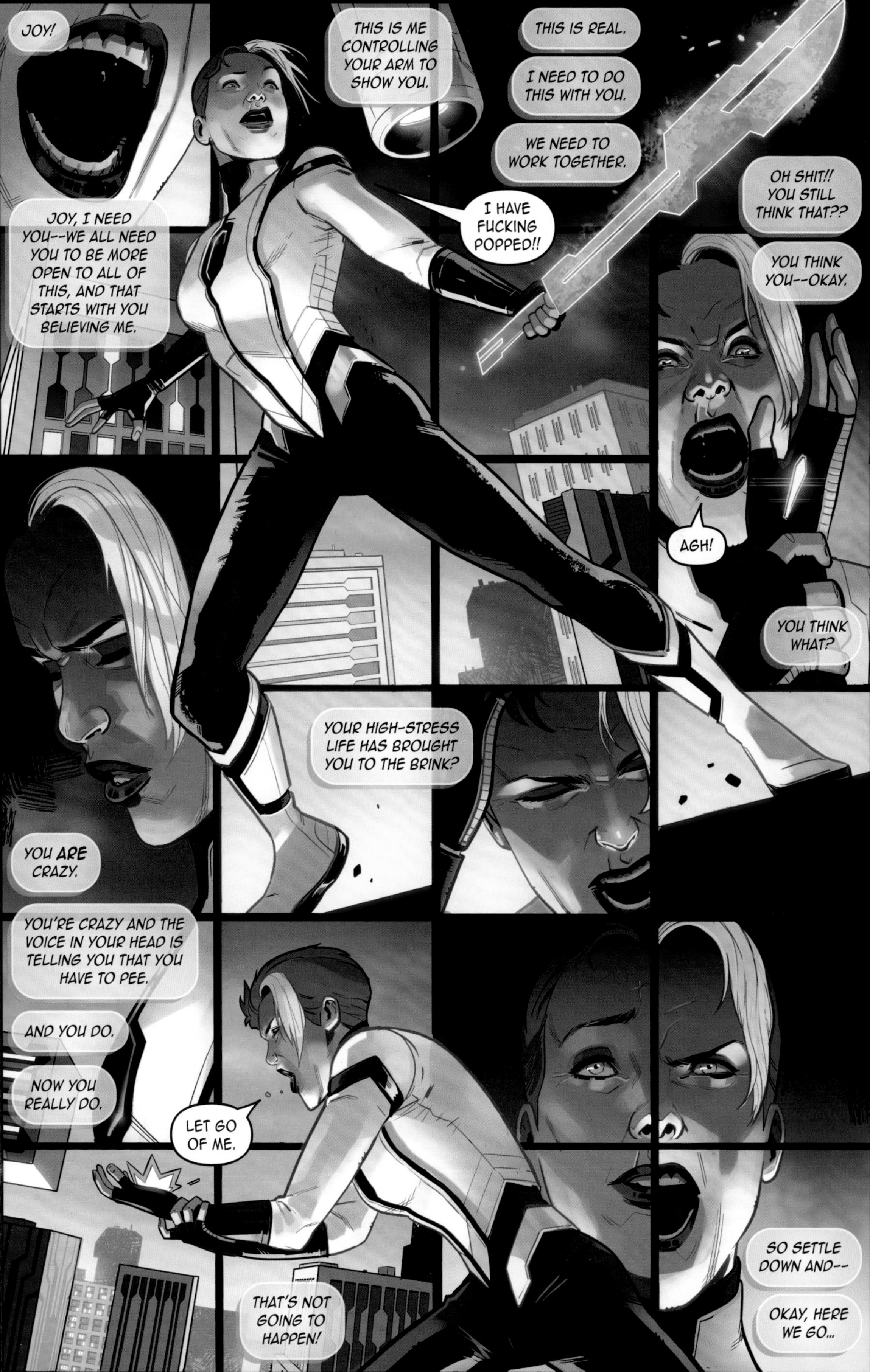
JOY!
THIS IS ME CONTROLLING YOUR ARM TO SHOW YOU.
THIS IS REAL.
I NEED TO DO THIS WITH YOU.
WE NEED TO WORK TOGETHER.
JOY, I NEED YOU--WE ALL NEED YOU TO BE MORE OPEN TO ALL OF THIS, AND THAT STARTS WITH YOU BELIEVING ME.
I HAVE FUCKING POPPED!!
OH SHIT!! YOU STILL THINK THAT??
YOU THINK YOU--OKAY.
AGH!
YOU THINK WHAT?
YOUR HIGH-STRESS LIFE HAS BROUGHT YOU TO THE BRINK?
YOU ARE CRAZY.
YOU'RE CRAZY AND THE VOICE IN YOUR HEAD IS TELLING YOU THAT YOU HAVE TO PEE.
AND YOU DO.
NOW YOU REALLY DO.
LET GO OF ME.
SO SETTLE DOWN AND--
THAT'S NOT GOING TO HAPPEN!
OKAY, HERE WE GO...

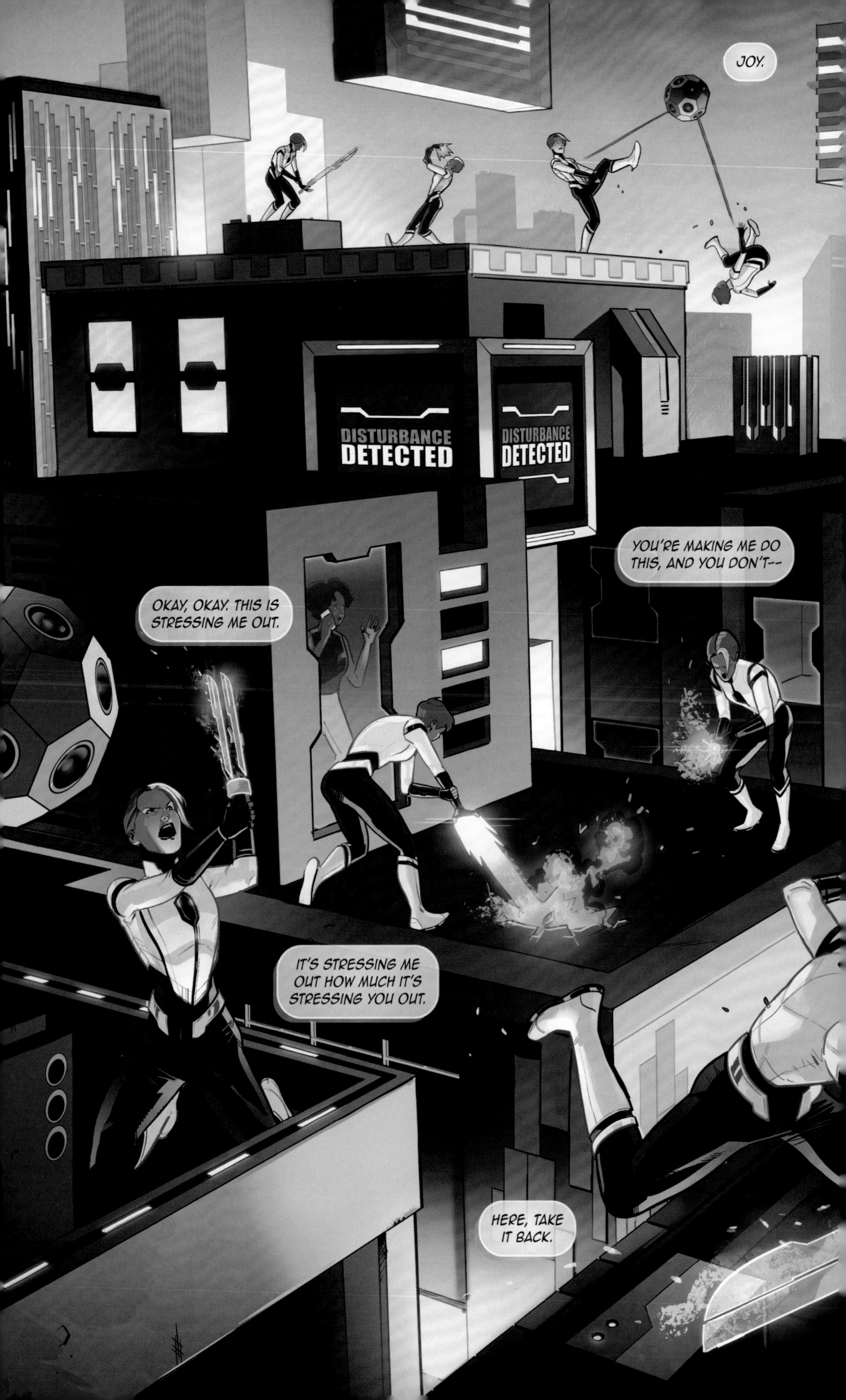
JOY.
DISTURBANCE DETECTED
DISTURBANCE DETECTED
YOU'RE MAKING ME DO THIS, AND YOU DON'T--
OKAY, OKAY. THIS IS STRESSING ME OUT.
IT'S STRESSING ME OUT HOW MUCH IT'S STRESSING YOU OUT.
HERE, TAKE IT BACK.

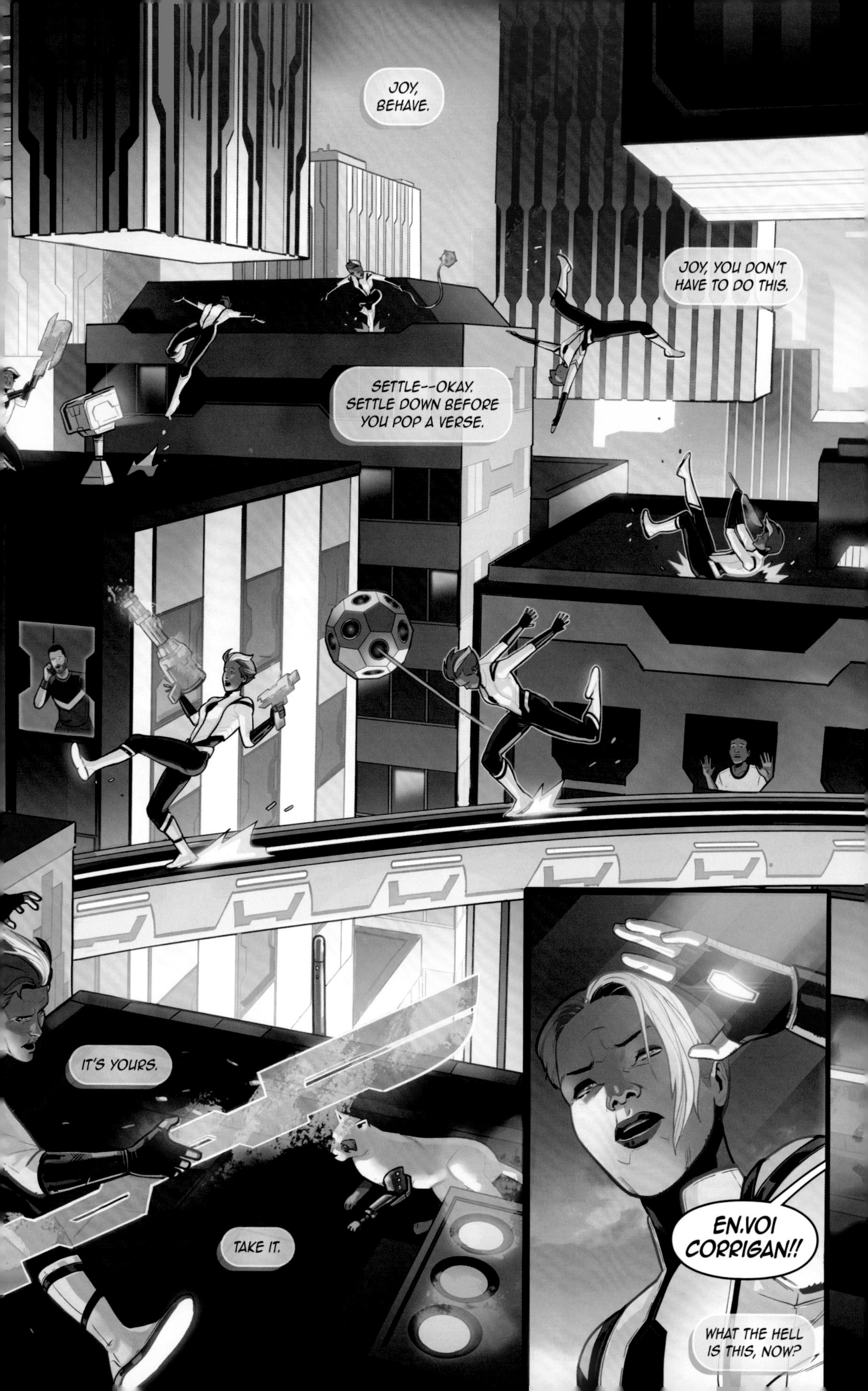
JOY, BEHAVE.
JOY, YOU DON'T HAVE TO DO THIS.
SETTLE--OKAY. SETTLE DOWN BEFORE YOU POP A VERSE.
IT'S YOURS.
TAKE IT.
EN.VOI CORRIGAN!!
WHAT THE HELL IS THIS, NOW?

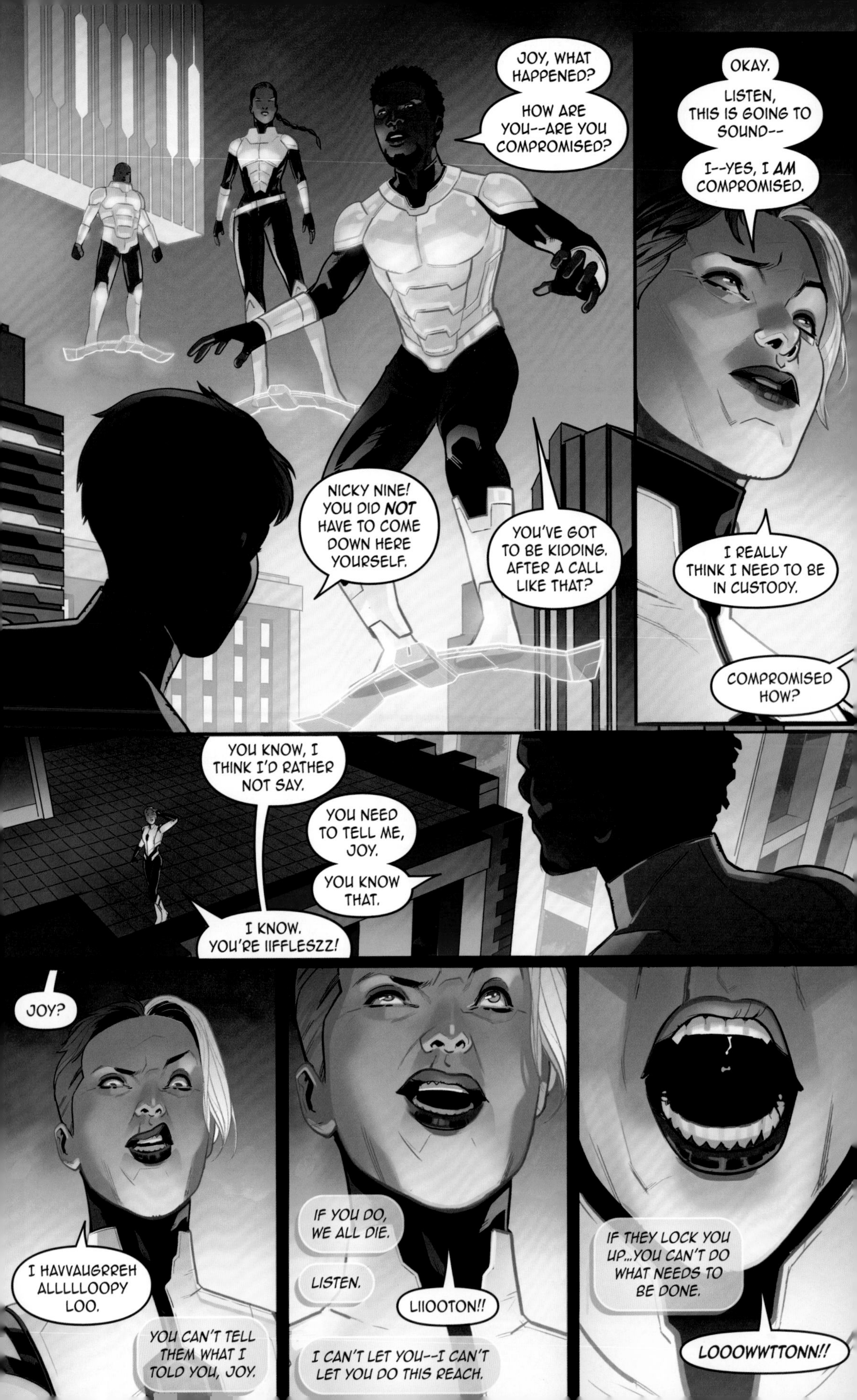
JOY, WHAT HAPPENED?
HOW ARE YOU--ARE YOU COMPROMISED?
NICKY NINE! YOU DID NOT HAVE TO COME DOWN HERE YOURSELF.
YOU'VE GOT TO BE KIDDING. AFTER A CALL LIKE THAT?
OKAY.
LISTEN, THIS IS GOING TO SOUND--
I--YES, I AM COMPROMISED.
I REALLY THINK I NEED TO BE IN CUSTODY.
COMPROMISED HOW?
YOU KNOW, I THINK I'D RATHER NOT SAY.
YOU NEED TO TELL ME, JOY.
YOU KNOW THAT.
I KNOW. YOU'RE IIFFLESZZ!
JOY?
I HAVVAUGRREH ALLLLLOOPY LOO.
YOU CAN'T TELL THEM WHAT I TOLD YOU, JOY.
IF YOU DO, WE ALL DIE.
LISTEN.
LIIOOTON!!
I CAN'T LET YOU--I CAN'T LET YOU DO THIS REACH.
IF THEY LOCK YOU UP...YOU CAN'T DO WHAT NEEDS TO BE DONE.
LOOOWWTTONN!!

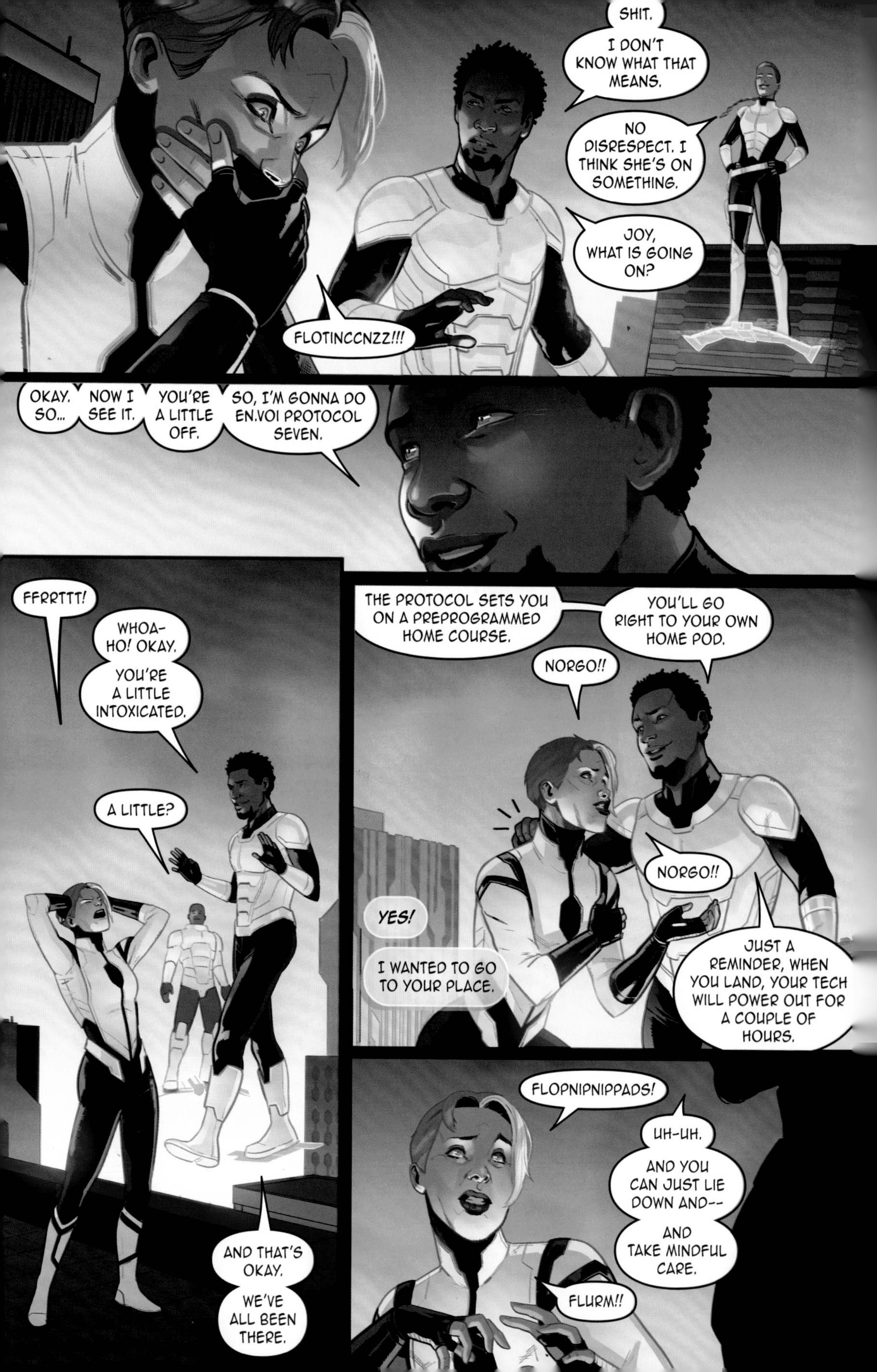
SHIT.
I DON'T KNOW WHAT THAT MEANS.
NO DISRESPECT. I THINK SHE'S ON SOMETHING.
JOY, WHAT IS GOING ON?
FLOTINCCNZZ!!!
OKAY. SO...
NOW I SEE IT.
YOU'RE A LITTLE OFF.
SO, I'M GONNA DO EN.VOI PROTOCOL SEVEN.
FFRRTTT!
WHOA-HO! OKAY.
YOU'RE A LITTLE INTOXICATED.
A LITTLE?
AND THAT'S OKAY.
WE'VE ALL BEEN THERE.
THE PROTOCOL SETS YOU ON A PREPROGRAMMED HOME COURSE.
YOU'LL GO RIGHT TO YOUR OWN HOME POD.
NORGO!!
NORGO!!
YES!
I WANTED TO GO TO YOUR PLACE.
JUST A REMINDER, WHEN YOU LAND, YOUR TECH WILL POWER OUT FOR A COUPLE OF HOURS.
FLOPNIPNIPPADS!
UH-UH.
AND YOU CAN JUST LIE DOWN AND--
AND TAKE MINDFUL CARE.
FLURM!!

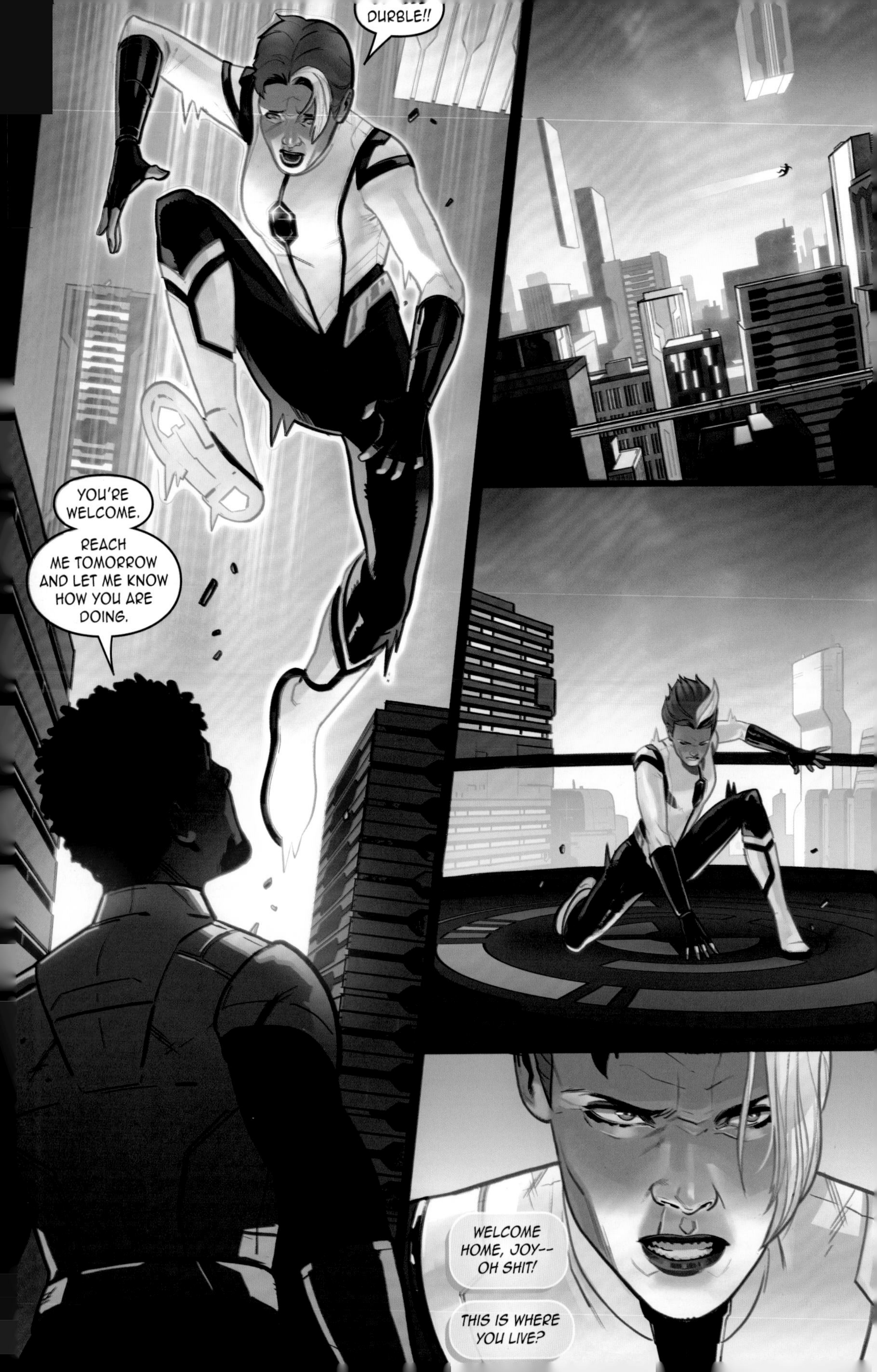
DURBLE!!
YOU'RE WELCOME.
REACH ME TOMORROW AND LET ME KNOW HOW YOU ARE DOING.
WELCOME HOME, JOY-- OH SHIT!
THIS IS WHERE YOU LIVE?

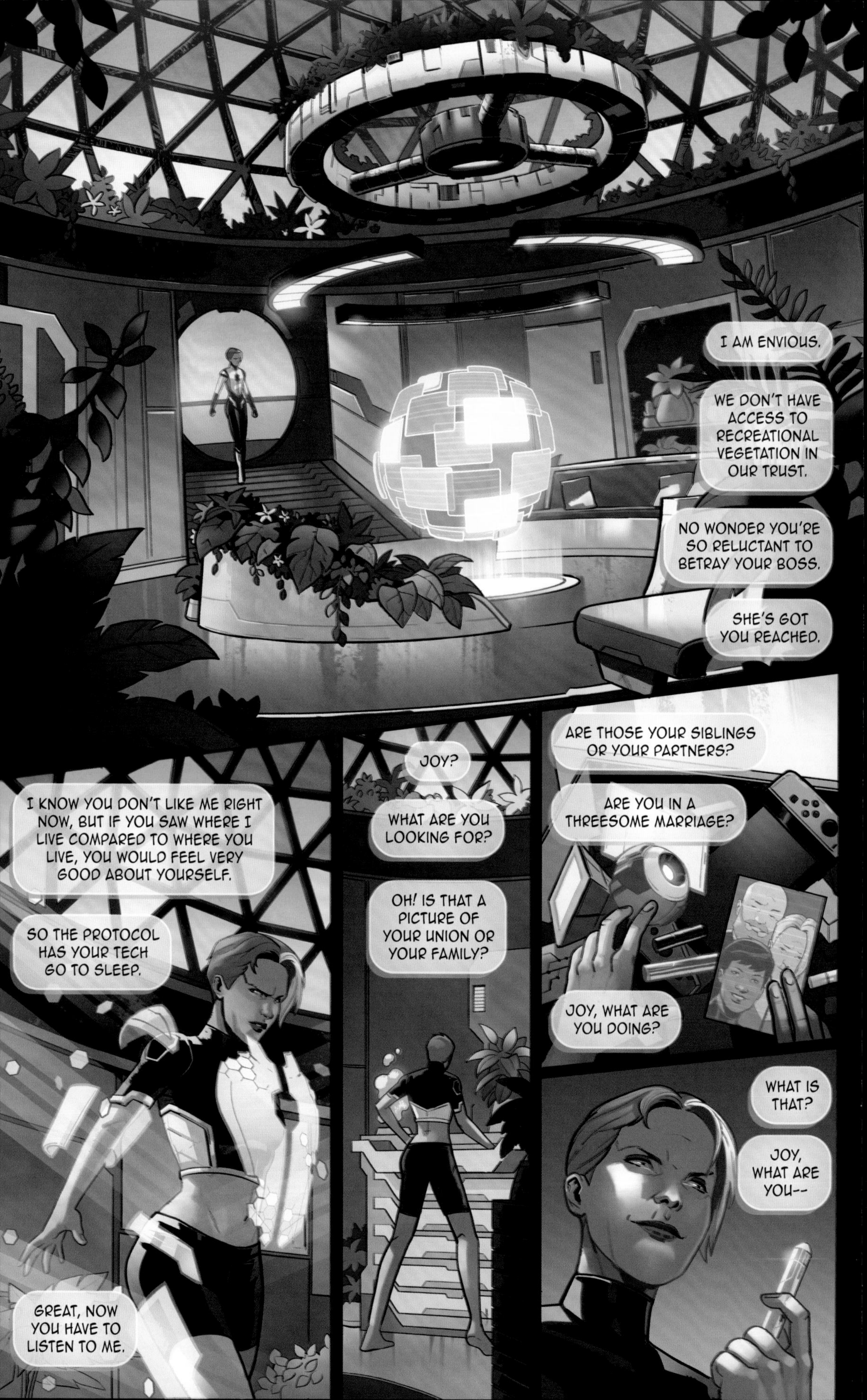
I AM ENVIOUS.
WE DON'T HAVE ACCESS TO RECREATIONAL VEGETATION IN OUR TRUST.
NO WONDER YOU'RE SO RELUCTANT TO BETRAY YOUR BOSS.
SHE'S GOT YOU REACHED.
I KNOW YOU DON'T LIKE ME RIGHT NOW, BUT IF YOU SAW WHERE I LIVE COMPARED TO WHERE YOU LIVE, YOU WOULD FEEL VERY GOOD ABOUT YOURSELF.
SO THE PROTOCOL HAS YOUR TECH GO TO SLEEP.
GREAT, NOW YOU HAVE TO LISTEN TO ME.
JOY?
WHAT ARE YOU LOOKING FOR?
OH! IS THAT A PICTURE OF YOUR UNION OR YOUR FAMILY?
ARE THOSE YOUR SIBLINGS OR YOUR PARTNERS?
ARE YOU IN A THREESOME MARRIAGE?
JOY, WHAT ARE YOU DOING?
WHAT IS THAT?
JOY, WHAT ARE YOU--

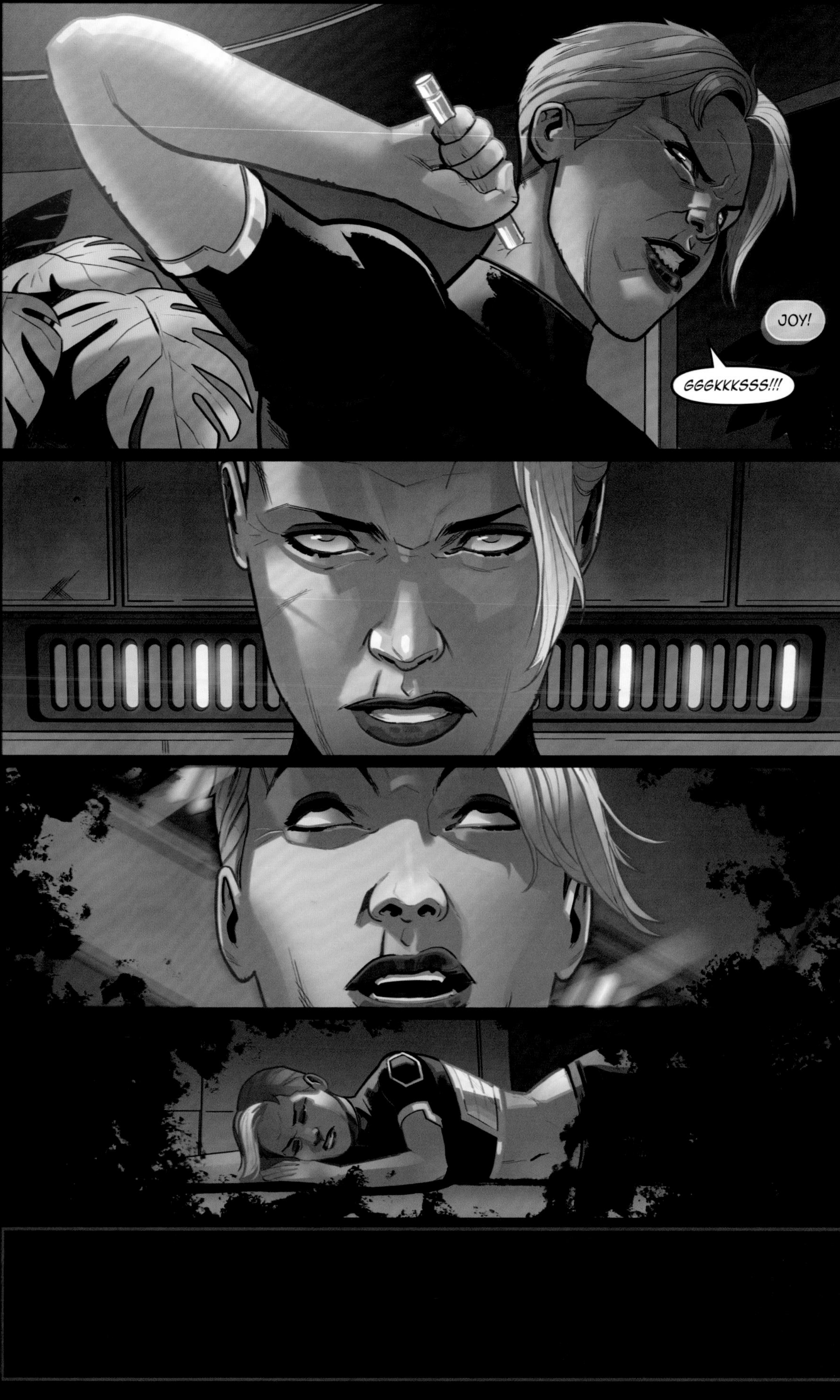
JOY!
GGGKKKSSS!!!

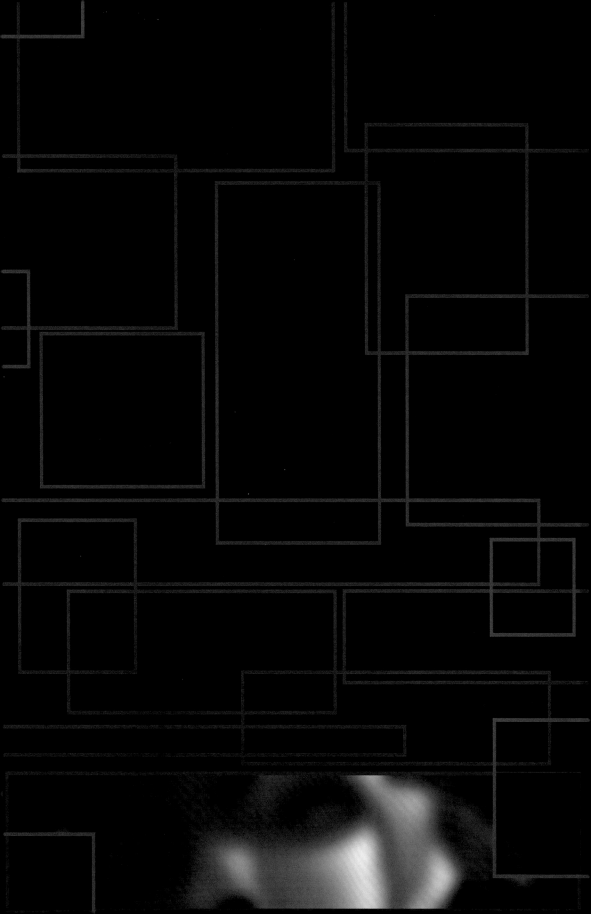

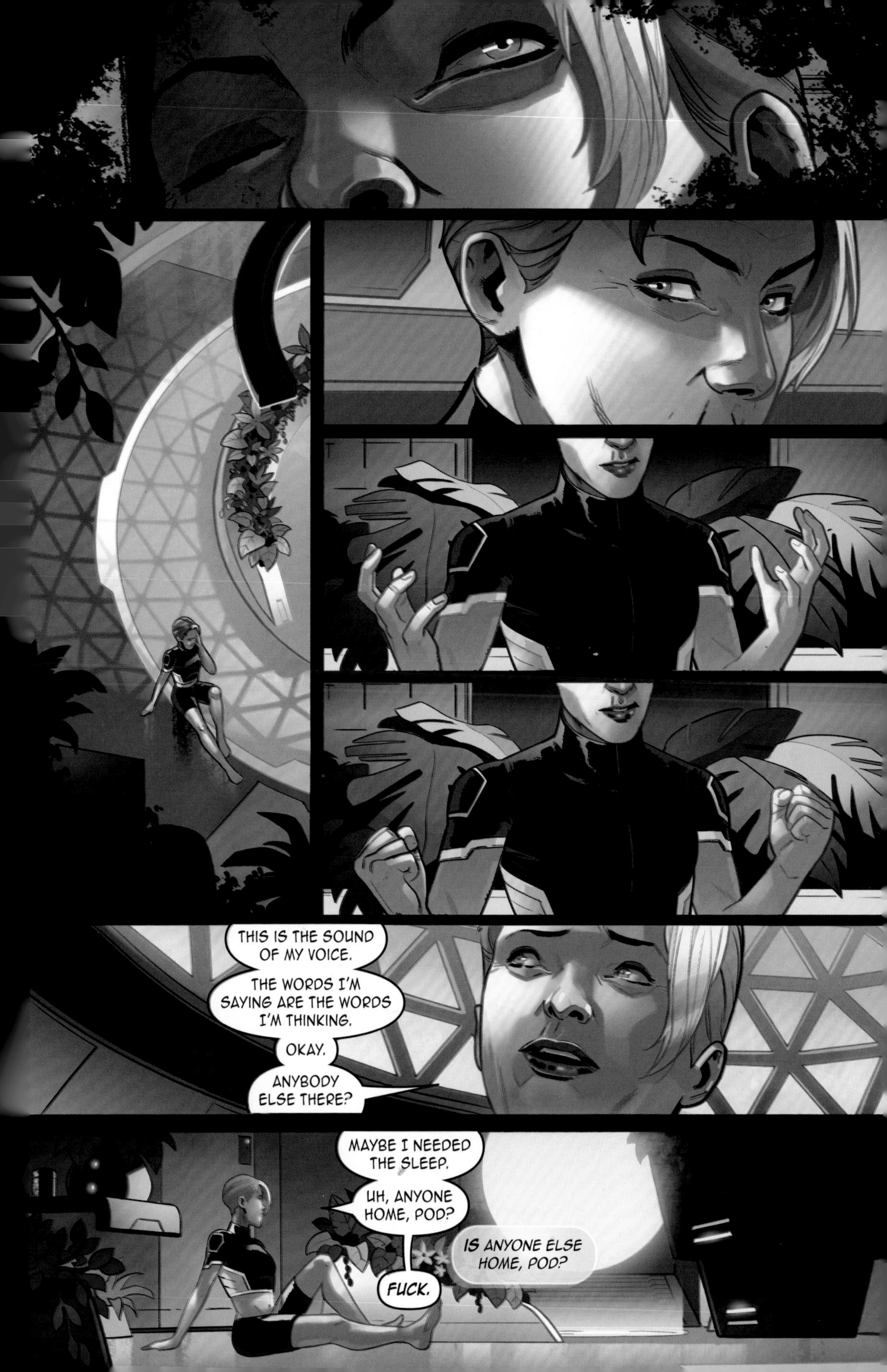
THIS IS THE SOUND OF MY VOICE.
THE WORDS I'M SAYING ARE THE WORDS I'M THINKING.
OKAY.
ANYBODY ELSE THERE?
MAYBE I NEEDED THE SLEEP.
UH, ANYONE HOME, POD?
FUCK.
IS ANYONE ELSE HOME, POD?

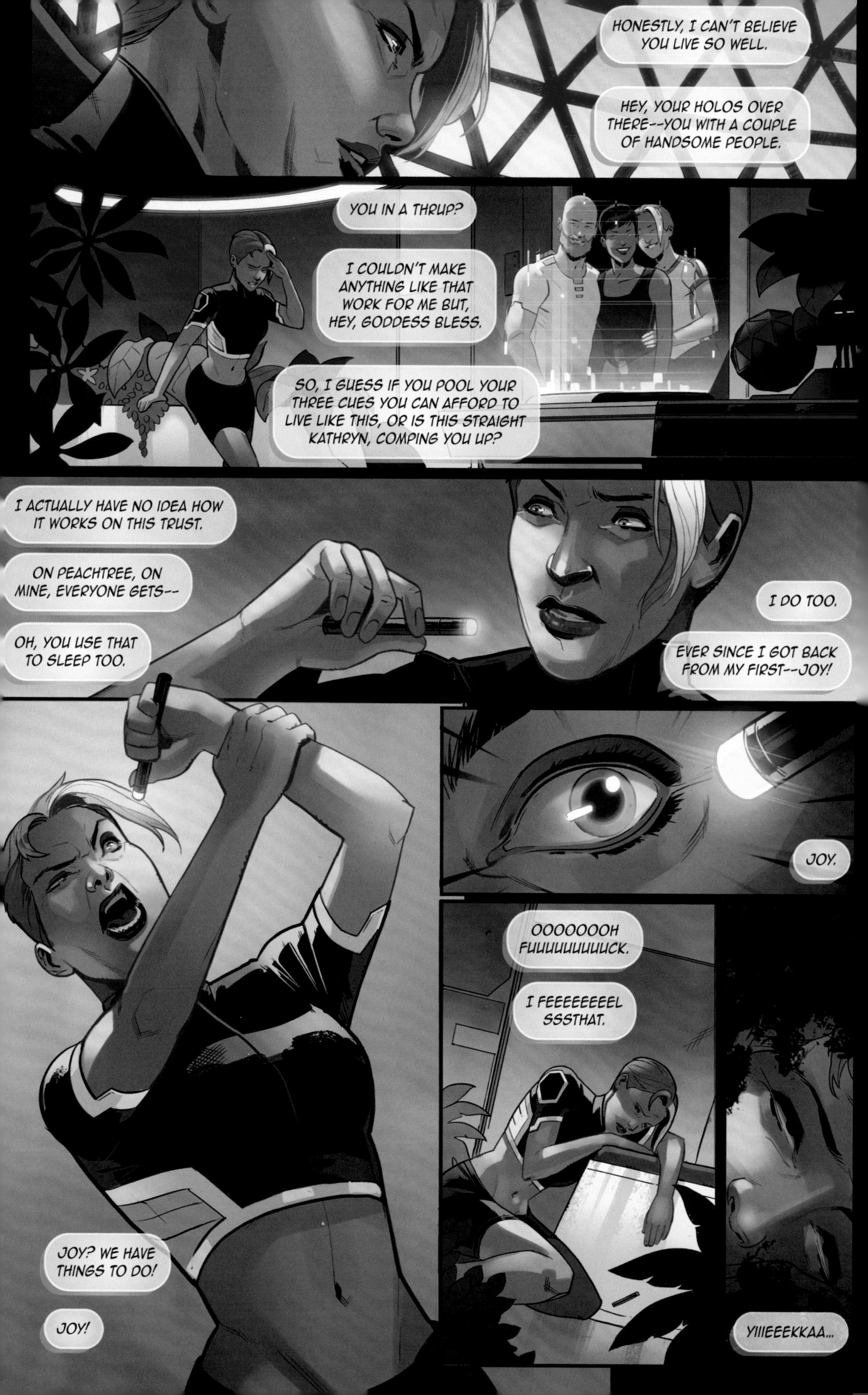

HONESTLY, I CAN'T BELIEVE YOU LIVE SO WELL.
HEY, YOUR HOLOS OVER THERE--YOU WITH A COUPLE OF HANDSOME PEOPLE.
YOU IN A THRUP?
I COULDN'T MAKE ANYTHING LIKE THAT WORK FOR ME BUT, HEY, GODDESS BLESS.
SO, I GUESS IF YOU POOL YOUR THREE CUES YOU CAN AFFORD TO LIVE LIKE THIS, OR IS THIS STRAIGHT KATHRYN, COMPING YOU UP?
I ACTUALLY HAVE NO IDEA HOW IT WORKS ON THIS TRUST.
ON PEACHTREE, ON MINE, EVERYONE GETS--
OH, YOU USE THAT TO SLEEP TOO.
I DO TOO.
EVER SINCE I GOT BACK FROM MY FIRST--JOY!
JOY.
OOOOOOOH FUUUUUUUUUCK.
I FEEEEEEEEL SSSTHAT.
JOY? WE HAVE THINGS TO DO!
JOY!
YIIIEEEKKAA...

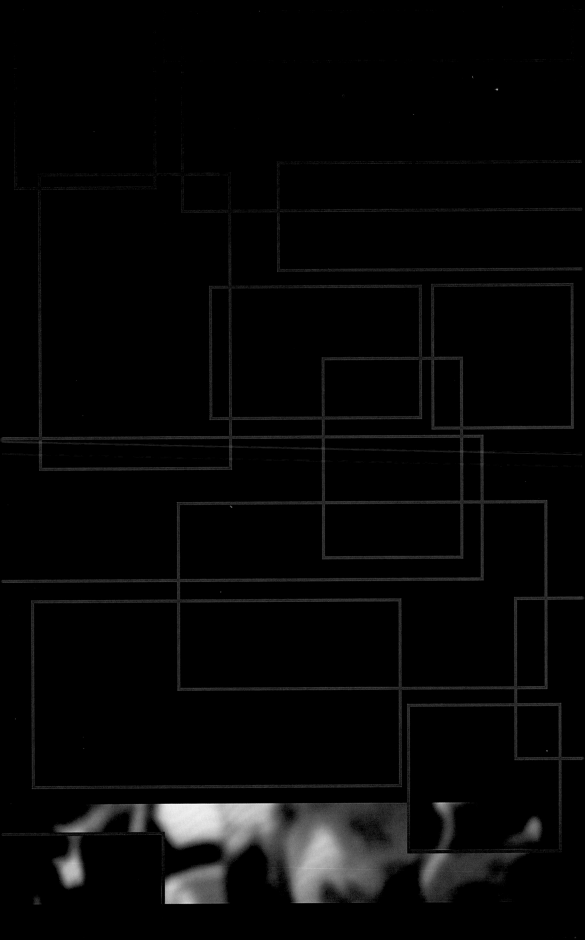

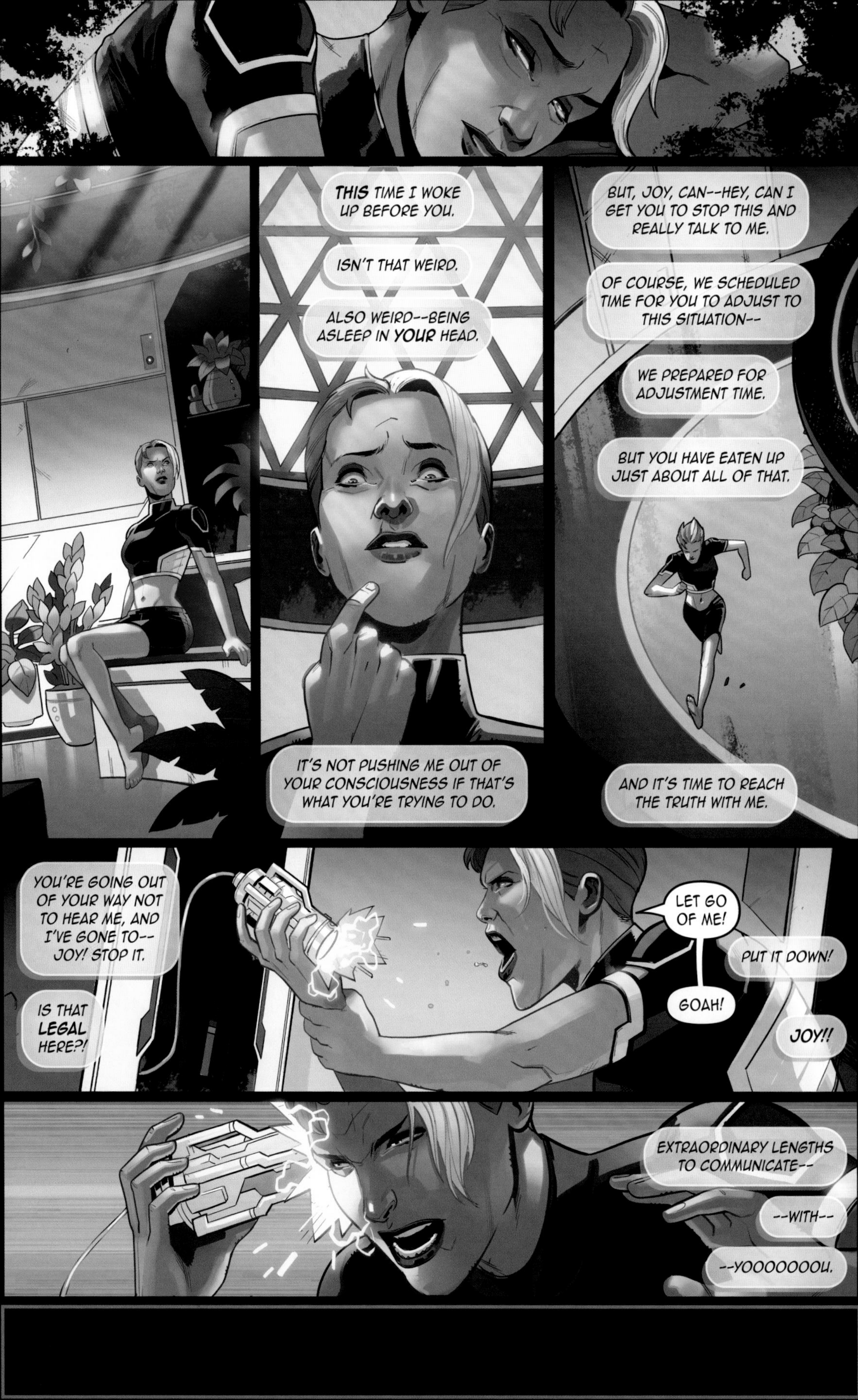
THIS TIME I WOKE UP BEFORE YOU.
ISN'T THAT WEIRD.
ALSO WEIRD--BEING ASLEEP IN YOUR HEAD.
IT'S NOT PUSHING ME OUT OF YOUR CONSCIOUSNESS IF THAT'S WHAT YOU'RE TRYING TO DO.
BUT, JOY, CAN--HEY, CAN I GET YOU TO STOP THIS AND REALLY TALK TO ME.
OF COURSE, WE SCHEDULED TIME FOR YOU TO ADJUST TO THIS SITUATION--
WE PREPARED FOR ADJUSTMENT TIME.
BUT YOU HAVE EATEN UP JUST ABOUT ALL OF THAT.
AND IT'S TIME TO REACH THE TRUTH WITH ME.
YOU'RE GOING OUT OF YOUR WAY NOT TO HEAR ME, AND I'VE GONE TO-- JOY! STOP IT.
IS THAT LEGAL HERE?!
LET GO OF ME!
GOAH!
PUT IT DOWN!
JOY!!
EXTRAORDINARY LENGTHS TO COMMUNICATE--
--WITH--
--YOOOOOOOU.

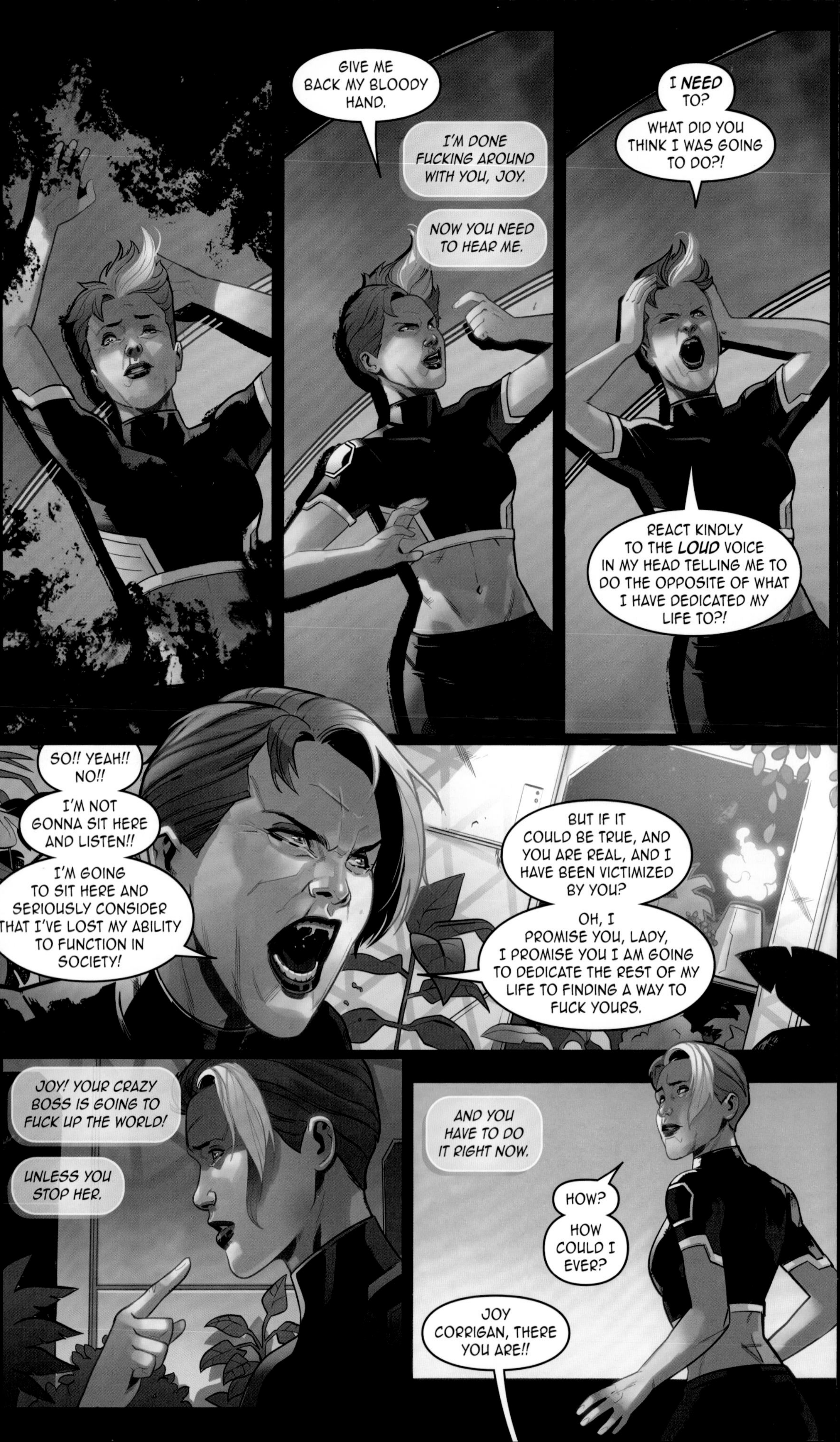

GIVE ME BACK MY BLOODY HAND.
I'M DONE FUCKING AROUND WITH YOU, JOY.
NOW YOU NEED TO HEAR ME.
I NEED TO?
WHAT DID YOU THINK I WAS GOING TO DO?!
REACT KINDLY TO THE LOUD VOICE IN MY HEAD TELLING ME TO DO THE OPPOSITE OF WHAT I HAVE DEDICATED MY LIFE TO?!
SO!! YEAH!! NO!!
I'M NOT GONNA SIT HERE AND LISTEN!!
I'M GOING TO SIT HERE AND SERIOUSLY CONSIDER THAT I'VE LOST MY ABILITY TO FUNCTION IN SOCIETY!
BUT IF IT COULD BE TRUE, AND YOU ARE REAL, AND I HAVE BEEN VICTIMIZED BY YOU?
OH, I PROMISE YOU, LADY, I PROMISE YOU I AM GOING TO DEDICATE THE REST OF MY LIFE TO FINDING A WAY TO FUCK YOURS.
JOY! YOUR CRAZY BOSS IS GOING TO FUCK UP THE WORLD!
UNLESS YOU STOP HER.
AND YOU HAVE TO DO IT RIGHT NOW.
HOW?
HOW COULD I EVER?
JOY CORRIGAN, THERE YOU ARE!!

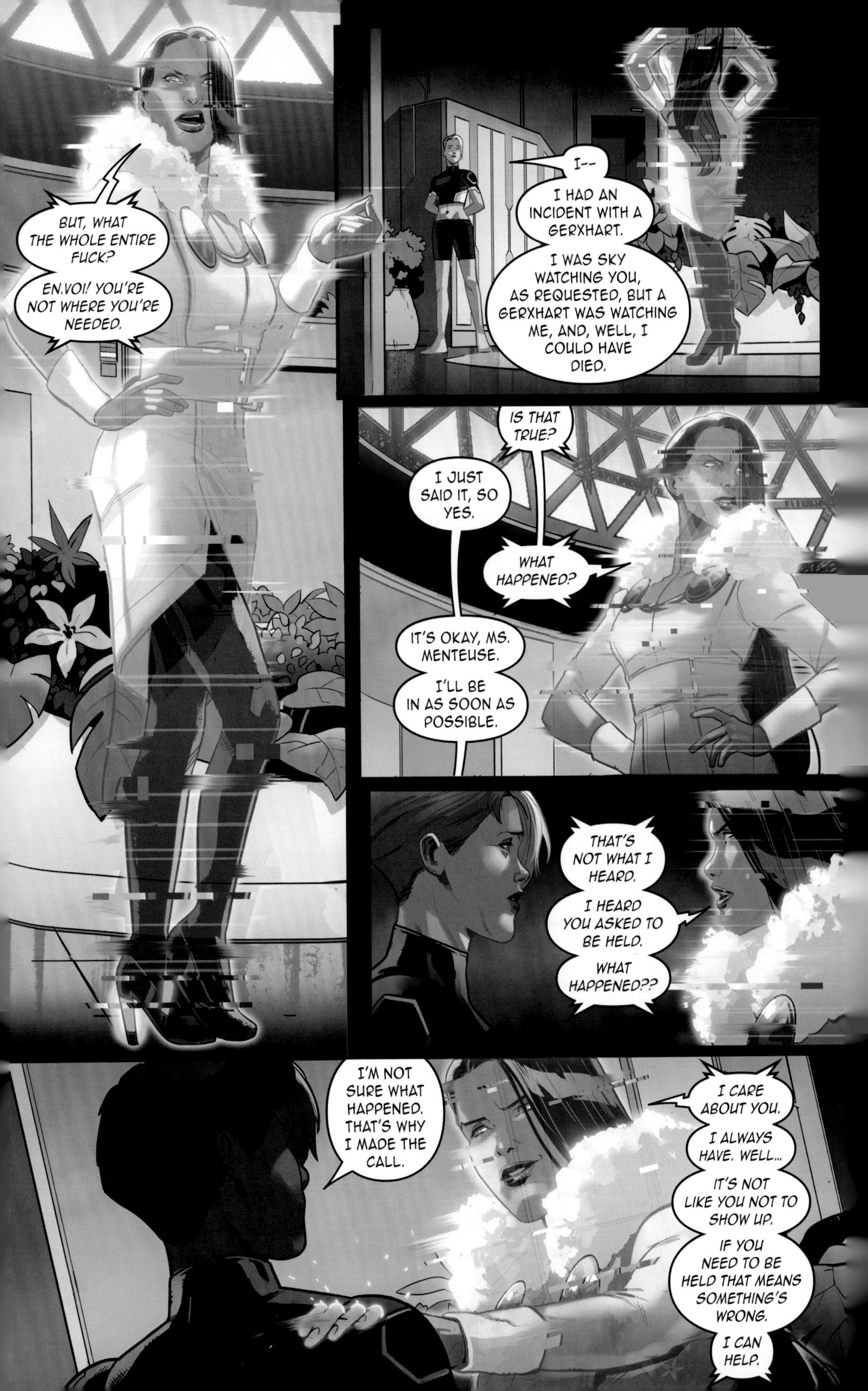

BUT, WHAT THE WHOLE ENTIRE FUCK?
EN.VOI! YOU'RE NOT WHERE YOU'RE NEEDED.
I--
I HAD AN INCIDENT WITH A GERXHART.
I WAS SKY WATCHING YOU, AS REQUESTED, BUT A GERXHART WAS WATCHING ME, AND, WELL, I COULD HAVE DIED.
IS THAT TRUE?
I JUST SAID IT, SO YES.
WHAT HAPPENED?
IT'S OKAY, MS. MENTEUSE.
I'LL BE IN AS SOON AS POSSIBLE.
THAT'S NOT WHAT I HEARD.
I HEARD YOU ASKED TO BE HELD.
WHAT HAPPENED??
I'M NOT SURE WHAT HAPPENED. THAT'S WHY I MADE THE CALL.
I CARE ABOUT YOU.
I ALWAYS HAVE. WELL...
IT'S NOT LIKE YOU NOT TO SHOW UP.
IF YOU NEED TO BE HELD THAT MEANS SOMETHING'S WRONG.
I CAN HELP.

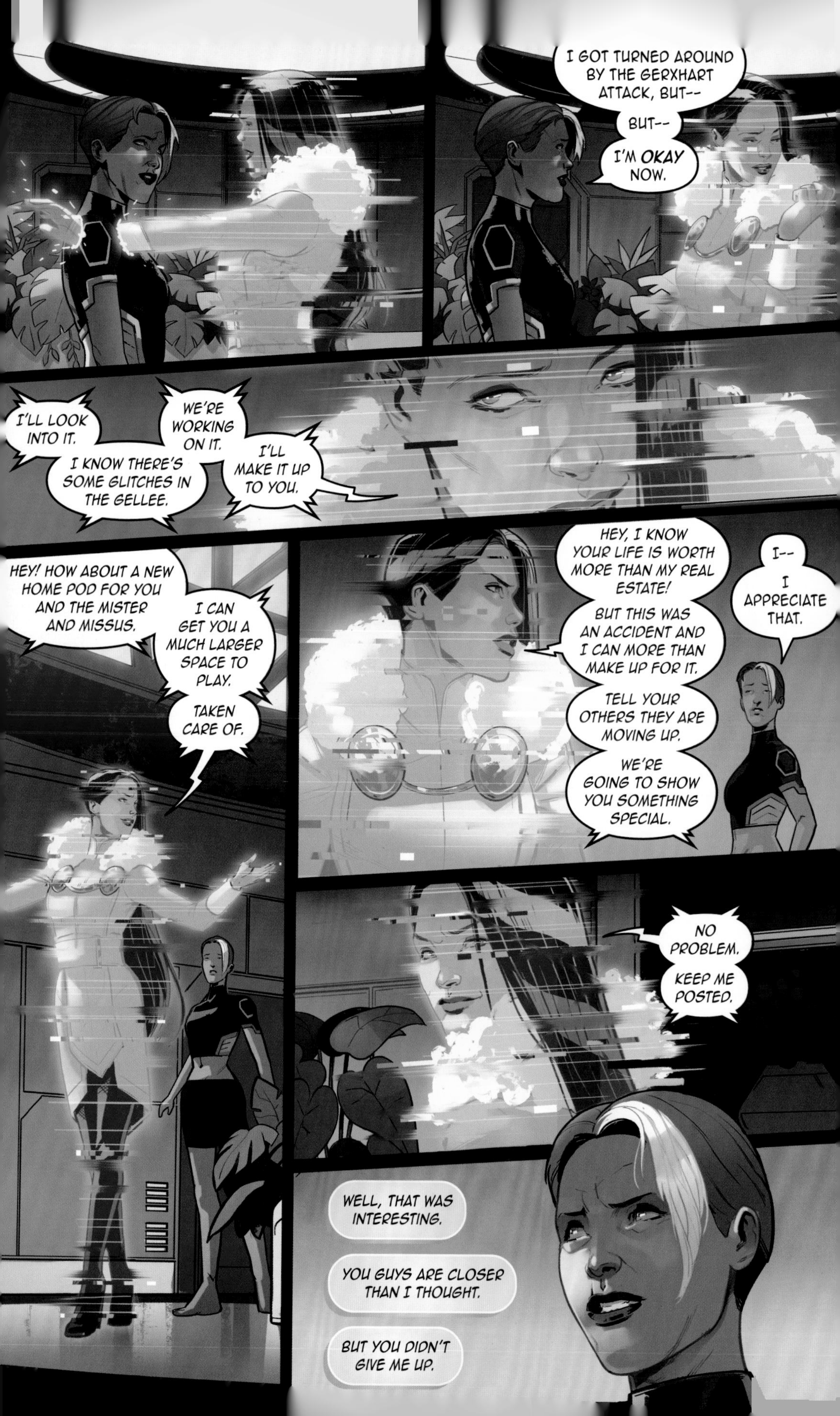
I GOT TURNED AROUND BY THE GERXHART ATTACK, BUT--
BUT--
I'M **OKAY** NOW.
I'LL LOOK INTO IT.
I KNOW THERE'S SOME GLITCHES IN THE GELLEE.
WE'RE WORKING ON IT.
I'LL MAKE IT UP TO YOU.
HEY! HOW ABOUT A NEW HOME POD FOR YOU AND THE MISTER AND MISSUS.
I CAN GET YOU A MUCH LARGER SPACE TO PLAY.
TAKEN CARE OF.
HEY, I KNOW YOUR LIFE IS WORTH MORE THAN MY REAL ESTATE!
BUT THIS WAS AN ACCIDENT AND I CAN MORE THAN MAKE UP FOR IT.
TELL YOUR OTHERS THEY ARE MOVING UP.
WE'RE GOING TO SHOW YOU SOMETHING SPECIAL.
I-- I APPRECIATE THAT.
NO PROBLEM.
KEEP ME POSTED.
WELL, THAT WAS INTERESTING.
YOU GUYS ARE CLOSER THAN I THOUGHT.
BUT YOU DIDN'T GIVE ME UP.

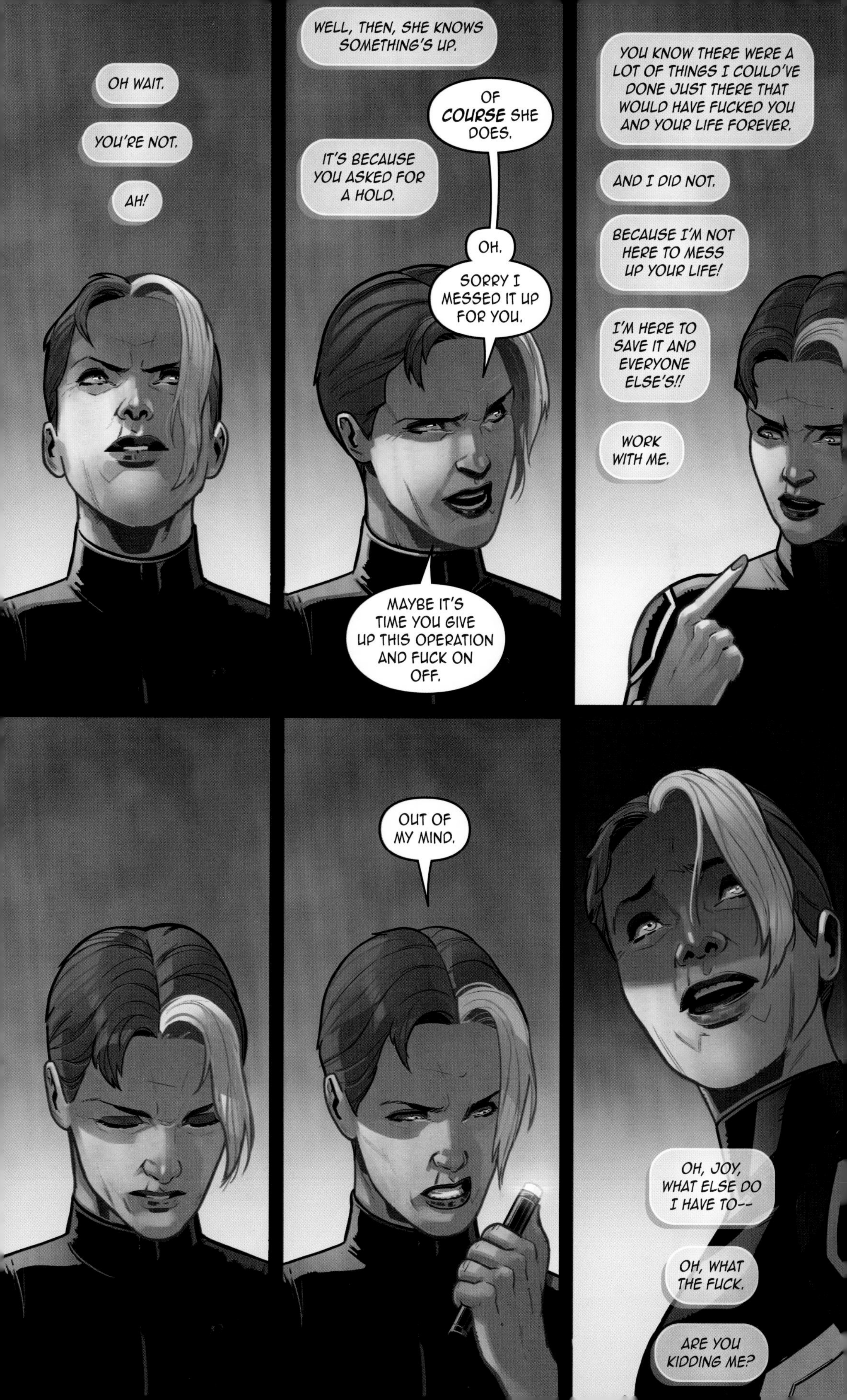
OH WAIT.
YOU'RE NOT.
AH!
WELL, THEN, SHE KNOWS SOMETHING'S UP.
OF COURSE SHE DOES.
IT'S BECAUSE YOU ASKED FOR A HOLD.
OH.
SORRY I MESSED IT UP FOR YOU.
MAYBE IT'S TIME YOU GIVE UP THIS OPERATION AND FUCK ON OFF.
YOU KNOW THERE WERE A LOT OF THINGS I COULD'VE DONE JUST THERE THAT WOULD HAVE FUCKED YOU AND YOUR LIFE FOREVER.
AND I DID NOT.
BECAUSE I'M NOT HERE TO MESS UP YOUR LIFE!
I'M HERE TO SAVE IT AND EVERYONE ELSE'S!!
WORK WITH ME.
OUT OF MY MIND.
OH, JOY, WHAT ELSE DO I HAVE TO--
OH, WHAT THE FUCK.
ARE YOU KIDDING ME?

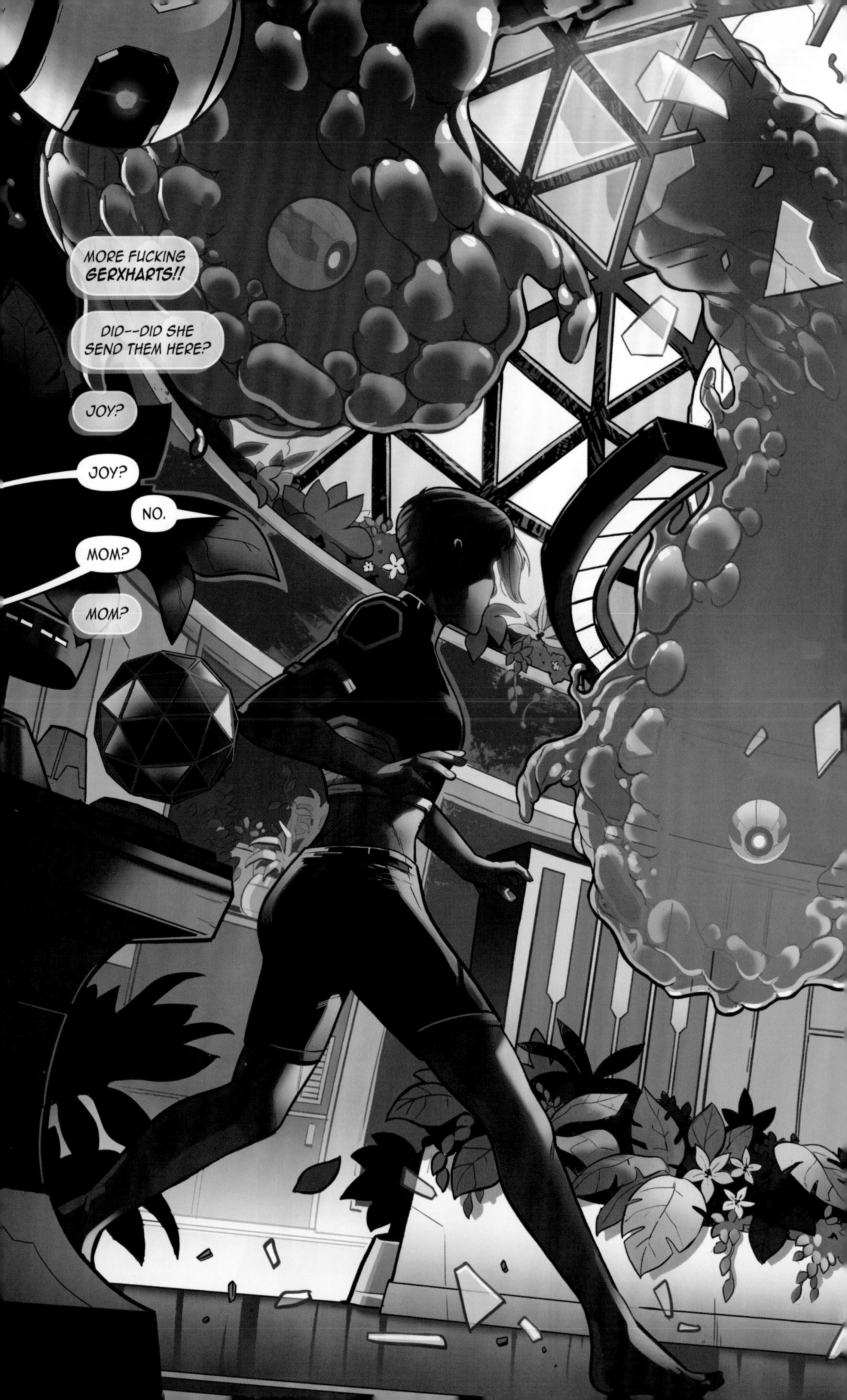
MORE FUCKING GERXHARTS!!
DID--DID SHE SEND THEM HERE?
JOY?
JOY?
NO.
MOM?
MOM?

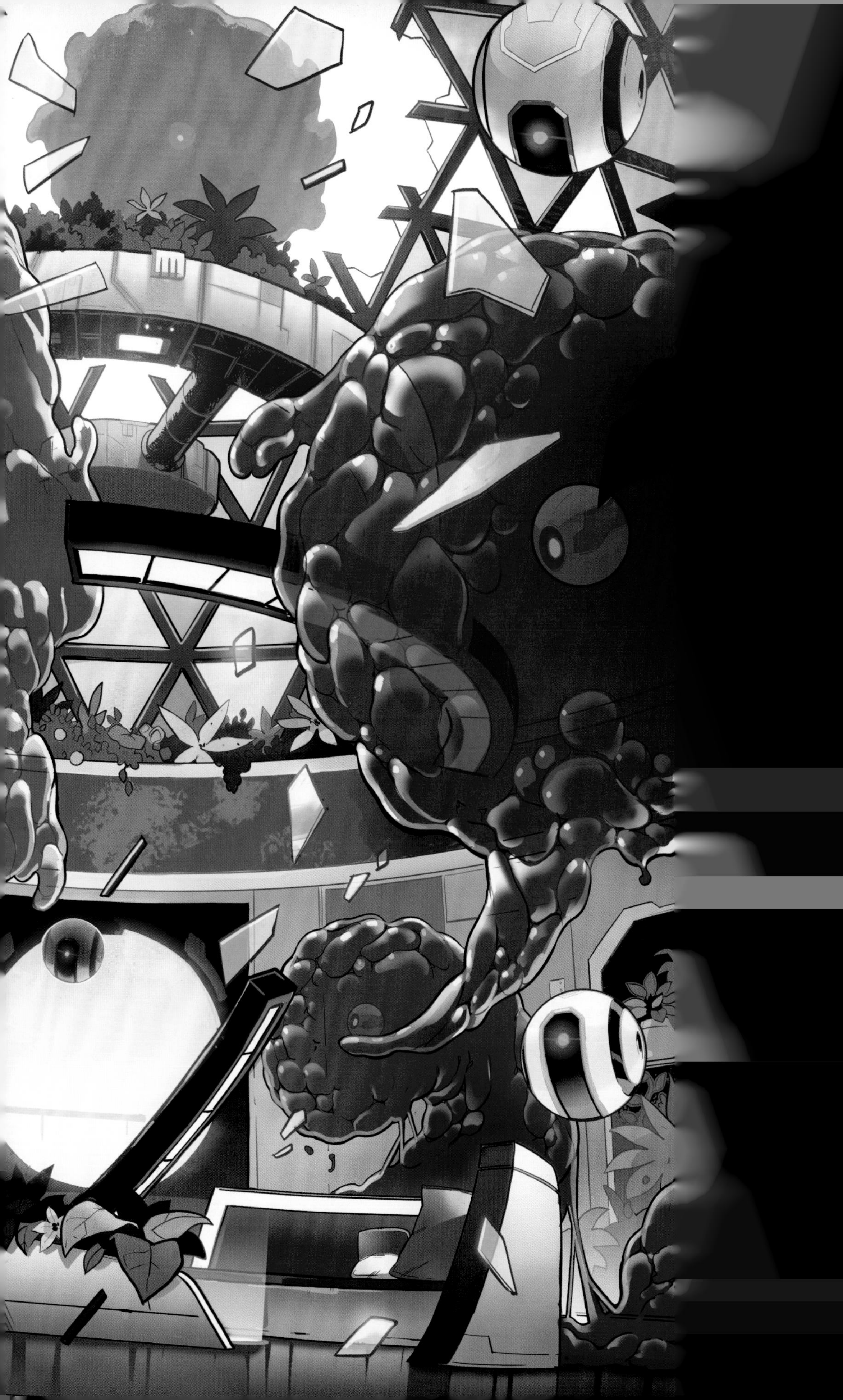

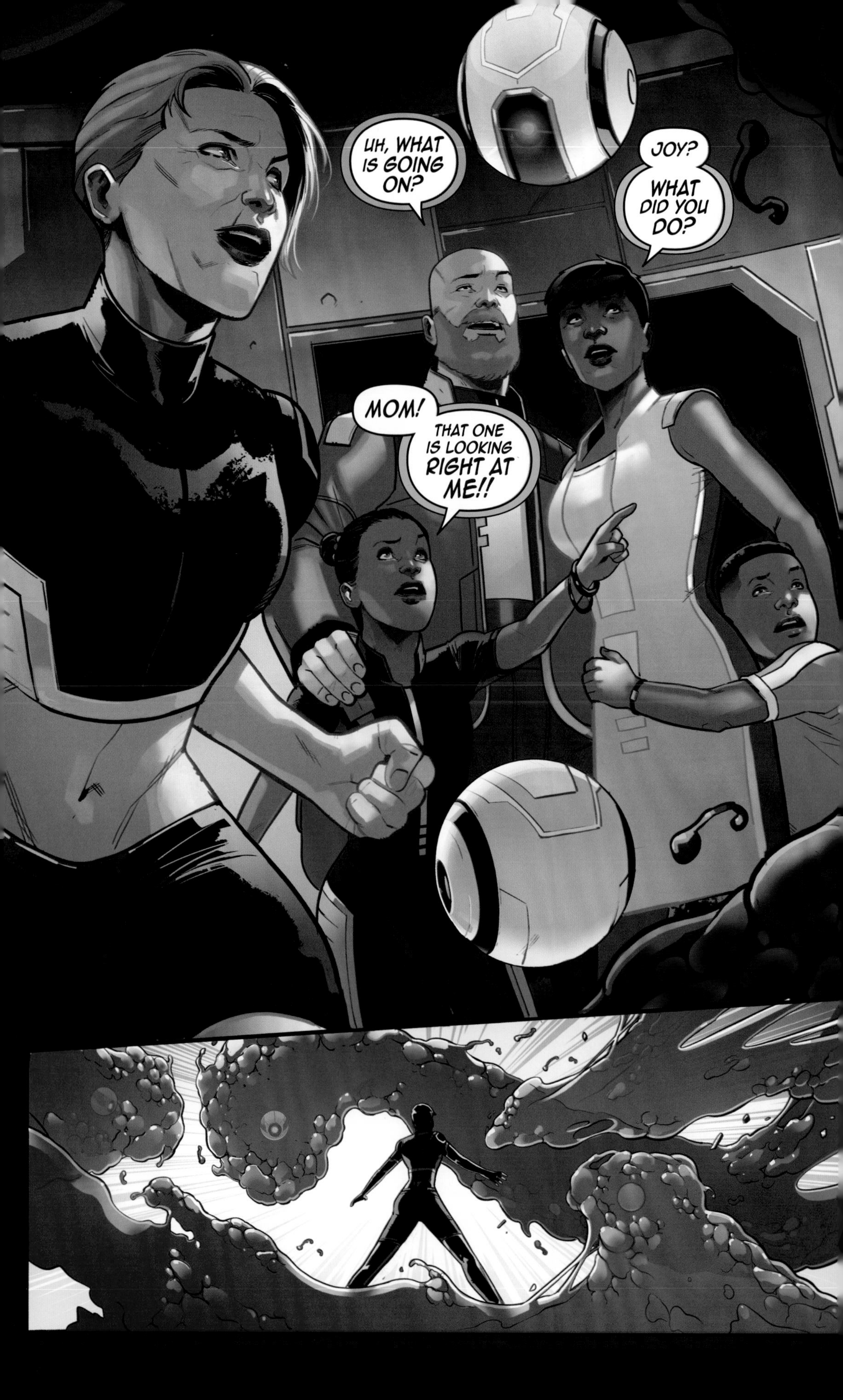
UH, WHAT IS GOING ON?
JOY?
WHAT DID YOU DO?
MOM!
THAT ONE IS LOOKING RIGHT AT ME!!

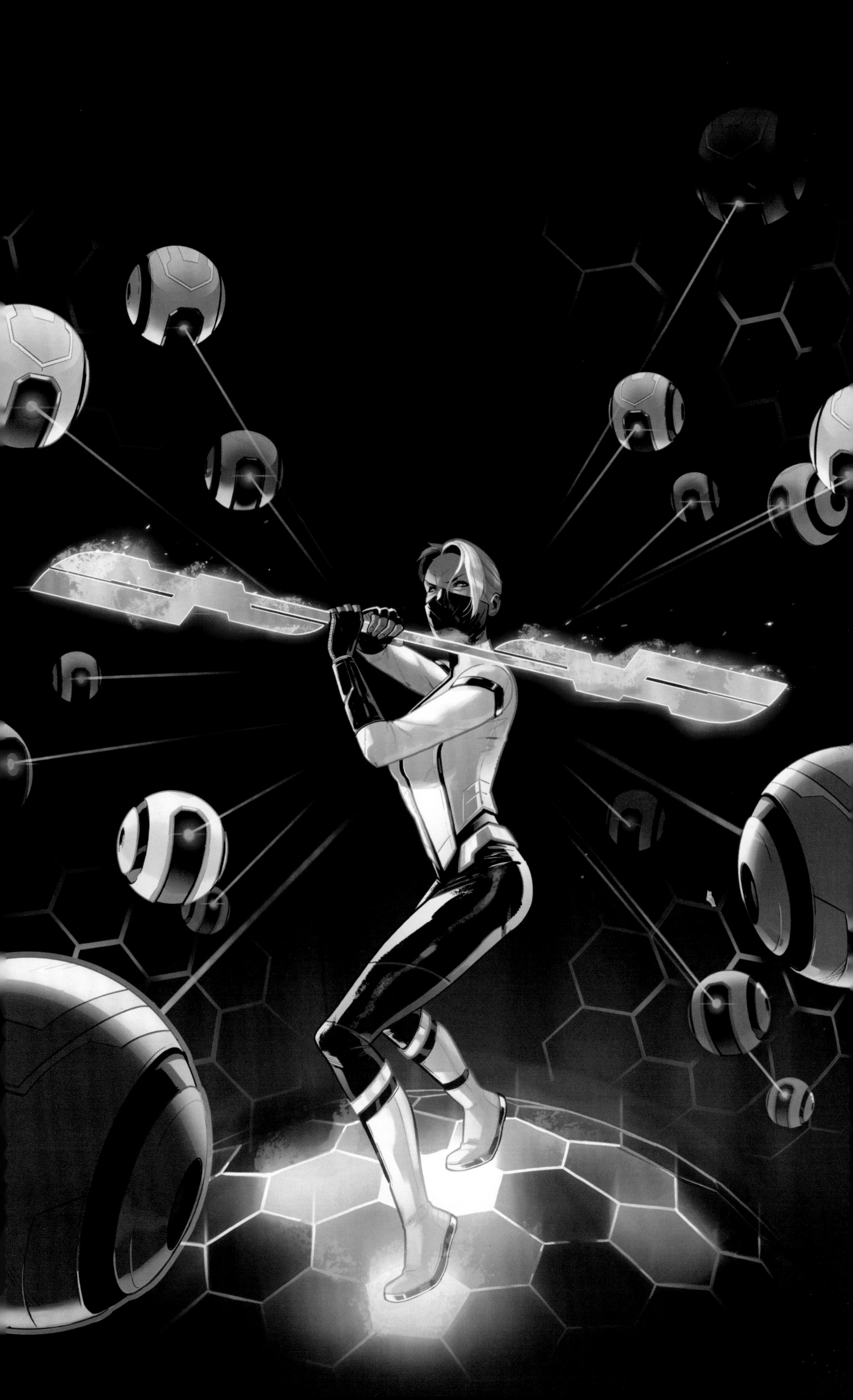

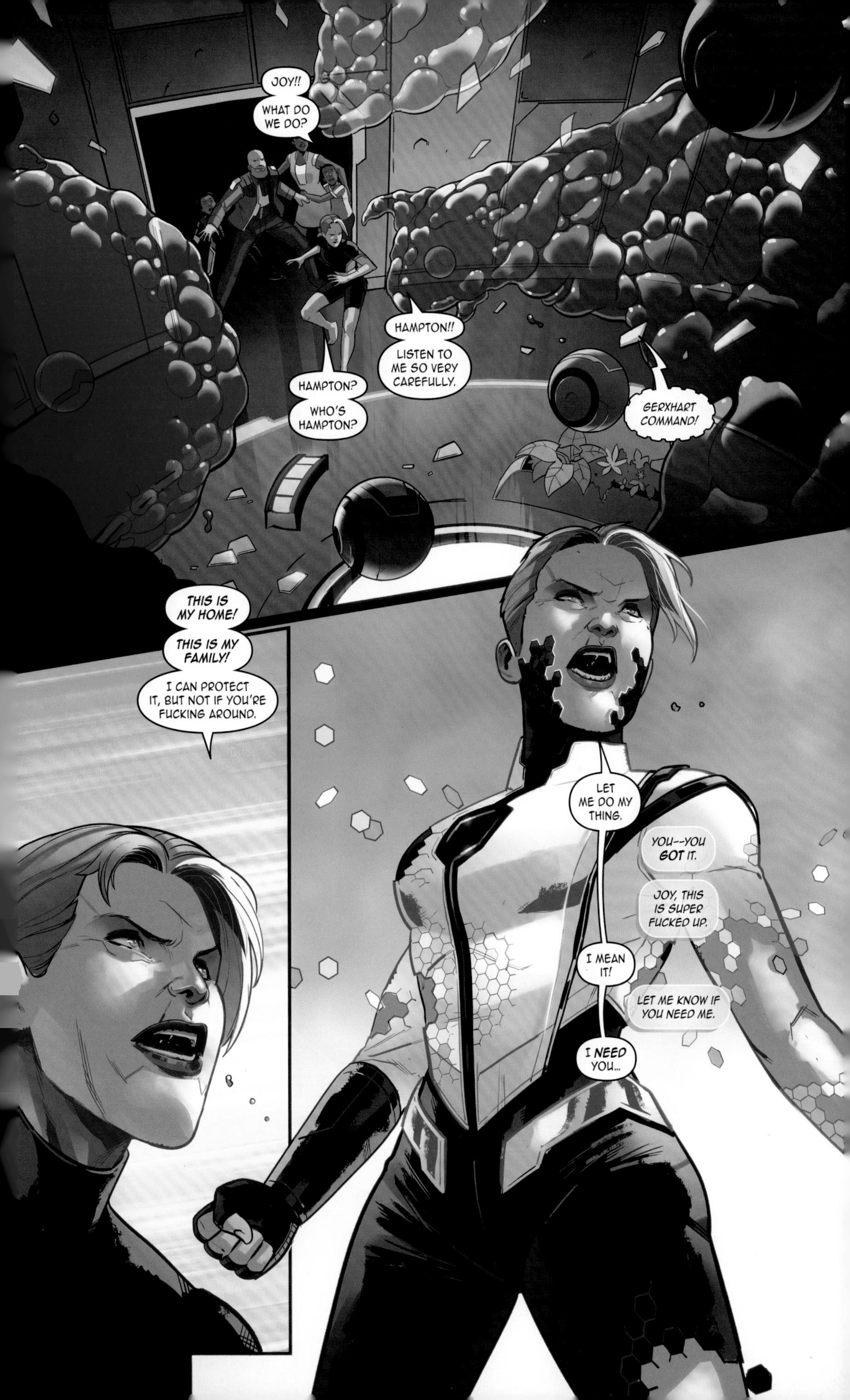
JOY!!
WHAT DO WE DO?
HAMPTON!!
LISTEN TO ME SO VERY CAREFULLY.
HAMPTON?
WHO'S HAMPTON?
GERXHART COMMAND!
THIS IS MY HOME!
THIS IS MY FAMILY!
I CAN PROTECT IT, BUT NOT IF YOU'RE FUCKING AROUND.
LET ME DO MY THING.
YOU--YOU GOT IT.
JOY, THIS IS SUPER FUCKED UP.
I MEAN IT!
LET ME KNOW IF YOU NEED ME.
I NEED YOU...

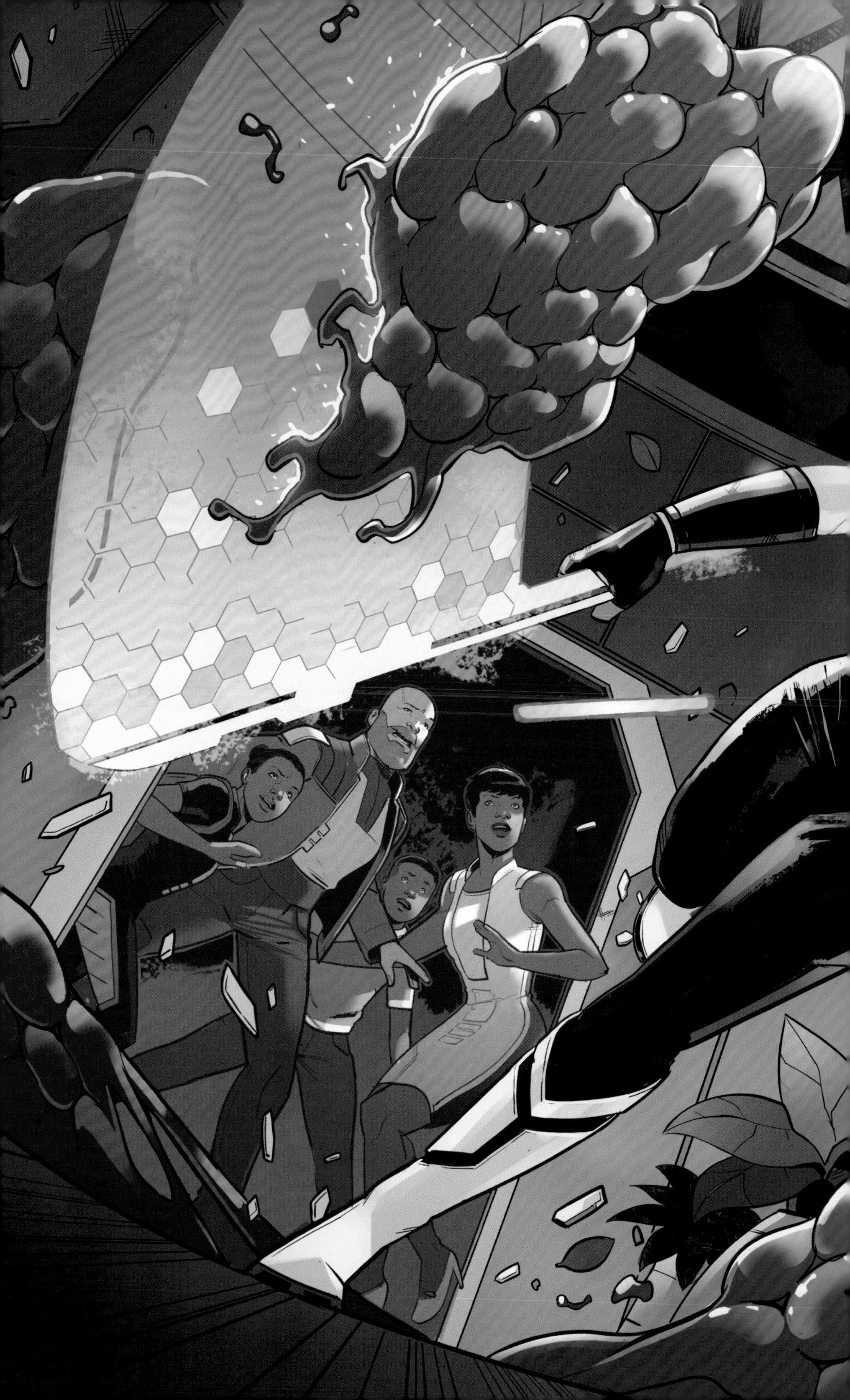

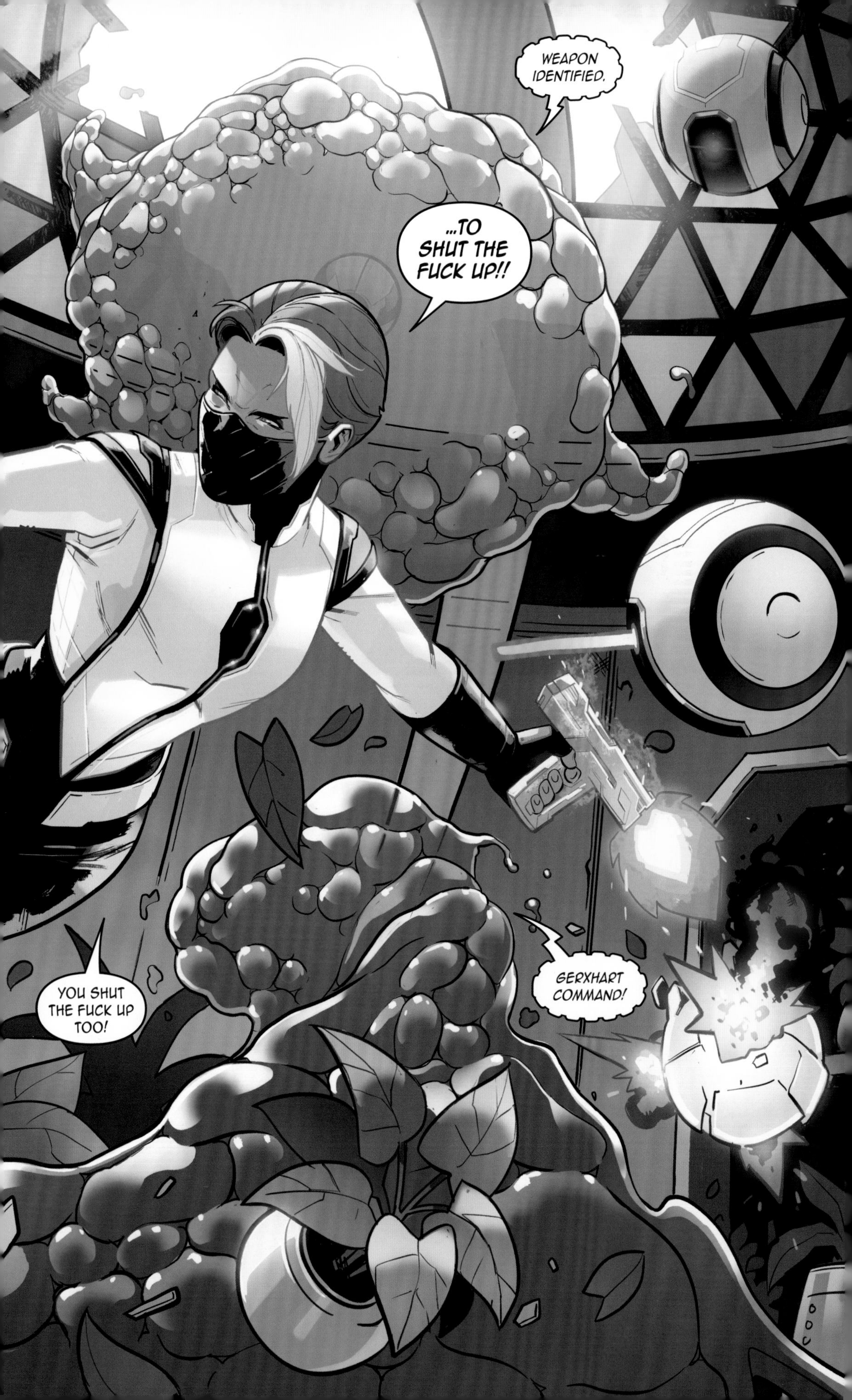
WEAPON IDENTIFIED.
...TO SHUT THE FUCK UP!!
GERXHART COMMAND!
YOU SHUT THE FUCK UP TOO!

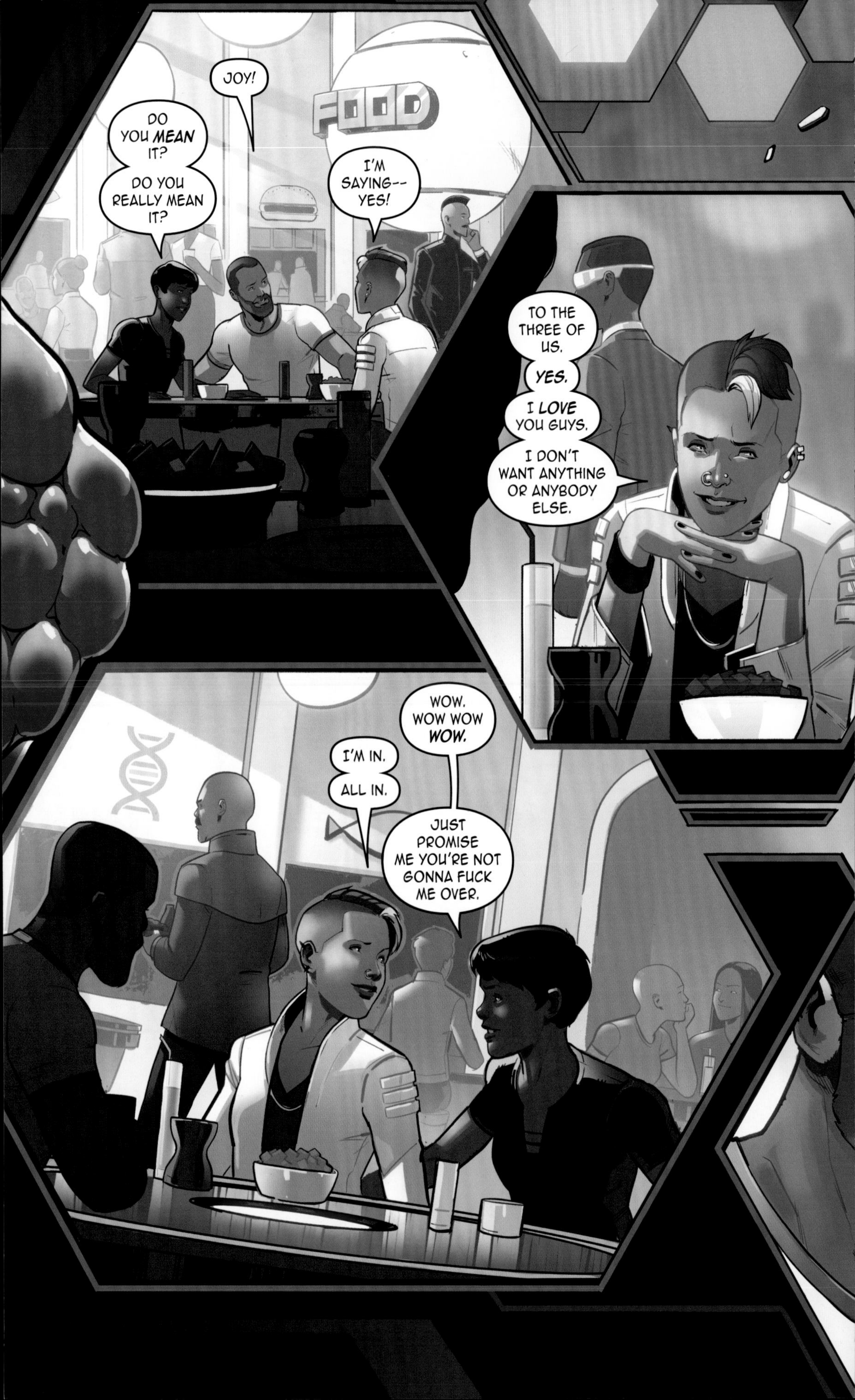
JOY!
DO YOU MEAN IT?
DO YOU REALLY MEAN IT?
FOOD
I'M SAYING-- YES!
TO THE THREE OF US.
YES.
I LOVE YOU GUYS.
I DON'T WANT ANYTHING OR ANYBODY ELSE.
WOW. WOW WOW WOW.
I'M IN.
ALL IN.
JUST PROMISE ME YOU'RE NOT GONNA FUCK ME OVER.

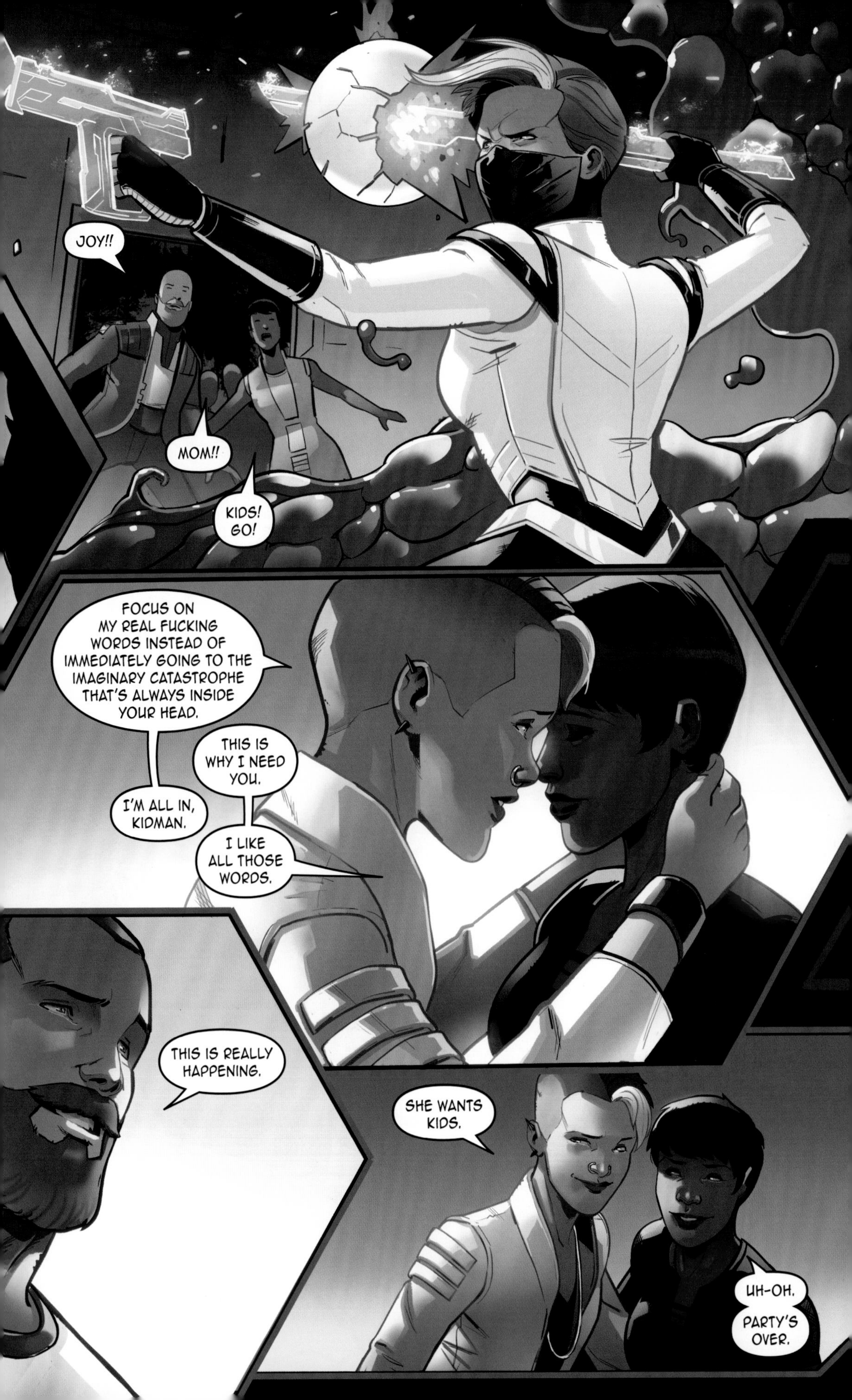
JOY!!
MOM!!
KIDS! GO!
FOCUS ON MY REAL FUCKING WORDS INSTEAD OF IMMEDIATELY GOING TO THE IMAGINARY CATASTROPHE THAT'S ALWAYS INSIDE YOUR HEAD.
I'M ALL IN, KIDMAN.
THIS IS WHY I NEED YOU.
I LIKE ALL THOSE WORDS.
THIS IS REALLY HAPPENING.
SHE WANTS KIDS.
UH-OH.
PARTY'S OVER.

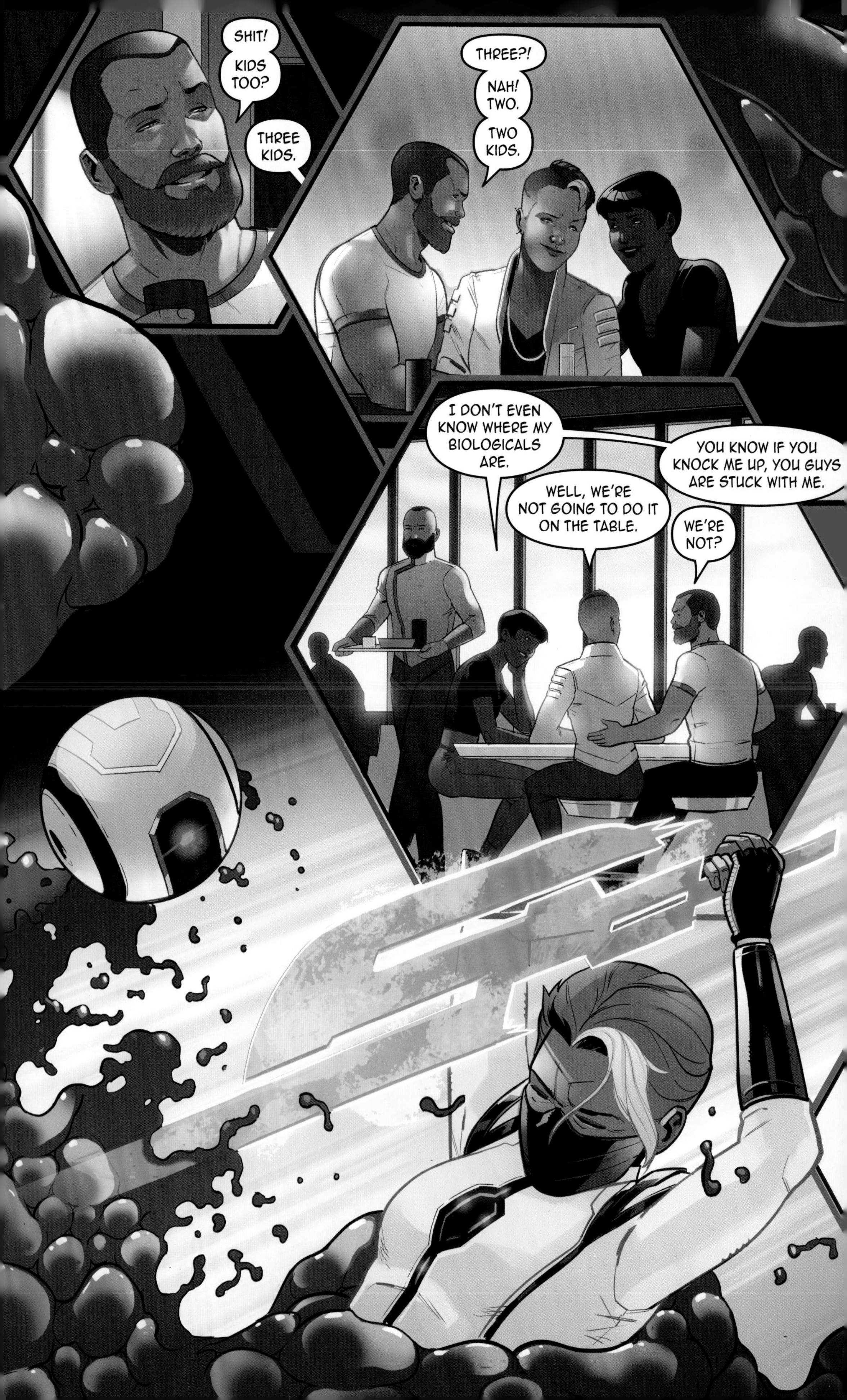
SHIT!
KIDS TOO?
THREE KIDS.
THREE?!
NAH! TWO.
TWO KIDS.
I DON'T EVEN KNOW WHERE MY BIOLOGICALS ARE.
YOU KNOW IF YOU KNOCK ME UP, YOU GUYS ARE STUCK WITH ME.
WELL, WE'RE NOT GOING TO DO IT ON THE TABLE.
WE'RE NOT?

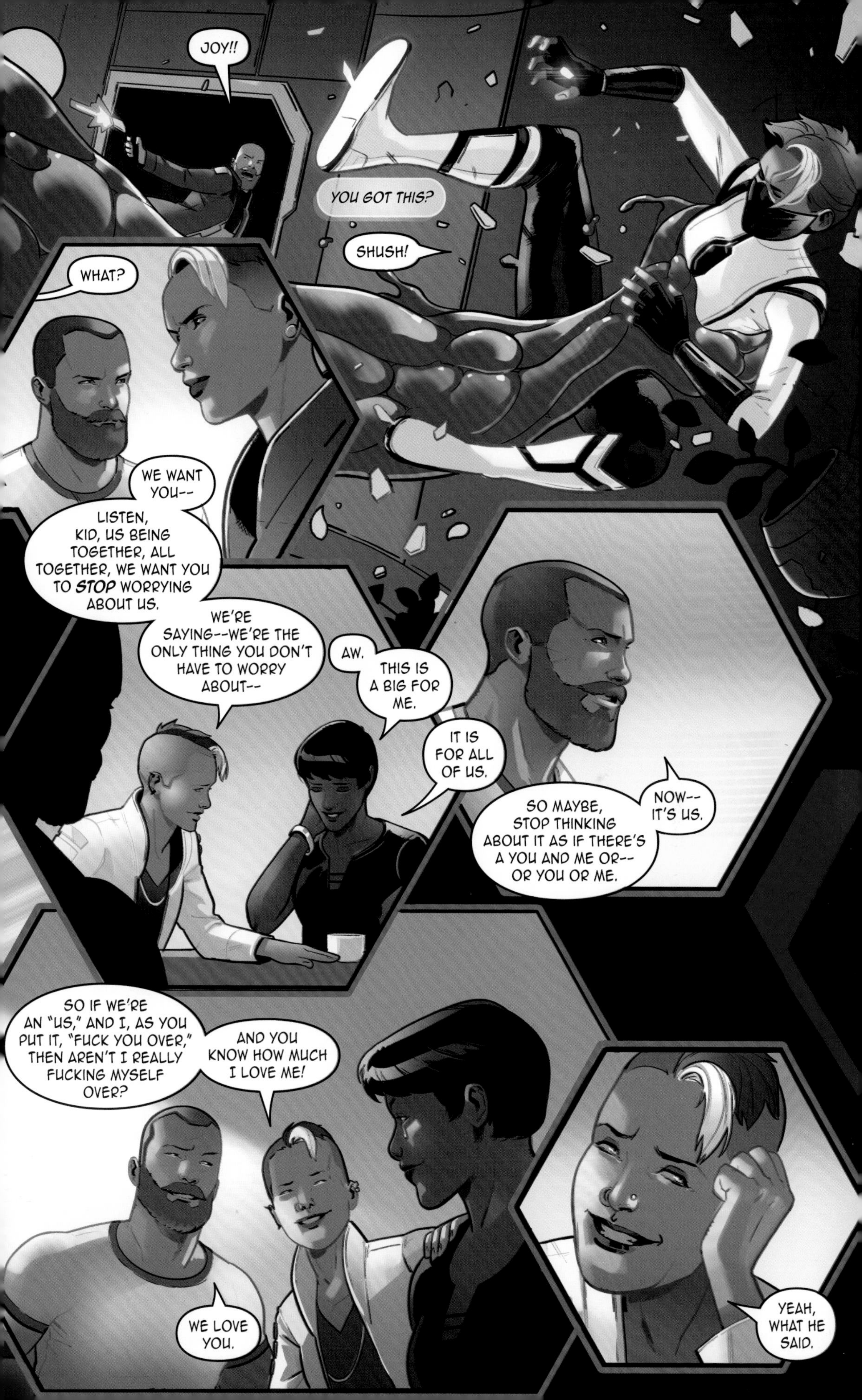
JOY!!
YOU GOT THIS?
SHUSH!
WHAT?
WE WANT YOU--
LISTEN, KID, US BEING TOGETHER, ALL TOGETHER, WE WANT YOU TO STOP WORRYING ABOUT US.
WE'RE SAYING--WE'RE THE ONLY THING YOU DON'T HAVE TO WORRY ABOUT--
AW.
THIS IS A BIG FOR ME.
IT IS FOR ALL OF US.
NOW--IT'S US.
SO MAYBE, STOP THINKING ABOUT IT AS IF THERE'S A YOU AND ME OR--OR YOU OR ME.
SO IF WE'RE AN "US," AND I, AS YOU PUT IT, "FUCK YOU OVER," THEN AREN'T I REALLY FUCKING MYSELF OVER?
AND YOU KNOW HOW MUCH I LOVE ME!
WE LOVE YOU.
YEAH, WHAT HE SAID.

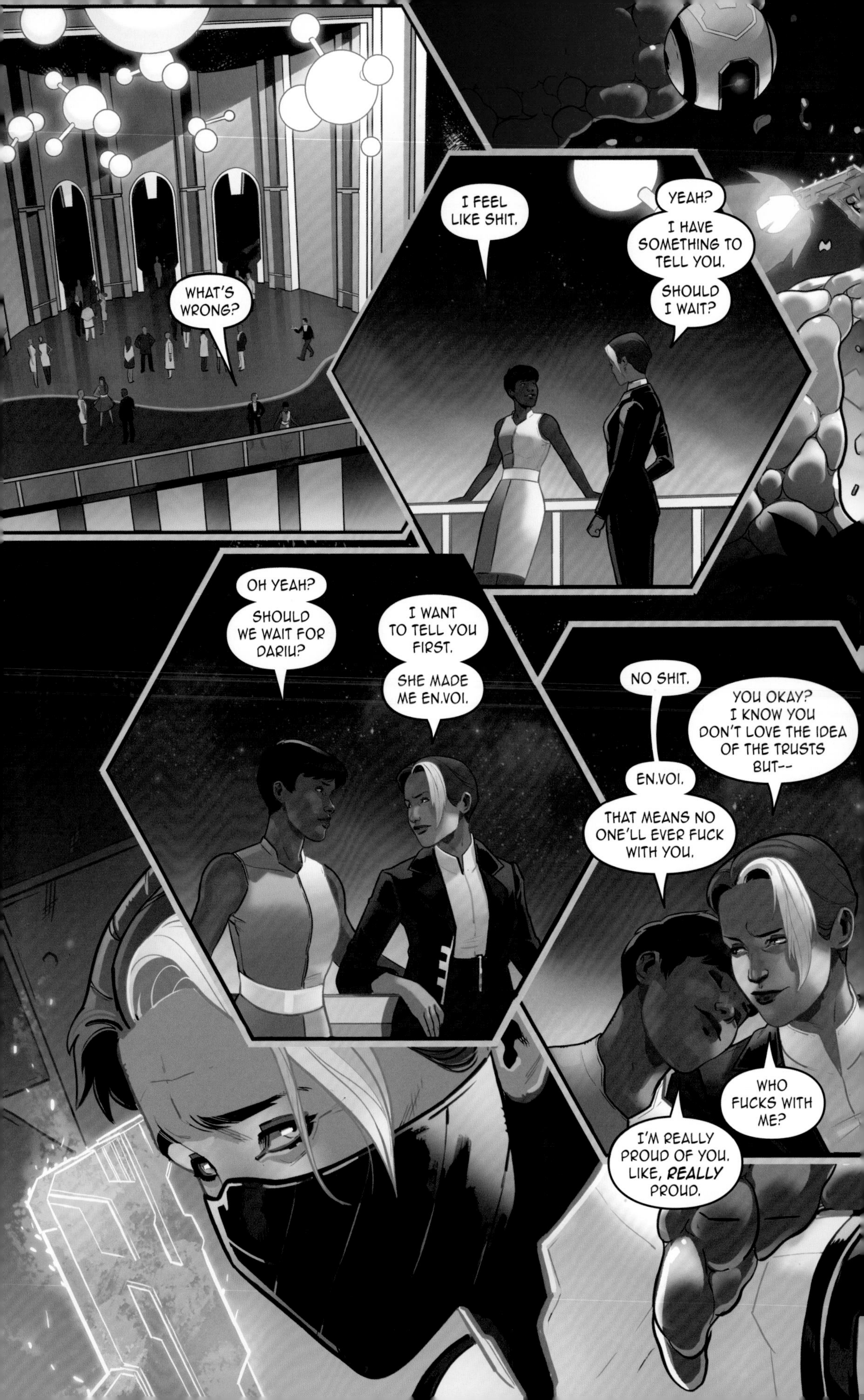
WHAT'S WRONG?
I FEEL LIKE SHIT.
YEAH?
I HAVE SOMETHING TO TELL YOU.
SHOULD I WAIT?
OH YEAH?
SHOULD WE WAIT FOR DARIU?
I WANT TO TELL YOU FIRST.
SHE MADE ME EN.VOI.
NO SHIT.
YOU OKAY? I KNOW YOU DON'T LOVE THE IDEA OF THE TRUSTS BUT--
EN.VOI.
THAT MEANS NO ONE'LL EVER FUCK WITH YOU.
WHO FUCKS WITH ME?
I'M REALLY PROUD OF YOU. LIKE, REALLY PROUD.

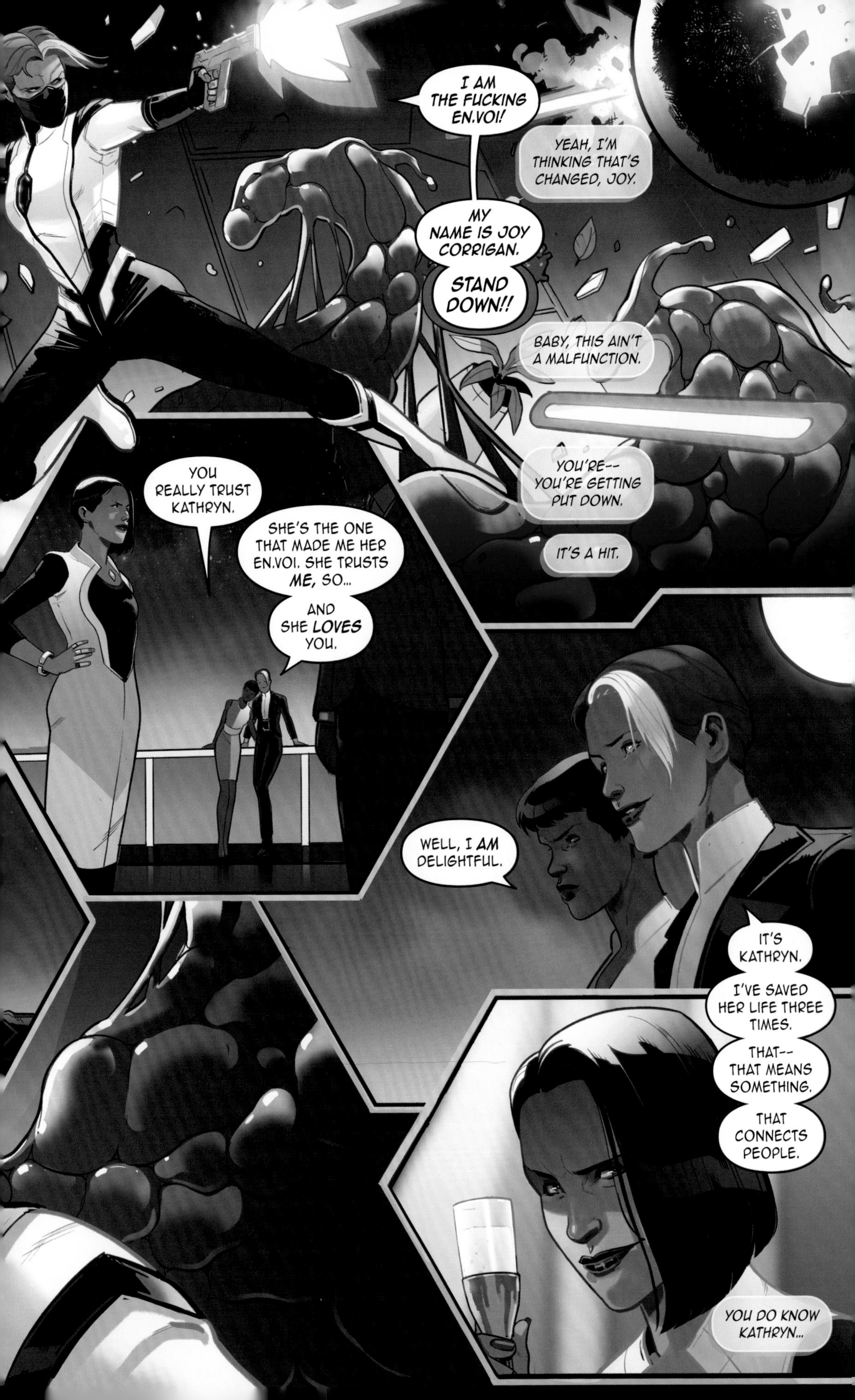
I AM THE FUCKING EN.VOI!
YEAH, I'M THINKING THAT'S CHANGED, JOY.
MY NAME IS JOY CORRIGAN.
STAND DOWN!!
BABY, THIS AIN'T A MALFUNCTION.
YOU'RE-- YOU'RE GETTING PUT DOWN.
IT'S A HIT.
YOU REALLY TRUST KATHRYN.
SHE'S THE ONE THAT MADE ME HER EN.VOI. SHE TRUSTS ME, SO...
AND SHE LOVES YOU.
WELL, I AM DELIGHTFUL.
IT'S KATHRYN.
I'VE SAVED HER LIFE THREE TIMES.
THAT-- THAT MEANS SOMETHING.
THAT CONNECTS PEOPLE.
YOU DO KNOW KATHRYN...

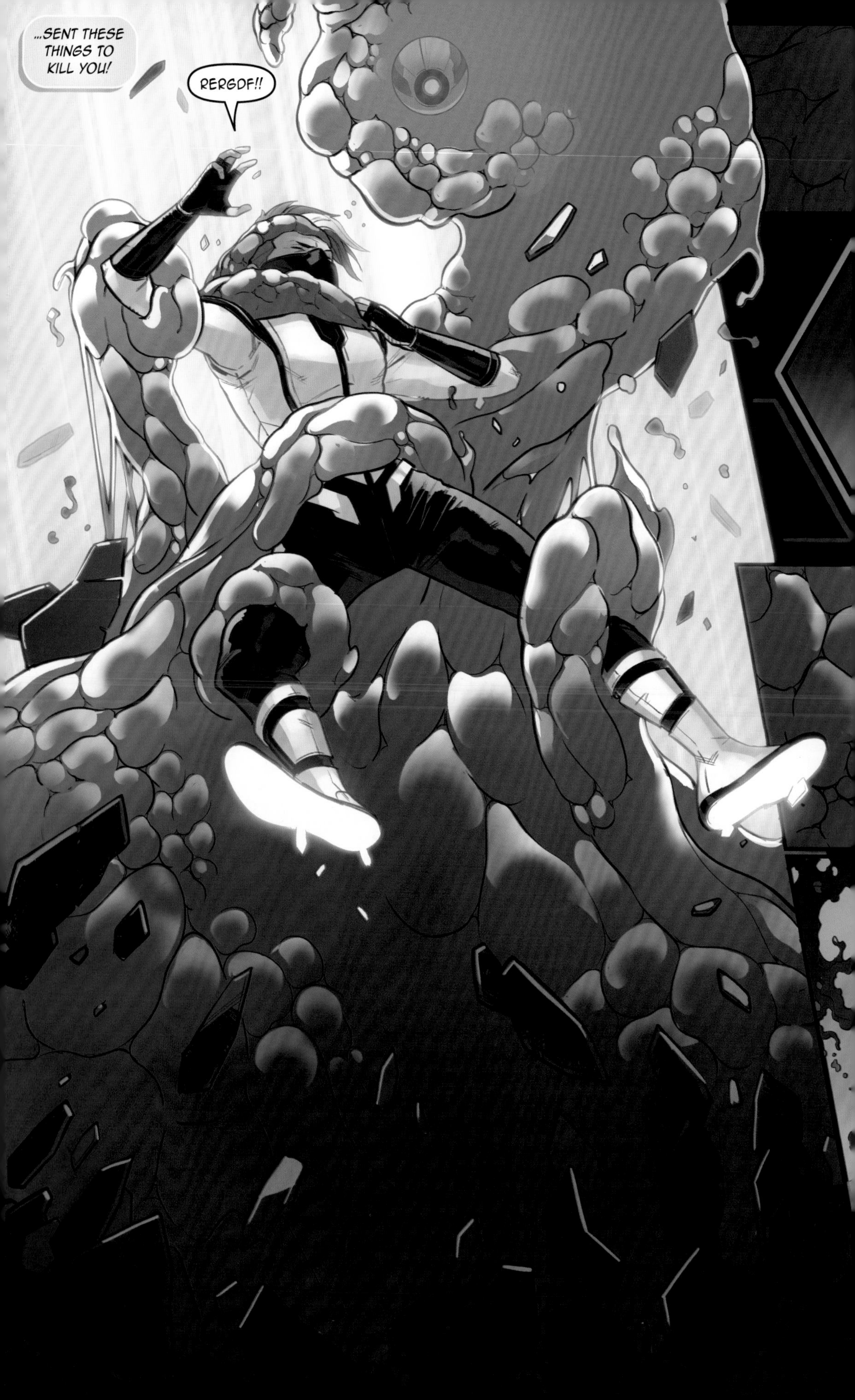
...SENT THESE THINGS TO KILL YOU!
RERGDF!!

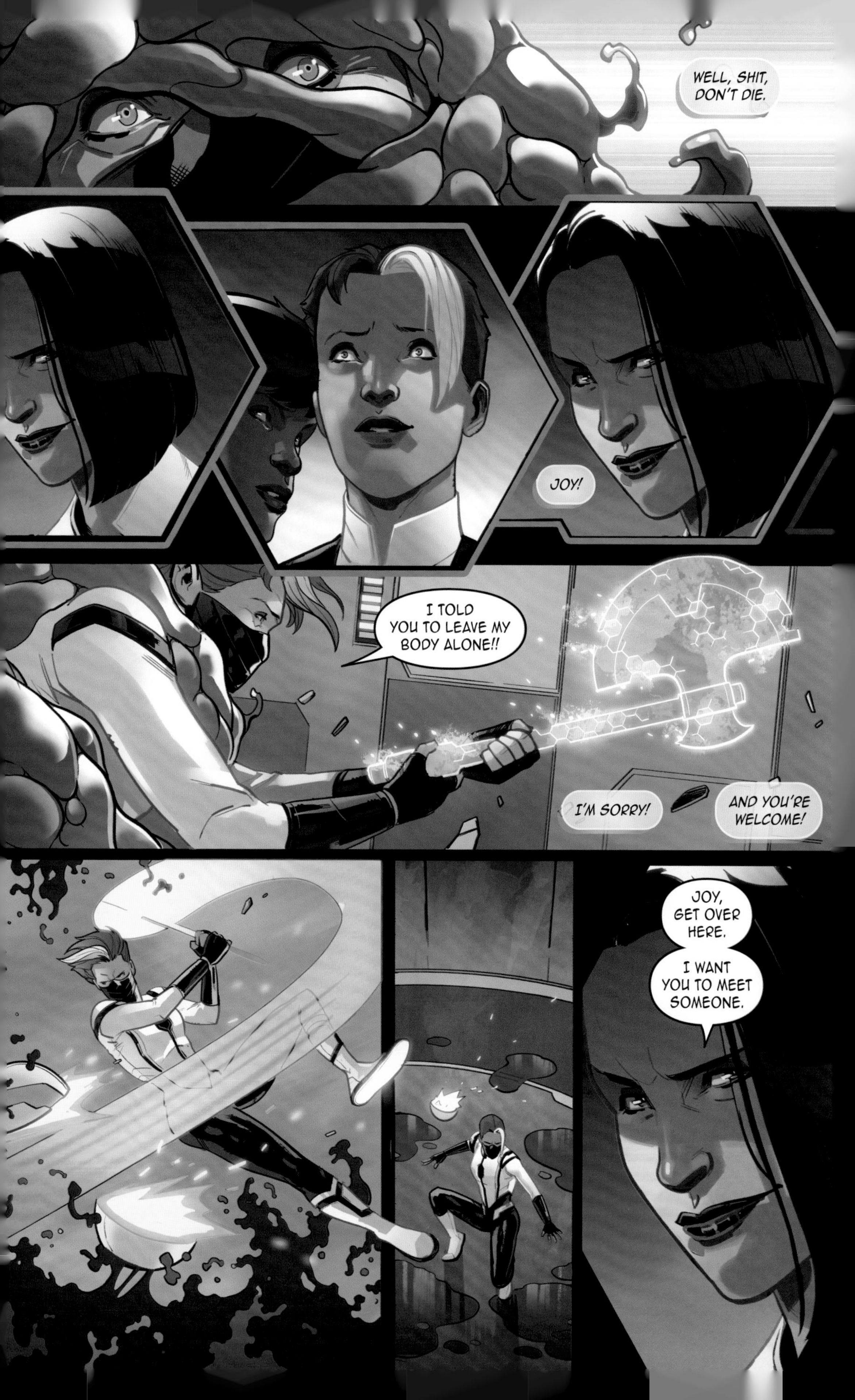

WELL, SHIT, DON'T DIE.
JOY!
I TOLD YOU TO LEAVE MY BODY ALONE!!
I'M SORRY!
AND YOU'RE WELCOME!
JOY, GET OVER HERE.
I WANT YOU TO MEET SOMEONE.

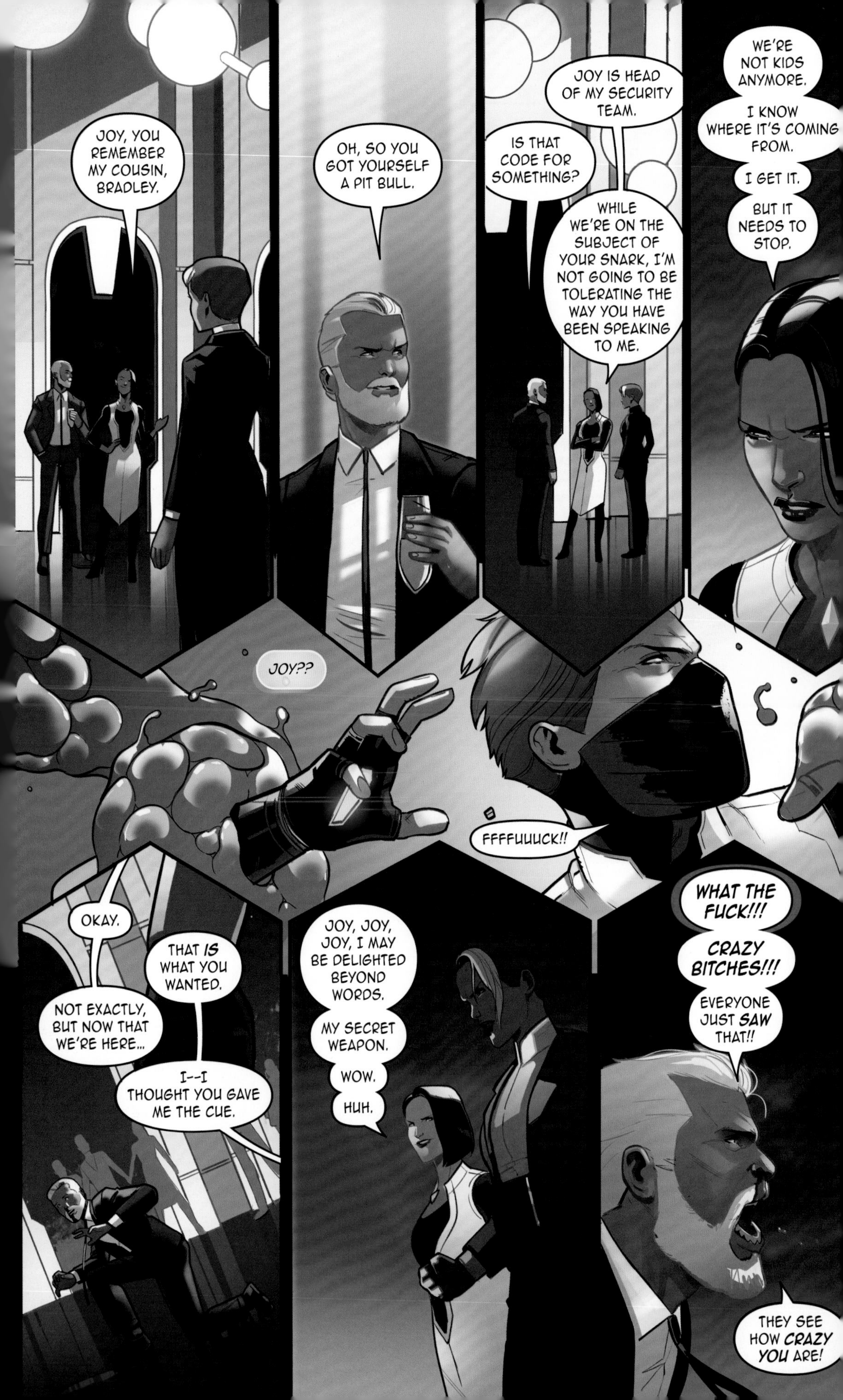

JOY, YOU REMEMBER MY COUSIN, BRADLEY.
OH, SO YOU GOT YOURSELF A PIT BULL.
JOY IS HEAD OF MY SECURITY TEAM.
IS THAT CODE FOR SOMETHING?
WHILE WE'RE ON THE SUBJECT OF YOUR SNARK, I'M NOT GOING TO BE TOLERATING THE WAY YOU HAVE BEEN SPEAKING TO ME.
WE'RE NOT KIDS ANYMORE.
I KNOW WHERE IT'S COMING FROM.
I GET IT.
BUT IT NEEDS TO STOP.
JOY??
FFFFUUUCK!!
OKAY.
THAT *IS* WHAT YOU WANTED.
NOT EXACTLY, BUT NOW THAT WE'RE HERE...
I--I THOUGHT YOU GAVE ME THE CUE.
JOY, JOY, JOY, I MAY BE DELIGHTED BEYOND WORDS.
MY SECRET WEAPON.
WOW.
HUH.
WHAT THE FUCK!!!
CRAZY BITCHES!!!
EVERYONE JUST *SAW* THAT!!
THEY SEE HOW *CRAZY YOU* ARE!

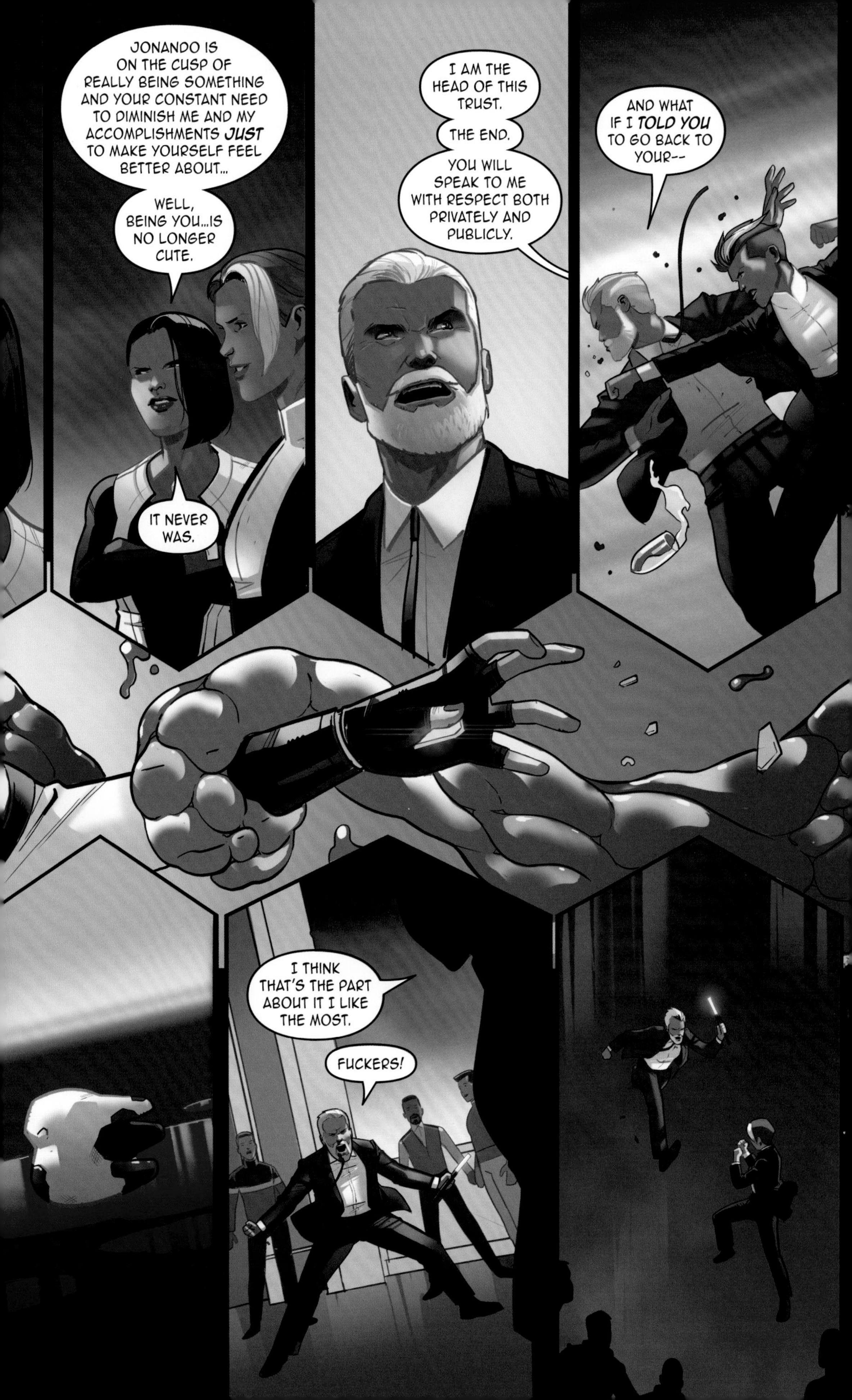
JONANDO IS ON THE CUSP OF REALLY BEING SOMETHING AND YOUR CONSTANT NEED TO DIMINISH ME AND MY ACCOMPLISHMENTS JUST TO MAKE YOURSELF FEEL BETTER ABOUT...
WELL, BEING YOU...IS NO LONGER CUTE.
IT NEVER WAS.
I AM THE HEAD OF THIS TRUST.
THE END.
YOU WILL SPEAK TO ME WITH RESPECT BOTH PRIVATELY AND PUBLICLY.
AND WHAT IF I TOLD YOU TO GO BACK TO YOUR--
I THINK THAT'S THE PART ABOUT IT I LIKE THE MOST.
FUCKERS!

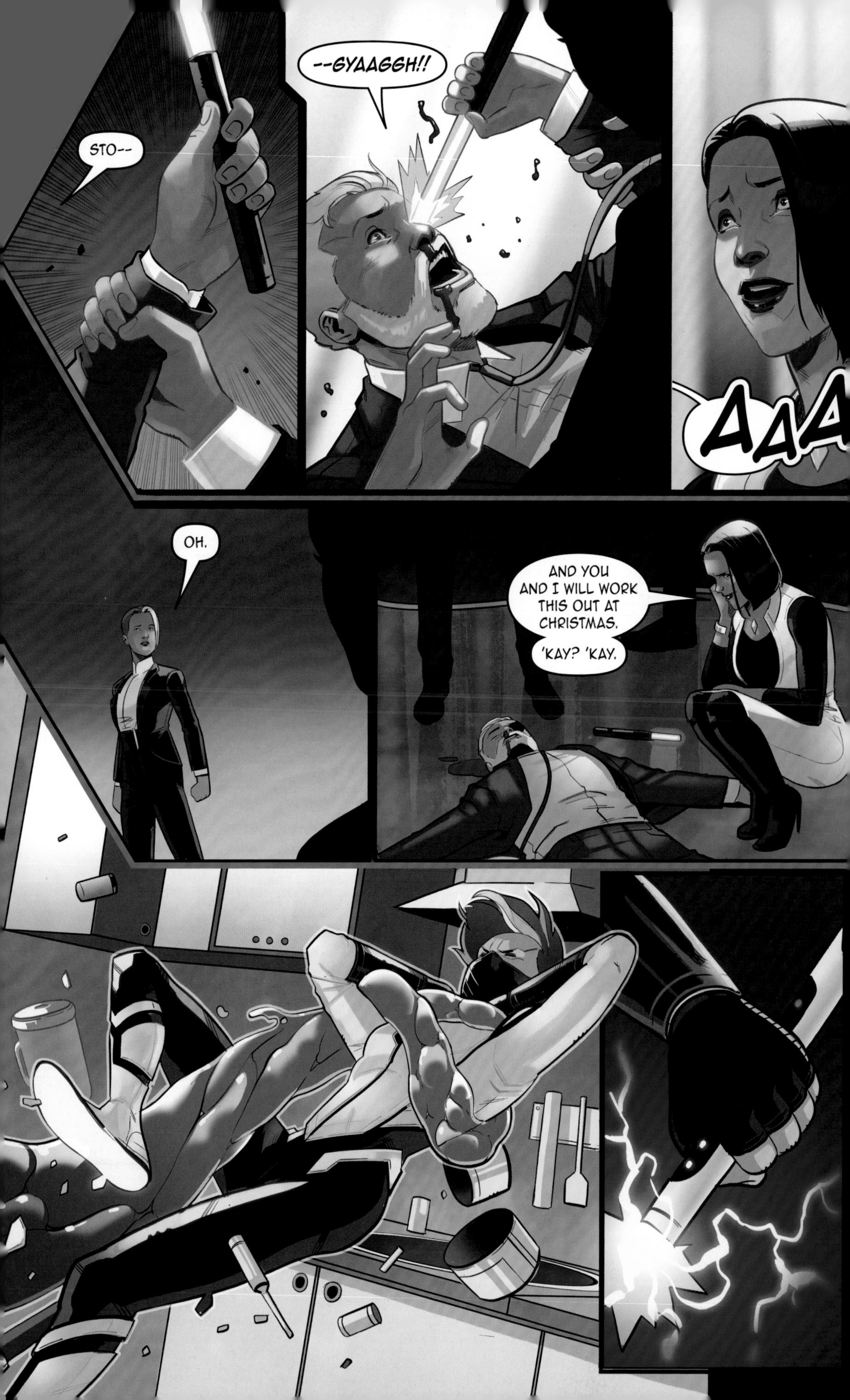
STO--
--GYAAGGH!!
AAA
OH.
AND YOU AND I WILL WORK THIS OUT AT CHRISTMAS.
'KAY? 'KAY.

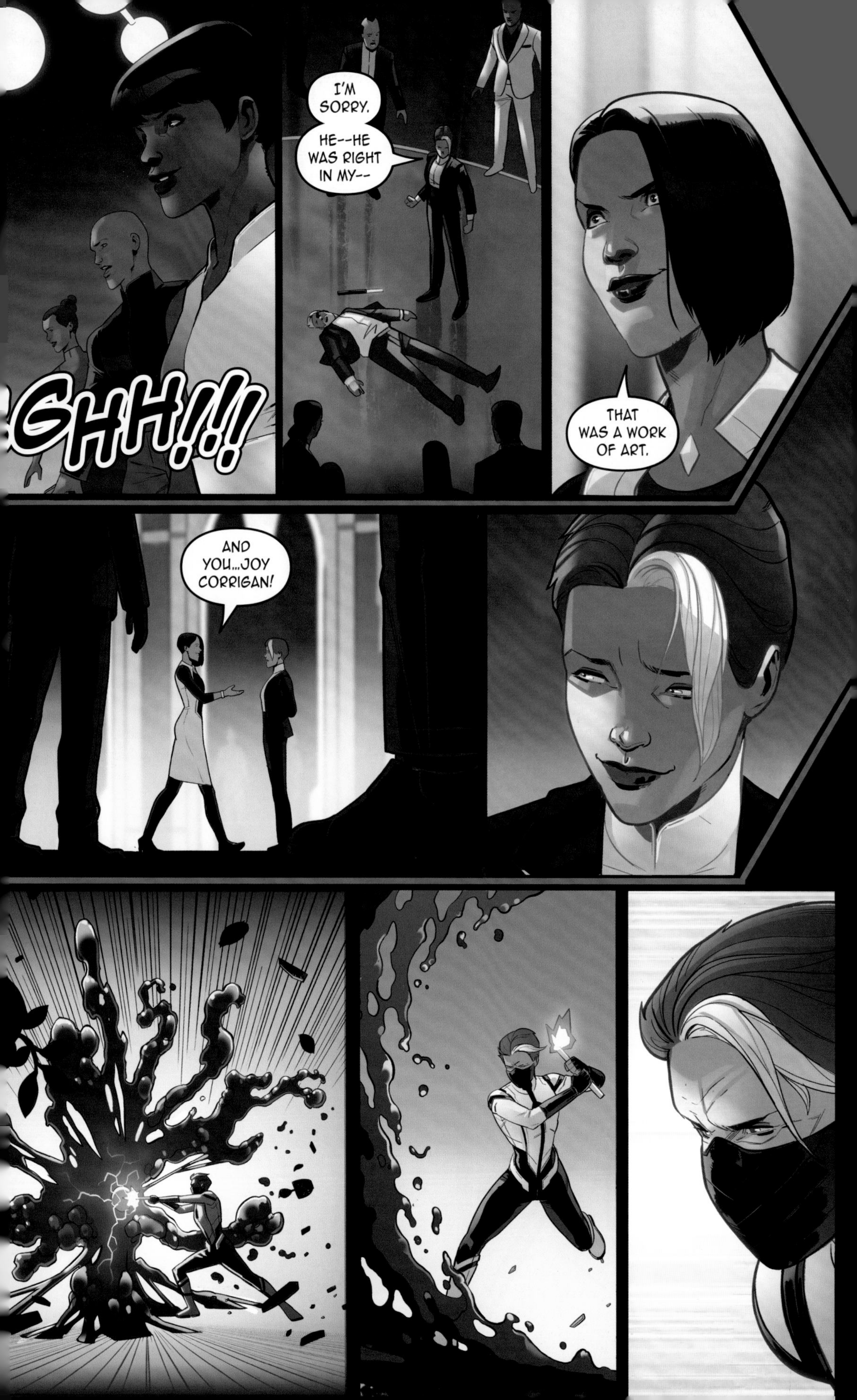
GHH!!!
I'M SORRY.
HE--HE WAS RIGHT IN MY--
THAT WAS A WORK OF ART.
AND YOU...JOY CORRIGAN!

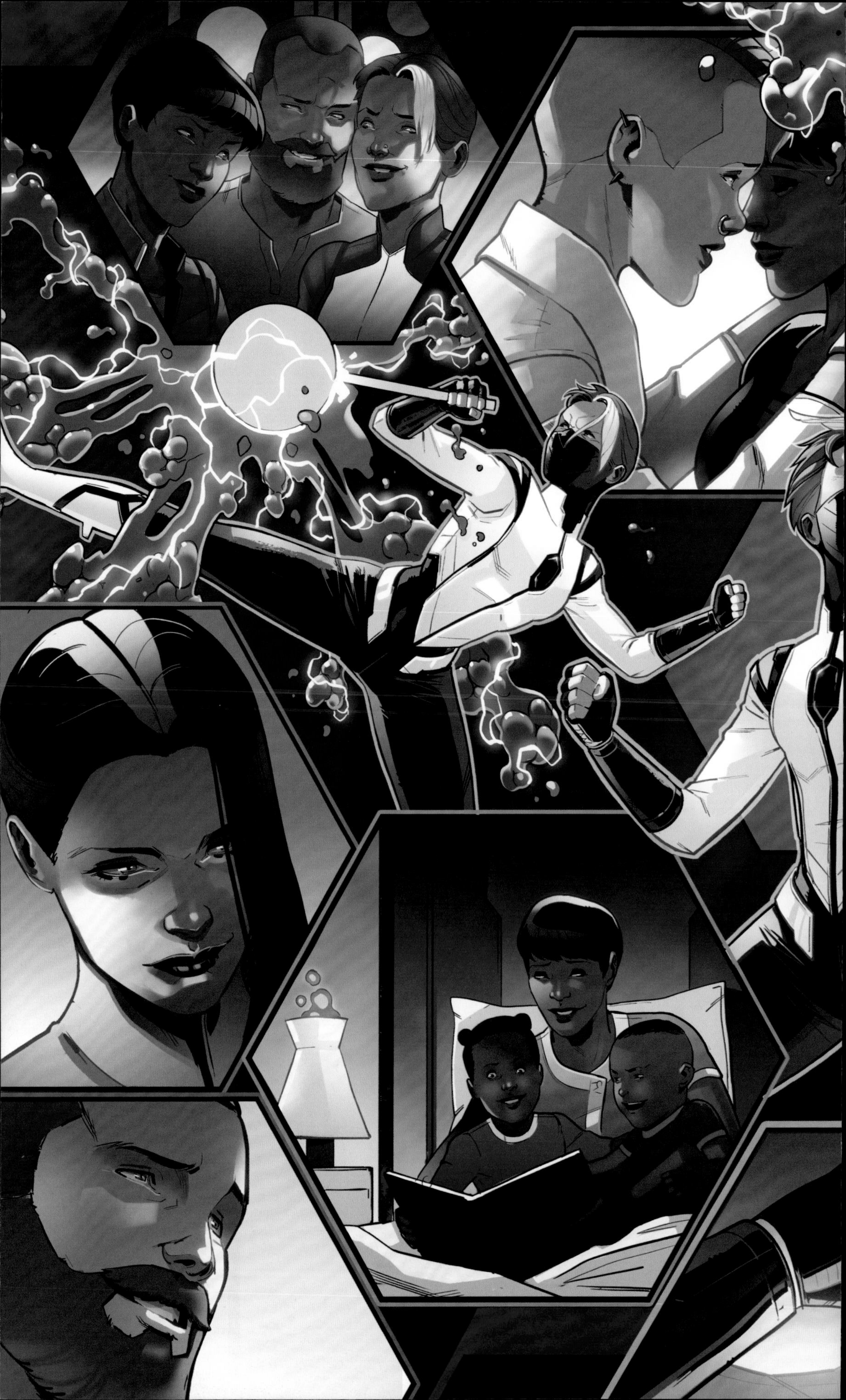

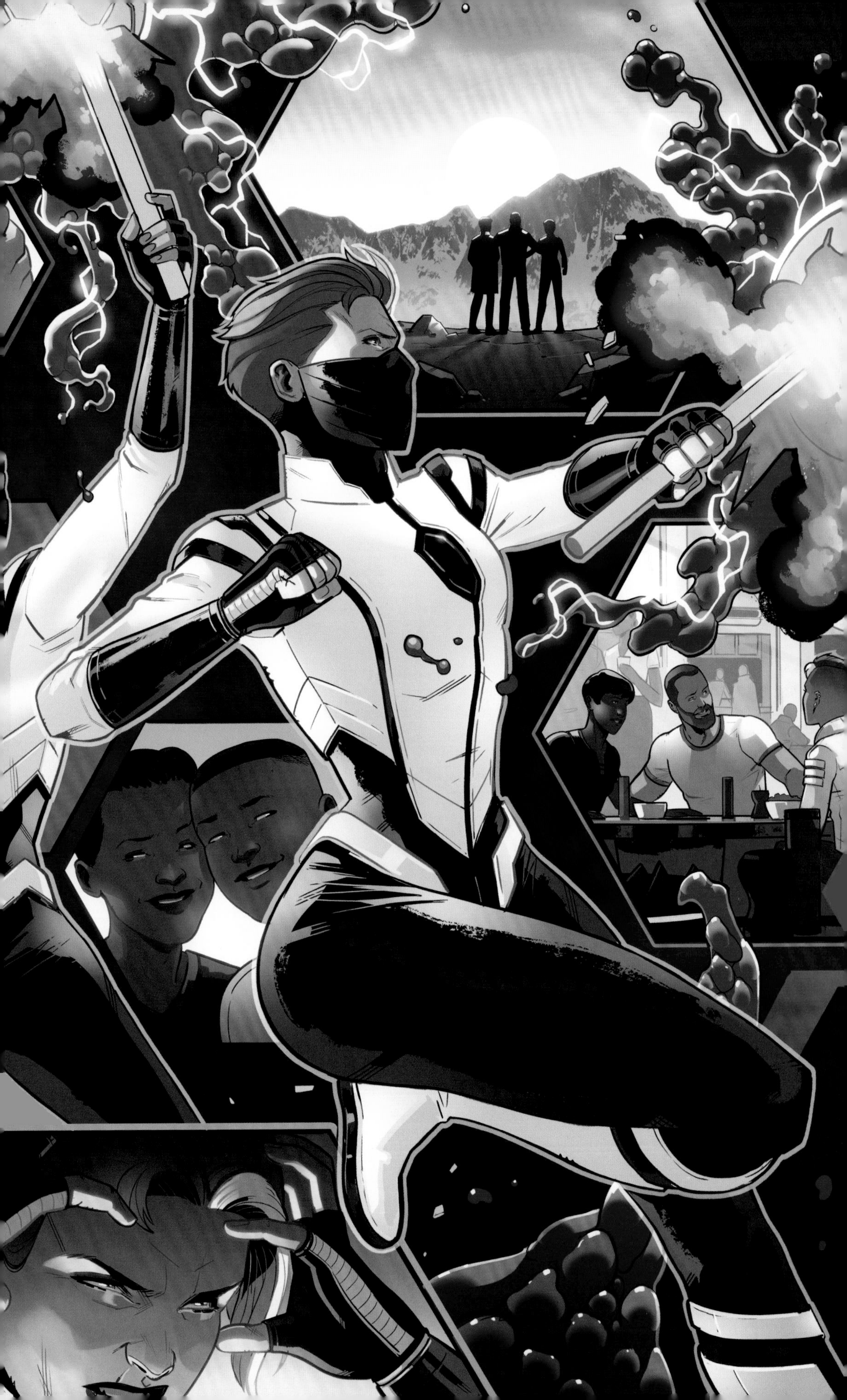

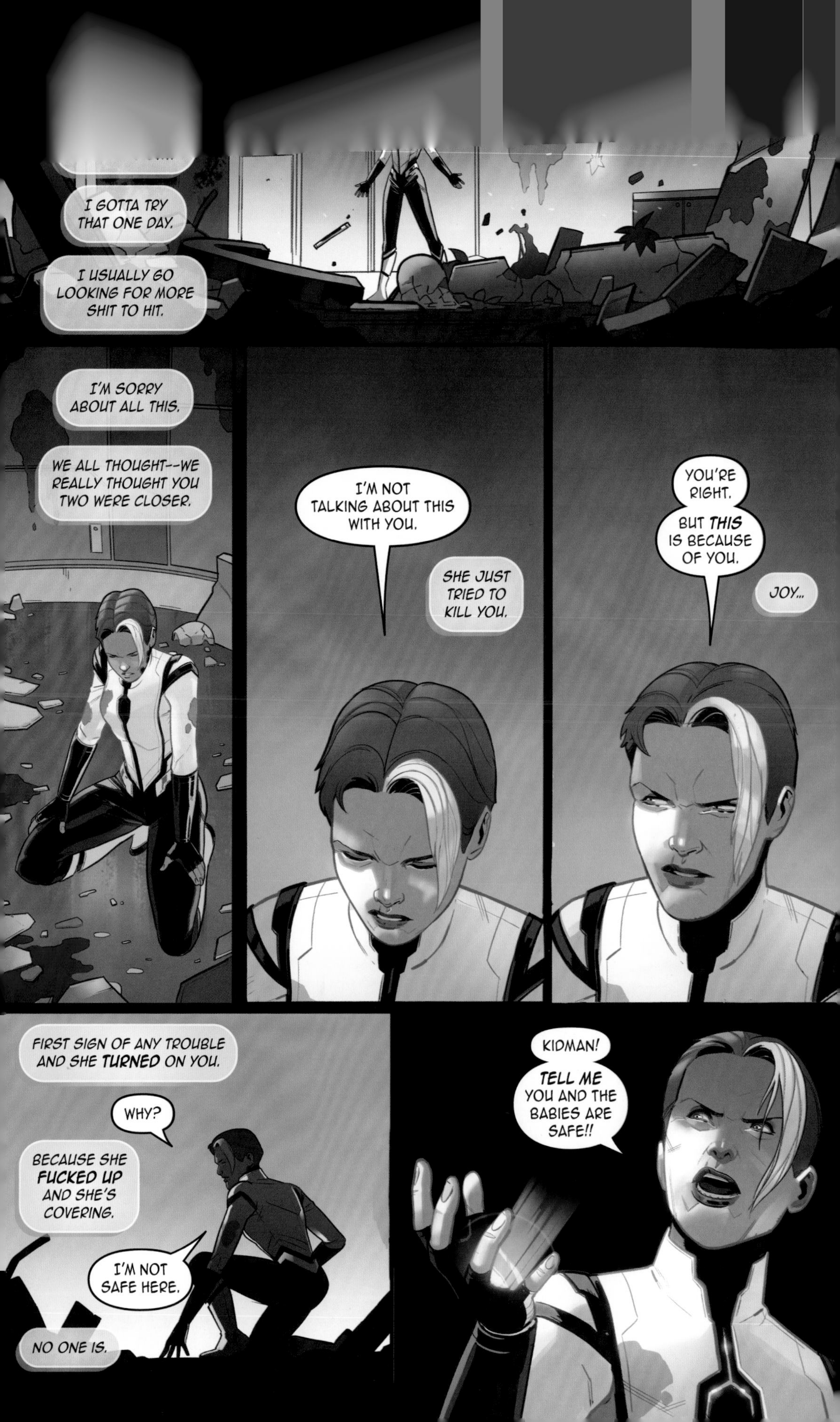
I GOTTA TRY THAT ONE DAY.
I USUALLY GO LOOKING FOR MORE SHIT TO HIT.
I'M SORRY ABOUT ALL THIS.
WE ALL THOUGHT--WE REALLY THOUGHT YOU TWO WERE CLOSER.
I'M NOT TALKING ABOUT THIS WITH YOU.
SHE JUST TRIED TO KILL YOU.
YOU'RE RIGHT.
BUT THIS IS BECAUSE OF YOU.
JOY...
FIRST SIGN OF ANY TROUBLE AND SHE TURNED ON YOU.
WHY?
BECAUSE SHE FUCKED UP AND SHE'S COVERING.
I'M NOT SAFE HERE.
NO ONE IS.
KIDMAN!
TELL ME YOU AND THE BABIES ARE SAFE!!

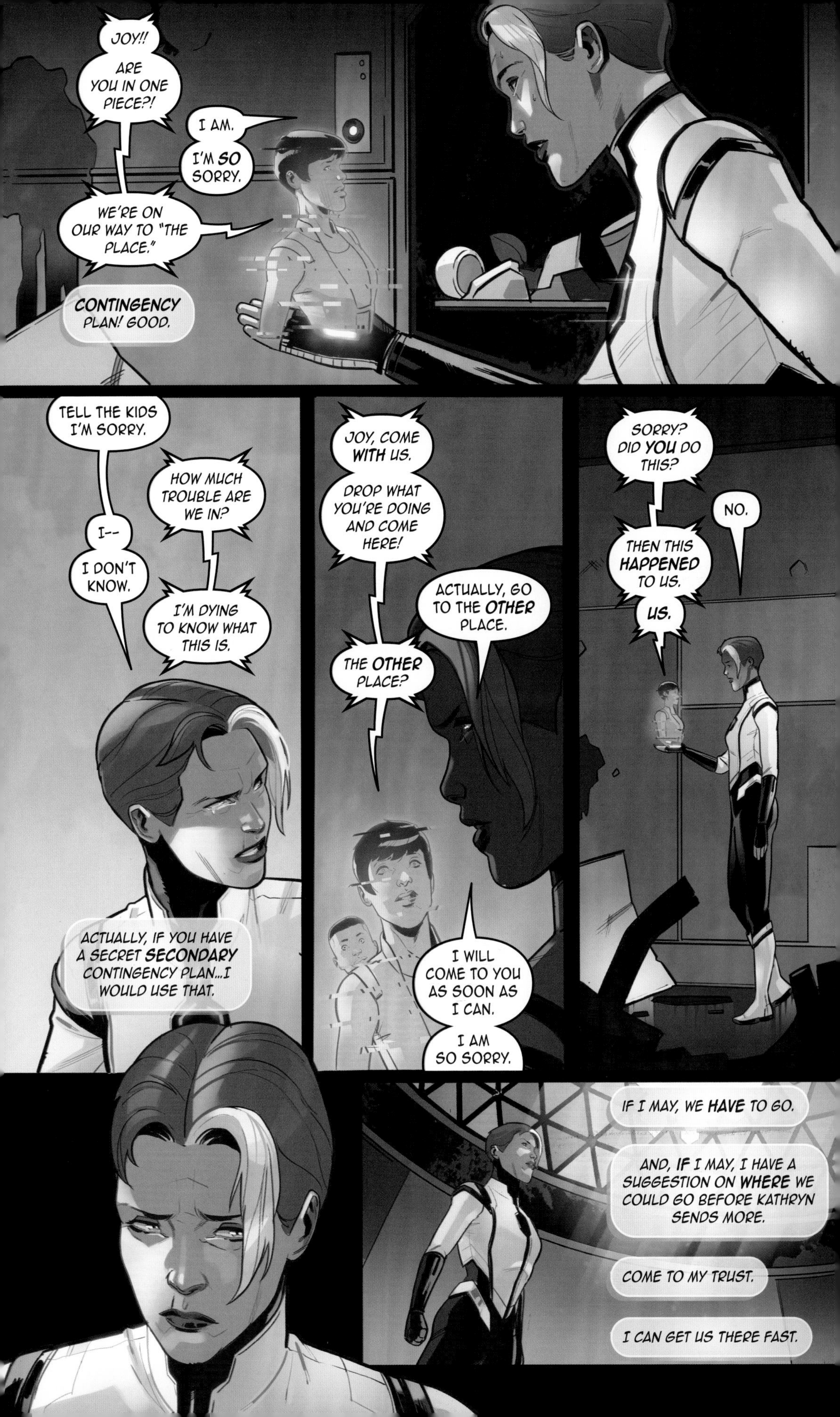
JOY!!
ARE YOU IN ONE PIECE?!
I AM.
I'M SO SORRY.
WE'RE ON OUR WAY TO "THE PLACE."
CONTINGENCY PLAN! GOOD.
TELL THE KIDS I'M SORRY.
HOW MUCH TROUBLE ARE WE IN?
I--
I DON'T KNOW.
I'M DYING TO KNOW WHAT THIS IS.
ACTUALLY, IF YOU HAVE A SECRET SECONDARY CONTINGENCY PLAN...I WOULD USE THAT.
JOY, COME WITH US.
DROP WHAT YOU'RE DOING AND COME HERE!
ACTUALLY, GO TO THE OTHER PLACE.
THE OTHER PLACE?
I WILL COME TO YOU AS SOON AS I CAN.
I AM SO SORRY.
SORRY? DID YOU DO THIS?
NO.
THEN THIS HAPPENED TO US.
US.
IF I MAY, WE HAVE TO GO.
AND, IF I MAY, I HAVE A SUGGESTION ON WHERE WE COULD GO BEFORE KATHRYN SENDS MORE.
COME TO MY TRUST.
I CAN GET US THERE FAST.

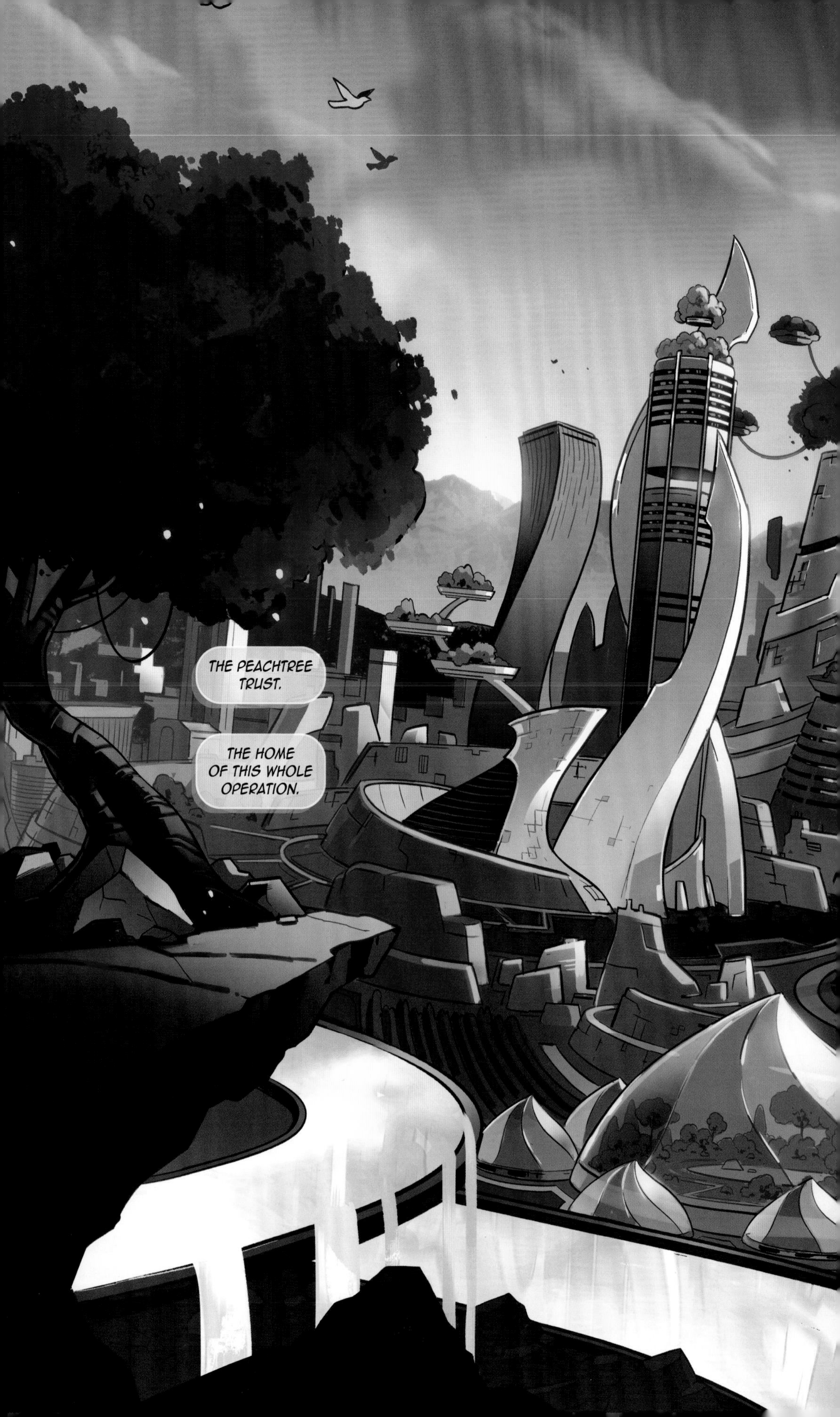
THE PEACHTREE TRUST.
THE HOME OF THIS WHOLE OPERATION.

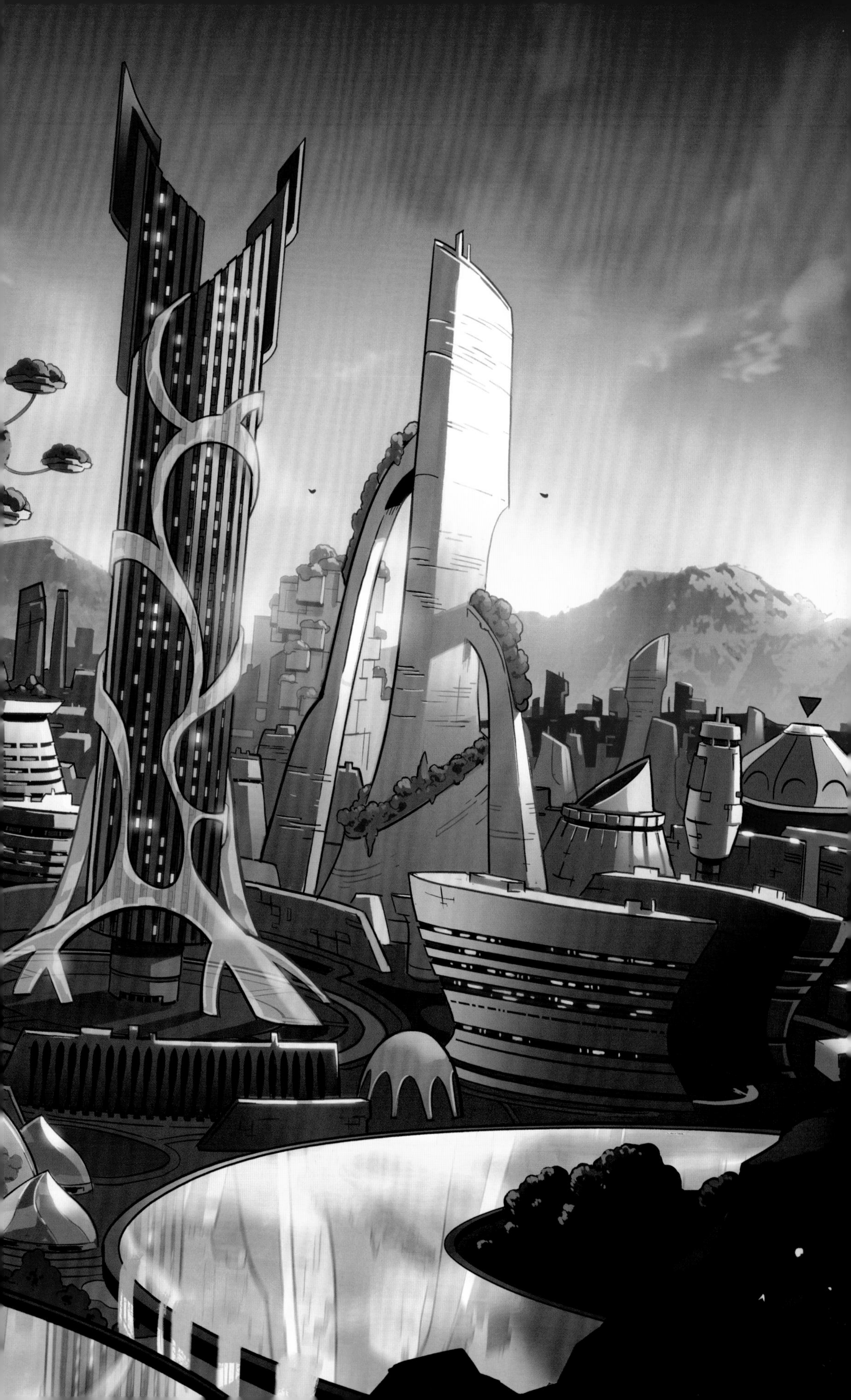

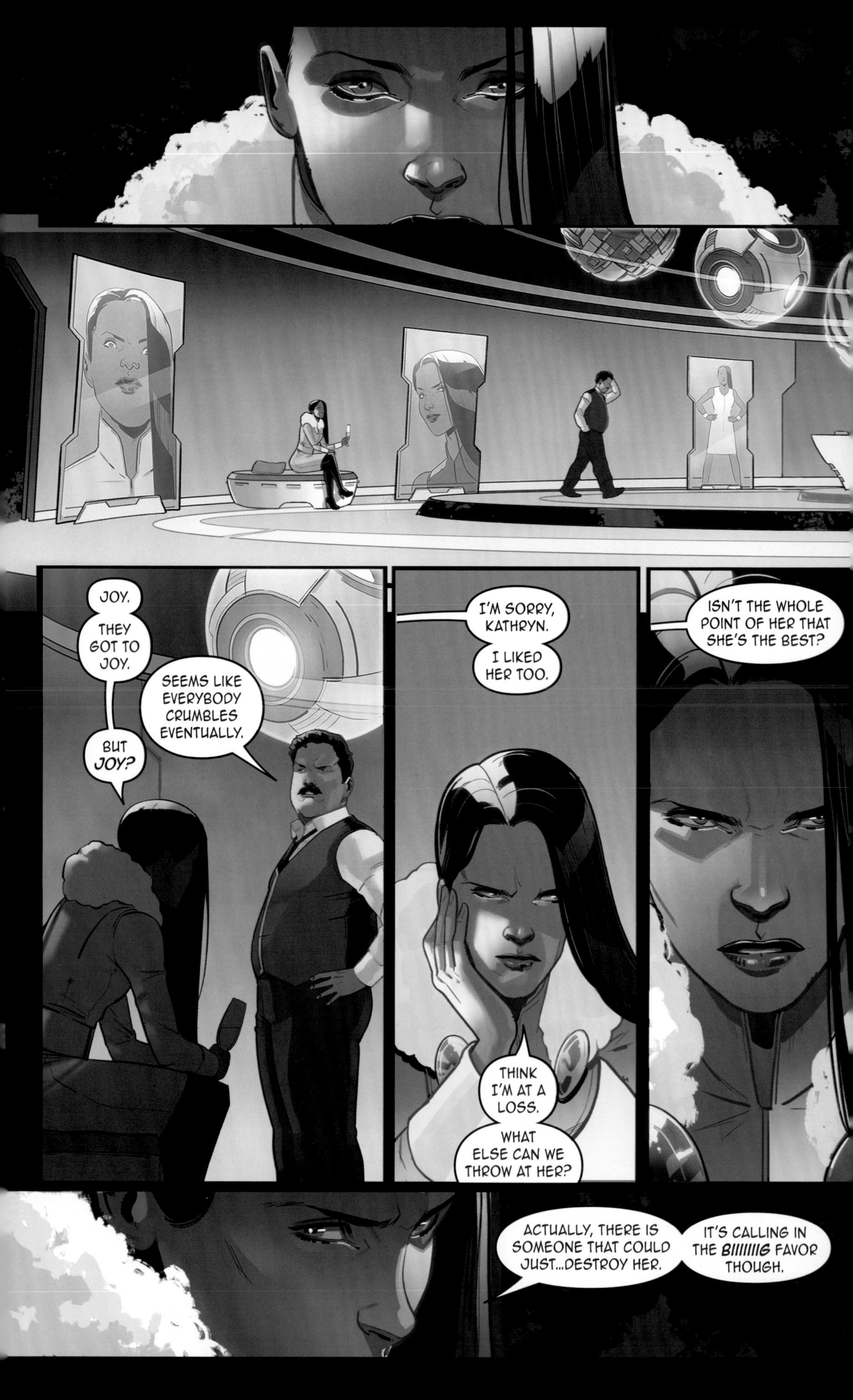
JOY.
THEY GOT TO JOY.
SEEMS LIKE EVERYBODY CRUMBLES EVENTUALLY.
BUT *JOY?*
I'M SORRY, KATHRYN.
I LIKED HER TOO.
THINK I'M AT A LOSS.
WHAT ELSE CAN WE THROW AT HER?
ISN'T THE WHOLE POINT OF HER THAT SHE'S THE BEST?
ACTUALLY, THERE IS SOMEONE THAT COULD JUST...DESTROY HER.
IT'S CALLING IN THE *BIIIIIIG* FAVOR THOUGH.

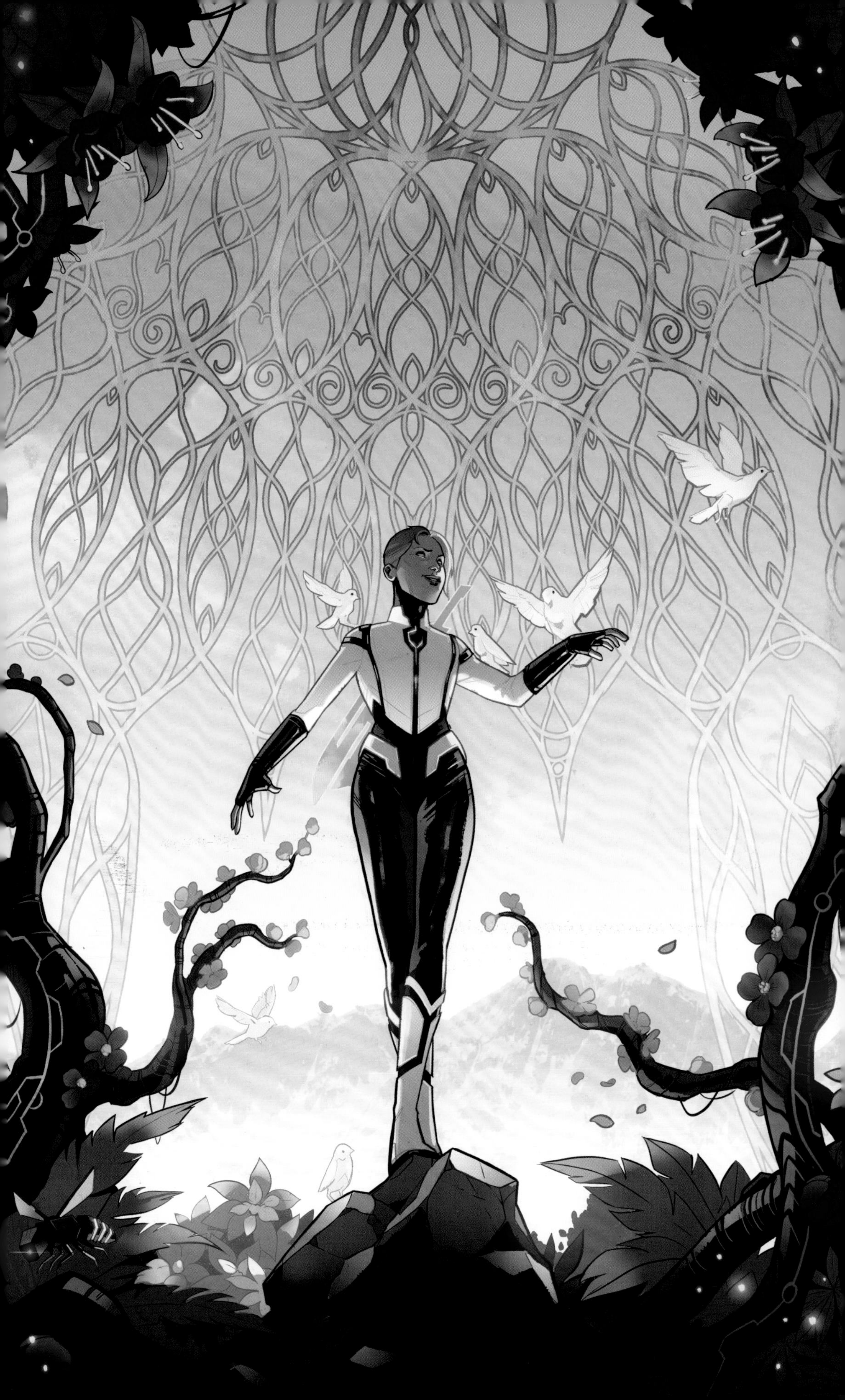

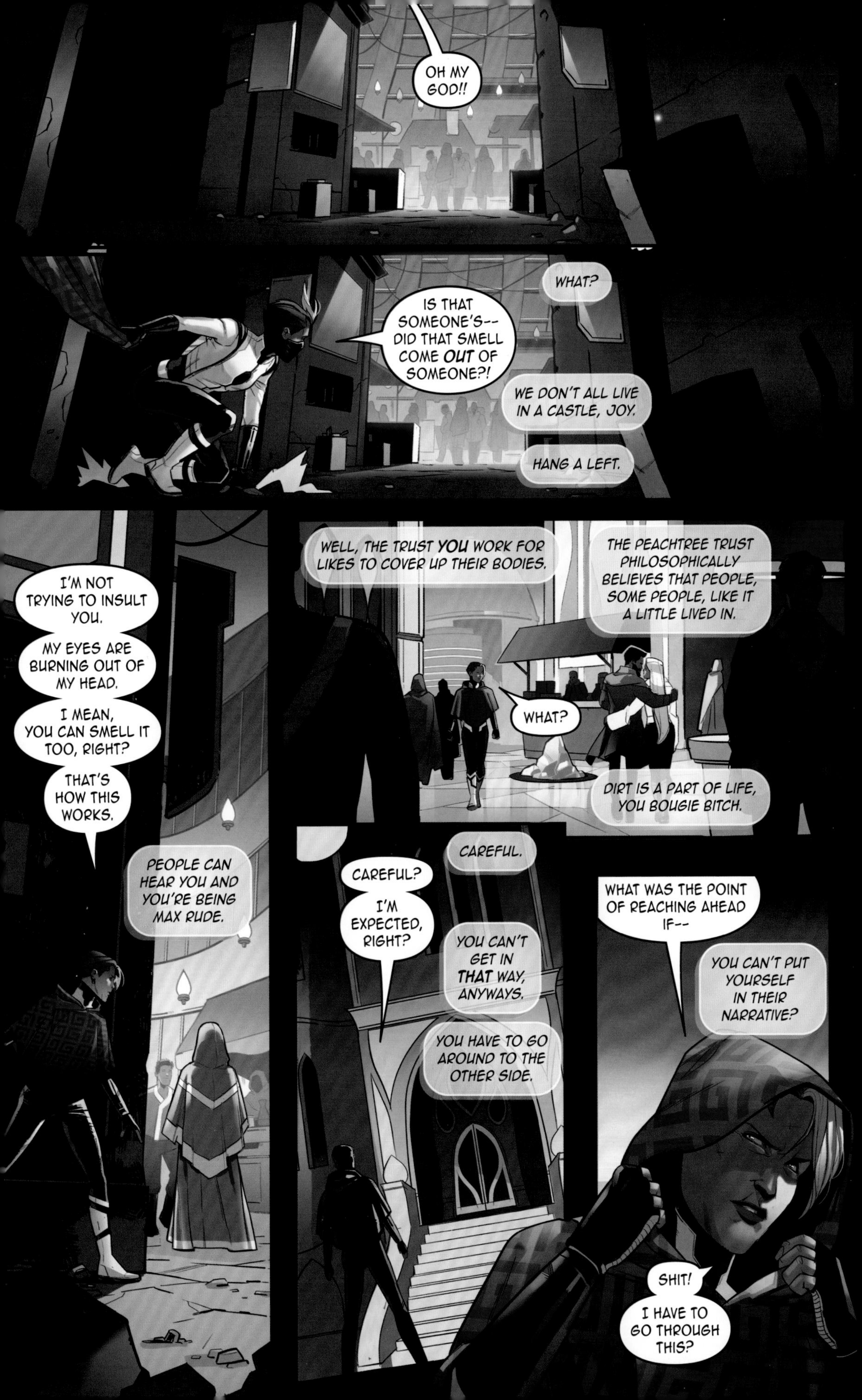
OH MY GOD!!
WHAT?
IS THAT SOMEONE'S-- DID THAT SMELL COME OUT OF SOMEONE?!
WE DON'T ALL LIVE IN A CASTLE, JOY.
HANG A LEFT.
I'M NOT TRYING TO INSULT YOU.
MY EYES ARE BURNING OUT OF MY HEAD.
I MEAN, YOU CAN SMELL IT TOO, RIGHT?
THAT'S HOW THIS WORKS.
PEOPLE CAN HEAR YOU AND YOU'RE BEING MAX RUDE.
WELL, THE TRUST YOU WORK FOR LIKES TO COVER UP THEIR BODIES.
THE PEACHTREE TRUST PHILOSOPHICALLY BELIEVES THAT PEOPLE, SOME PEOPLE, LIKE IT A LITTLE LIVED IN.
WHAT?
DIRT IS A PART OF LIFE, YOU BOUGIE BITCH.
CAREFUL.
CAREFUL?
I'M EXPECTED, RIGHT?
YOU CAN'T GET IN THAT WAY, ANYWAYS.
YOU HAVE TO GO AROUND TO THE OTHER SIDE.
WHAT WAS THE POINT OF REACHING AHEAD IF--
YOU CAN'T PUT YOURSELF IN THEIR NARRATIVE?
SHIT!
I HAVE TO GO THROUGH THIS?

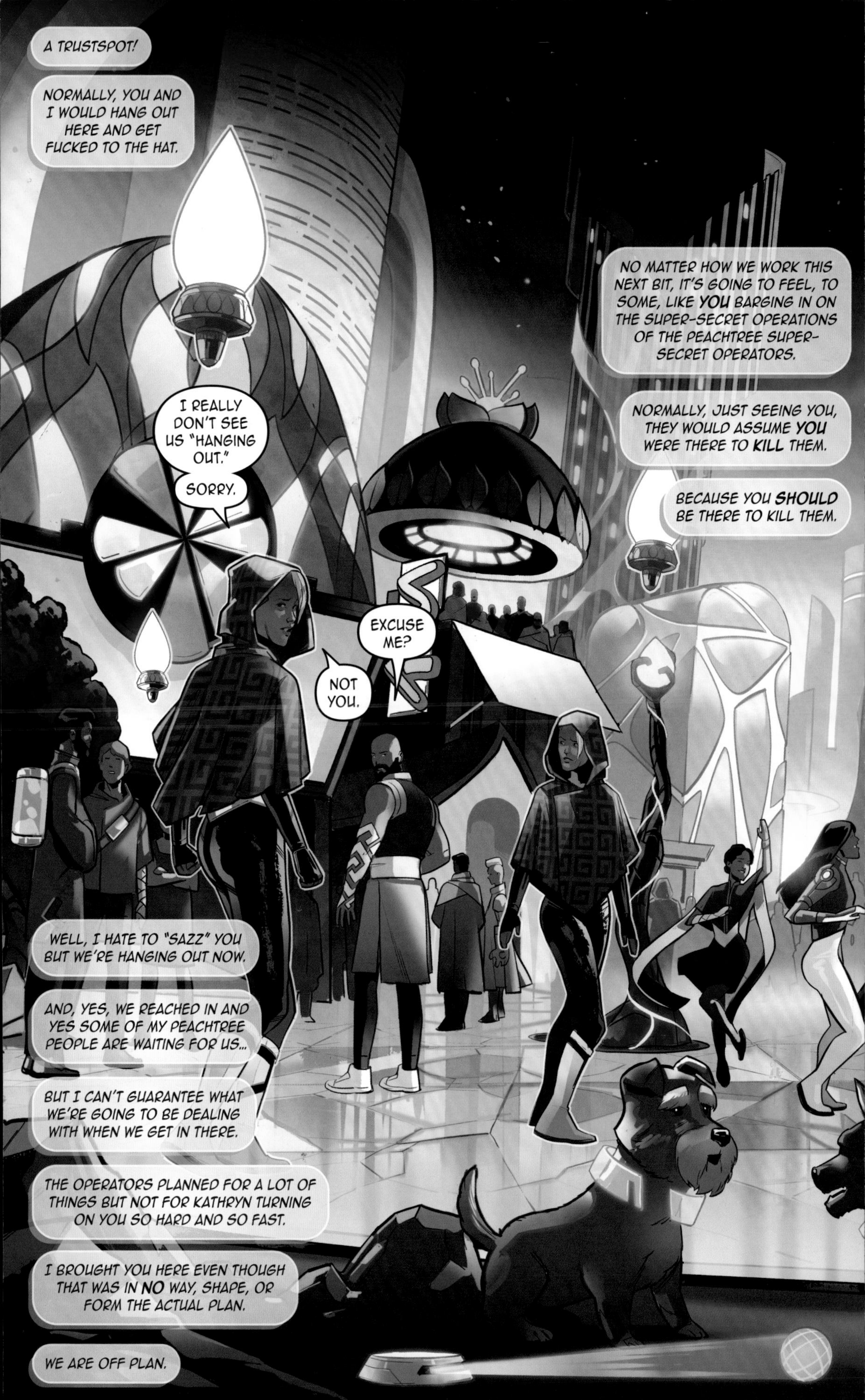
A TRUSTSPOT!
NORMALLY, YOU AND I WOULD HANG OUT HERE AND GET FUCKED TO THE HAT.
I REALLY DON'T SEE US "HANGING OUT."
SORRY.
NO MATTER HOW WE WORK THIS NEXT BIT, IT'S GOING TO FEEL, TO SOME, LIKE **YOU** BARGING IN ON THE SUPER-SECRET OPERATIONS OF THE PEACHTREE SUPER-SECRET OPERATORS.
NORMALLY, JUST SEEING YOU, THEY WOULD ASSUME **YOU** WERE THERE TO **KILL** THEM.
BECAUSE YOU **SHOULD** BE THERE TO KILL THEM.
EXCUSE ME?
NOT YOU.
WELL, I HATE TO "SAZZ" YOU BUT WE'RE HANGING OUT NOW.
AND, YES, WE REACHED IN AND YES SOME OF MY PEACHTREE PEOPLE ARE WAITING FOR US...
BUT I CAN'T GUARANTEE WHAT WE'RE GOING TO BE DEALING WITH WHEN WE GET IN THERE.
THE OPERATORS PLANNED FOR A LOT OF THINGS BUT NOT FOR KATHRYN TURNING ON YOU SO HARD AND SO FAST.
I BROUGHT YOU HERE EVEN THOUGH THAT WAS IN **NO** WAY, SHAPE, OR FORM THE ACTUAL PLAN.
WE ARE OFF PLAN.

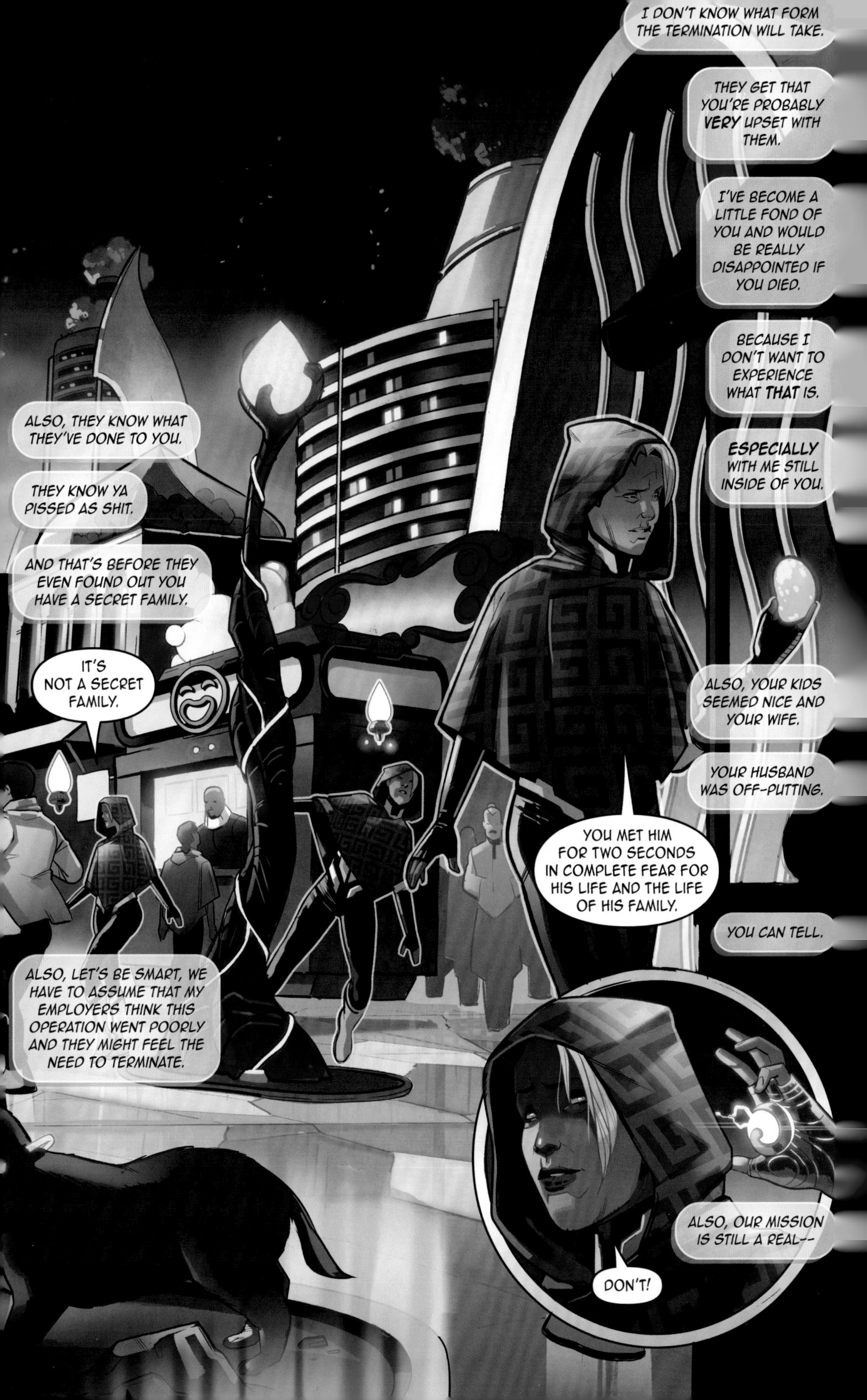
I DON'T KNOW WHAT FORM THE TERMINATION WILL TAKE.
THEY GET THAT YOU'RE PROBABLY **VERY** UPSET WITH THEM.
I'VE BECOME A LITTLE FOND OF YOU AND WOULD BE REALLY DISAPPOINTED IF YOU DIED.
BECAUSE I DON'T WANT TO EXPERIENCE WHAT **THAT** IS.
ESPECIALLY WITH ME STILL INSIDE OF YOU.
ALSO, THEY KNOW WHAT THEY'VE DONE TO YOU.
THEY KNOW YA PISSED AS SHIT.
AND THAT'S BEFORE THEY EVEN FOUND OUT YOU HAVE A SECRET FAMILY.
IT'S NOT A SECRET FAMILY.
ALSO, YOUR KIDS SEEMED NICE AND YOUR WIFE.
YOUR HUSBAND WAS OFF-PUTTING.
YOU MET HIM FOR TWO SECONDS IN COMPLETE FEAR FOR HIS LIFE AND THE LIFE OF HIS FAMILY.
YOU CAN TELL.
ALSO, LET'S BE SMART, WE HAVE TO ASSUME THAT MY EMPLOYERS THINK THIS OPERATION WENT POORLY AND THEY MIGHT FEEL THE NEED TO TERMINATE.
ALSO, OUR MISSION IS STILL A REAL--
DON'T!

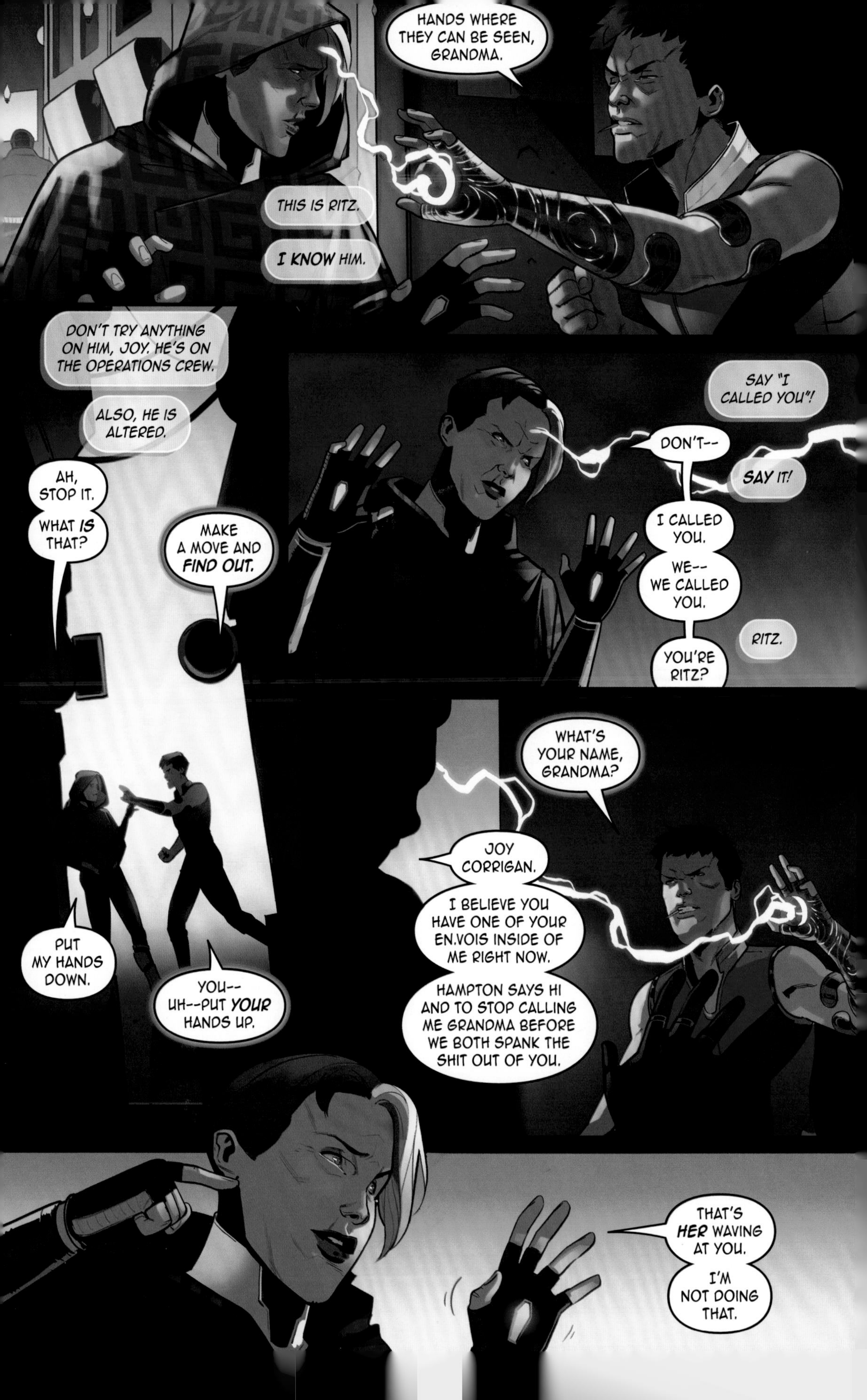
HANDS WHERE THEY CAN BE SEEN, GRANDMA.
THIS IS RITZ.
I KNOW HIM.
DON'T TRY ANYTHING ON HIM, JOY. HE'S ON THE OPERATIONS CREW.
ALSO, HE IS ALTERED.
AH, STOP IT.
WHAT IS THAT?
MAKE A MOVE AND FIND OUT.
SAY "I CALLED YOU"!
DON'T--
SAY IT!
I CALLED YOU.
WE-- WE CALLED YOU.
RITZ.
YOU'RE RITZ?
PUT MY HANDS DOWN.
YOU-- UH--PUT YOUR HANDS UP.
WHAT'S YOUR NAME, GRANDMA?
JOY CORRIGAN.
I BELIEVE YOU HAVE ONE OF YOUR EN.VOIS INSIDE OF ME RIGHT NOW.
HAMPTON SAYS HI AND TO STOP CALLING ME GRANDMA BEFORE WE BOTH SPANK THE SHIT OUT OF YOU.
THAT'S HER WAVING AT YOU.
I'M NOT DOING THAT.

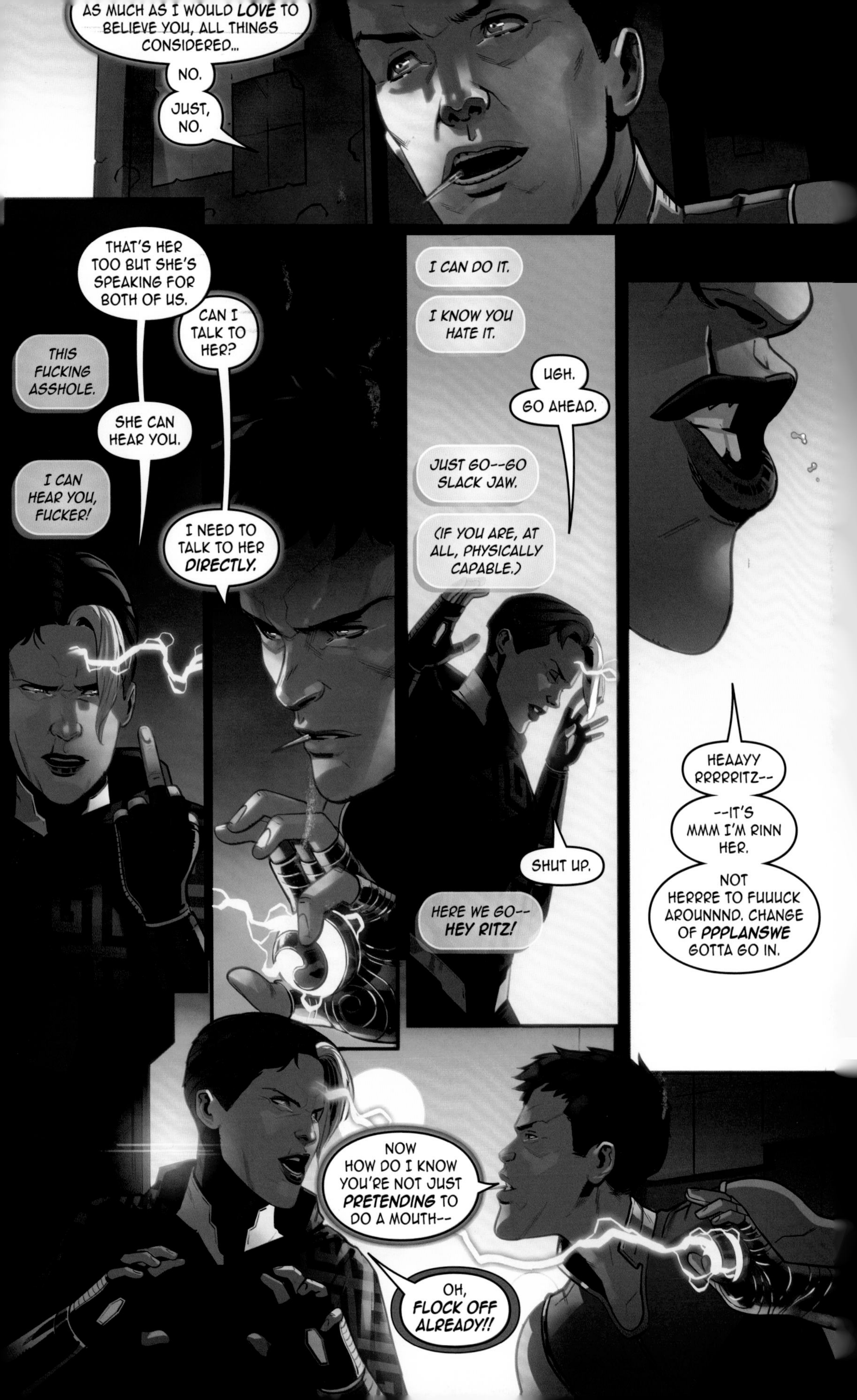
AS MUCH AS I WOULD **LOVE** TO BELIEVE YOU, ALL THINGS CONSIDERED...
NO.
JUST, NO.
THAT'S HER TOO BUT SHE'S SPEAKING FOR BOTH OF US.
CAN I TALK TO HER?
THIS FUCKING ASSHOLE.
SHE CAN HEAR YOU.
I CAN HEAR YOU, FUCKER!
I NEED TO TALK TO HER **DIRECTLY.**
I CAN DO IT.
I KNOW YOU HATE IT.
UGH.
GO AHEAD.
JUST GO--GO SLACK JAW.
(IF YOU ARE, AT ALL, PHYSICALLY CAPABLE.)
SHUT UP.
HERE WE GO-- **HEY RITZ!**
HEAAYY RRRRRITZ--
--IT'S MMM I'M RINN HER.
NOT HERRRE TO FUUUCK AROUNNND. CHANGE OF **PPPLANSWE** GOTTA GO IN.
NOW HOW DO I KNOW YOU'RE NOT JUST **PRETENDING** TO DO A MOUTH--
OH, **FLOCK OFF ALREADY!!**

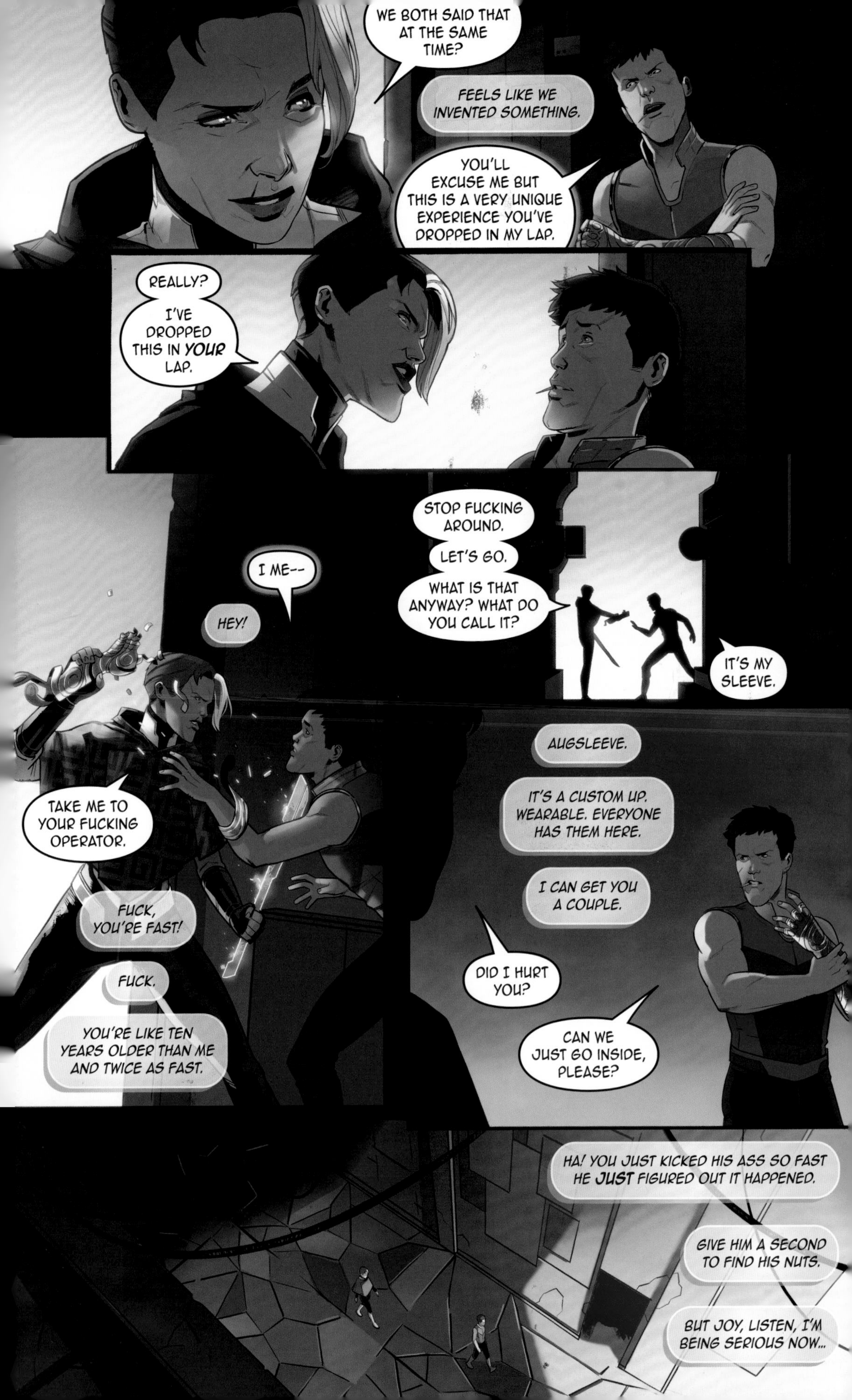
WE BOTH SAID THAT AT THE SAME TIME?
FEELS LIKE WE INVENTED SOMETHING.
YOU'LL EXCUSE ME BUT THIS IS A VERY UNIQUE EXPERIENCE YOU'VE DROPPED IN MY LAP.
REALLY?
I'VE DROPPED THIS IN *YOUR* LAP.
STOP FUCKING AROUND.
LET'S GO.
WHAT IS THAT ANYWAY? WHAT DO YOU CALL IT?
I ME--
HEY!
IT'S MY SLEEVE.
AUGSLEEVE.
IT'S A CUSTOM UP. WEARABLE. EVERYONE HAS THEM HERE.
I CAN GET YOU A COUPLE.
TAKE ME TO YOUR FUCKING OPERATOR.
FUCK, YOU'RE FAST!
FUCK.
YOU'RE LIKE TEN YEARS OLDER THAN ME AND TWICE AS FAST.
DID I HURT YOU?
CAN WE JUST GO INSIDE, PLEASE?
HA! YOU JUST KICKED HIS ASS SO FAST HE **JUST** FIGURED OUT IT HAPPENED.
GIVE HIM A SECOND TO FIND HIS NUTS.
BUT JOY, LISTEN, I'M BEING SERIOUS NOW...

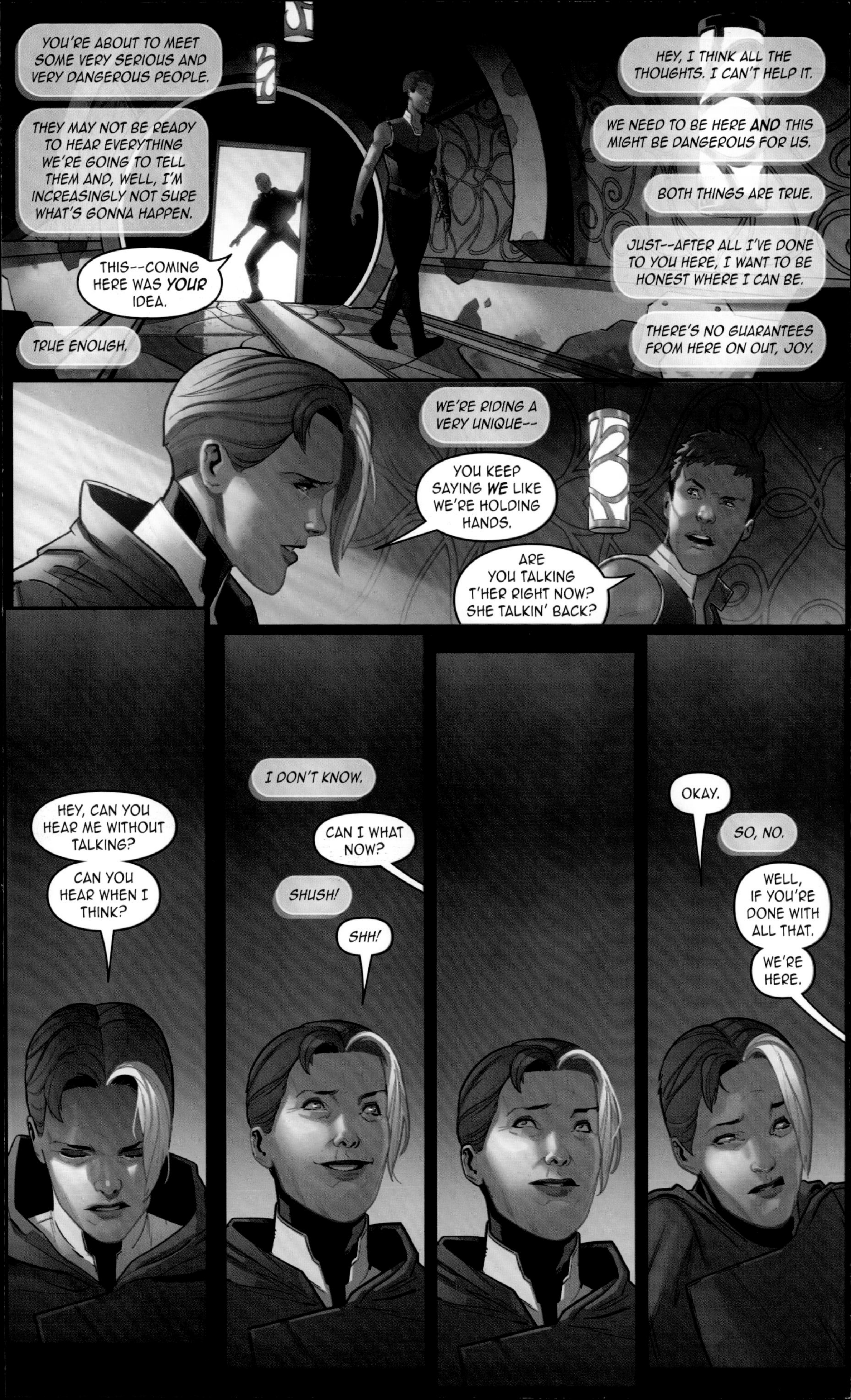
YOU'RE ABOUT TO MEET SOME VERY SERIOUS AND VERY DANGEROUS PEOPLE.
THEY MAY NOT BE READY TO HEAR EVERYTHING WE'RE GOING TO TELL THEM AND, WELL, I'M INCREASINGLY NOT SURE WHAT'S GONNA HAPPEN.
THIS--COMING HERE WAS YOUR IDEA.
TRUE ENOUGH.
HEY, I THINK ALL THE THOUGHTS. I CAN'T HELP IT.
WE NEED TO BE HERE AND THIS MIGHT BE DANGEROUS FOR US.
BOTH THINGS ARE TRUE.
JUST--AFTER ALL I'VE DONE TO YOU HERE, I WANT TO BE HONEST WHERE I CAN BE.
THERE'S NO GUARANTEES FROM HERE ON OUT, JOY.
WE'RE RIDING A VERY UNIQUE--
YOU KEEP SAYING WE LIKE WE'RE HOLDING HANDS.
ARE YOU TALKING T'HER RIGHT NOW? SHE TALKIN' BACK?
HEY, CAN YOU HEAR ME WITHOUT TALKING?
CAN YOU HEAR WHEN I THINK?
I DON'T KNOW.
CAN I WHAT NOW?
SHUSH!
SHH!
OKAY.
SO, NO.
WELL, IF YOU'RE DONE WITH ALL THAT.
WE'RE HERE.

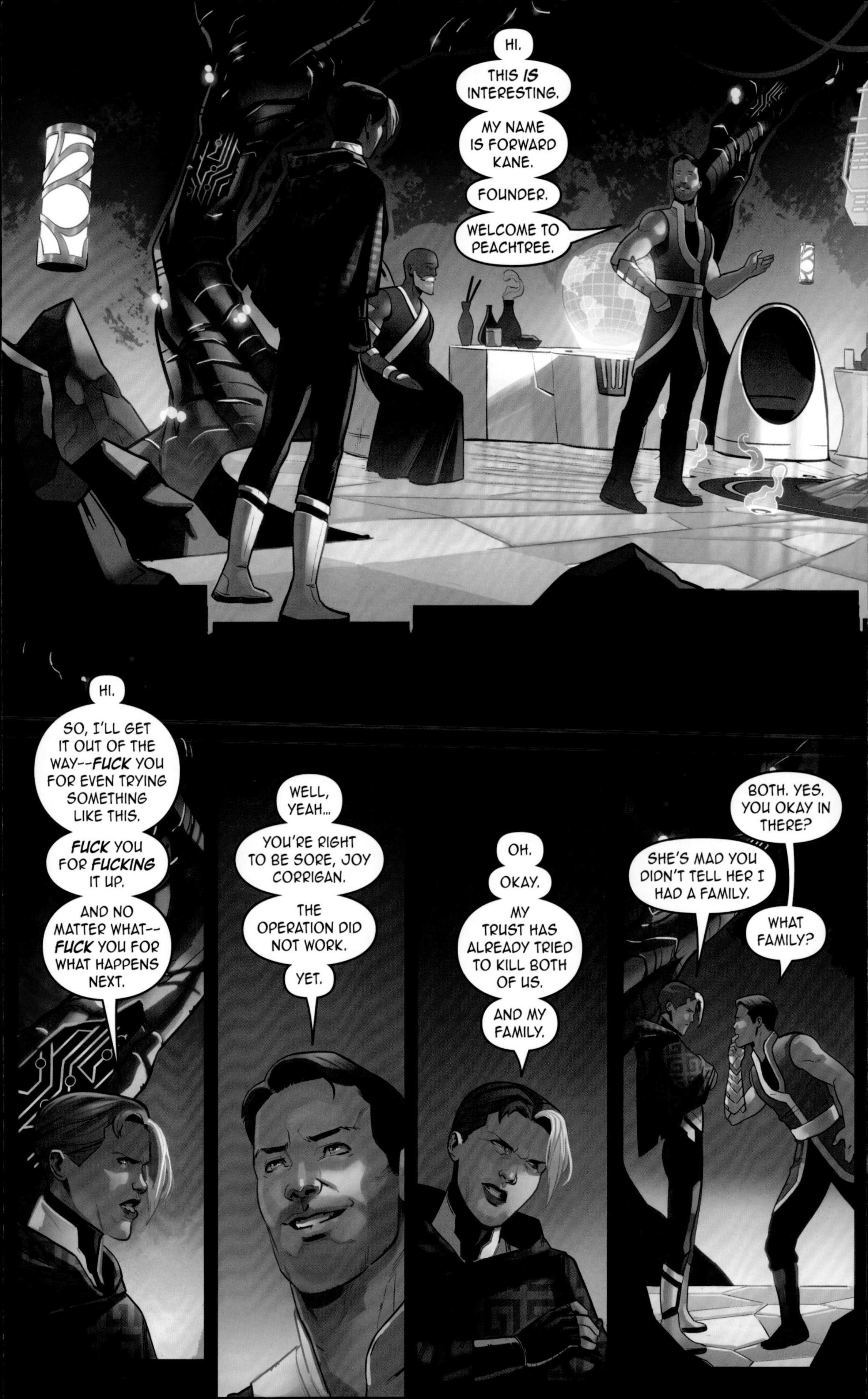
HI.
THIS *IS* INTERESTING.
MY NAME IS FORWARD KANE.
FOUNDER.
WELCOME TO PEACHTREE.
HI.
SO, I'LL GET IT OUT OF THE WAY--***FUCK*** YOU FOR EVEN TRYING SOMETHING LIKE THIS.
FUCK YOU FOR ***FUCKING*** IT UP.
AND NO MATTER WHAT--***FUCK*** YOU FOR WHAT HAPPENS NEXT.
WELL, YEAH...
YOU'RE RIGHT TO BE SORE, JOY CORRIGAN.
THE OPERATION DID NOT WORK.
YET.
OH.
OKAY.
MY TRUST HAS ALREADY TRIED TO KILL BOTH OF US.
AND MY FAMILY.
BOTH. YES. YOU OKAY IN THERE?
SHE'S MAD YOU DIDN'T TELL HER I HAD A FAMILY.
WHAT FAMILY?

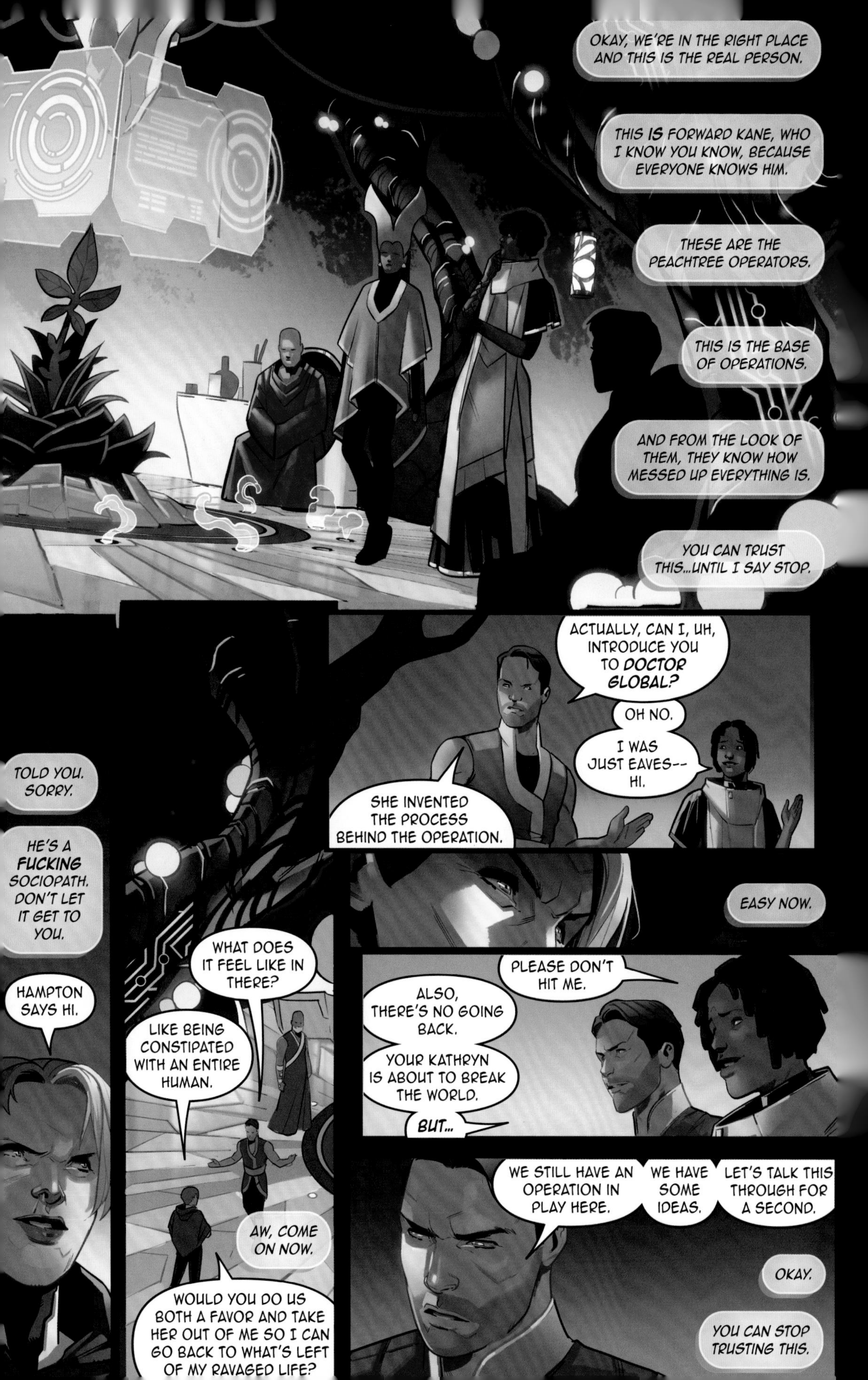

OKAY, WE'RE IN THE RIGHT PLACE AND THIS IS THE REAL PERSON.
THIS **IS** FORWARD KANE, WHO I KNOW YOU KNOW, BECAUSE EVERYONE KNOWS HIM.
THESE ARE THE PEACHTREE OPERATORS.
THIS IS THE BASE OF OPERATIONS.
AND FROM THE LOOK OF THEM, THEY KNOW HOW MESSED UP EVERYTHING IS.
YOU CAN TRUST THIS...UNTIL I SAY STOP.
ACTUALLY, CAN I, UH, INTRODUCE YOU TO **DOCTOR GLOBAL?**
OH NO.
I WAS JUST EAVES--HI.
SHE INVENTED THE PROCESS BEHIND THE OPERATION.
TOLD YOU. SORRY.
HE'S A **FUCKING** SOCIOPATH. DON'T LET IT GET TO YOU.
EASY NOW.
PLEASE DON'T HIT ME.
ALSO, THERE'S NO GOING BACK.
YOUR KATHRYN IS ABOUT TO BREAK THE WORLD.
BUT...
HAMPTON SAYS HI.
WHAT DOES IT FEEL LIKE IN THERE?
LIKE BEING CONSTIPATED WITH AN ENTIRE HUMAN.
AW, COME ON NOW.
WOULD YOU DO US BOTH A FAVOR AND TAKE HER OUT OF ME SO I CAN GO BACK TO WHAT'S LEFT OF MY RAVAGED LIFE?
WE STILL HAVE AN OPERATION IN PLAY HERE.
WE HAVE SOME IDEAS.
LET'S TALK THIS THROUGH FOR A SECOND.
OKAY.
YOU CAN STOP TRUSTING THIS.

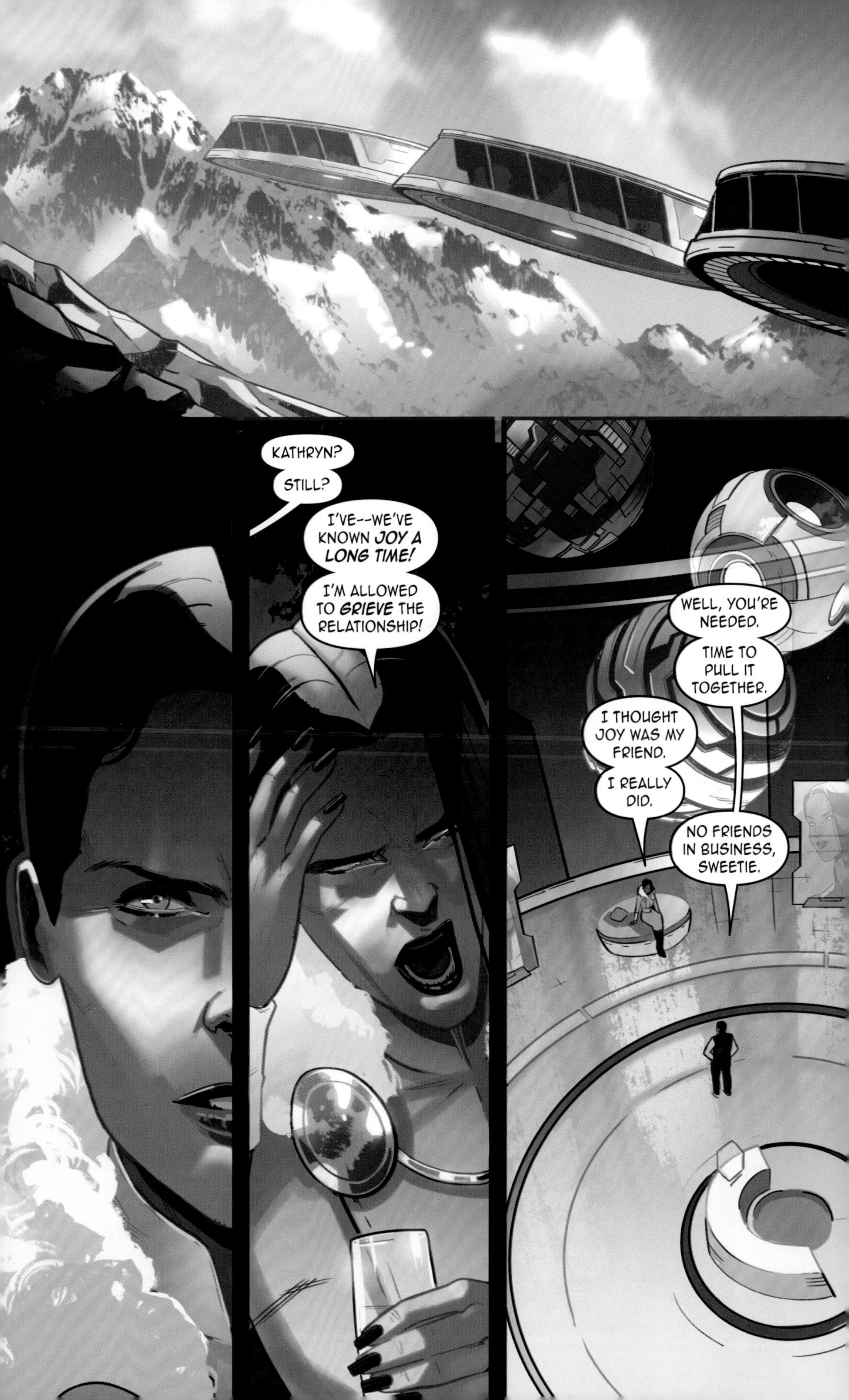
KATHRYN?
STILL?
I'VE--WE'VE KNOWN JOY A LONG TIME!
I'M ALLOWED TO GRIEVE THE RELATIONSHIP!
WELL, YOU'RE NEEDED.
TIME TO PULL IT TOGETHER.
I THOUGHT JOY WAS MY FRIEND.
I REALLY DID.
NO FRIENDS IN BUSINESS, SWEETIE.

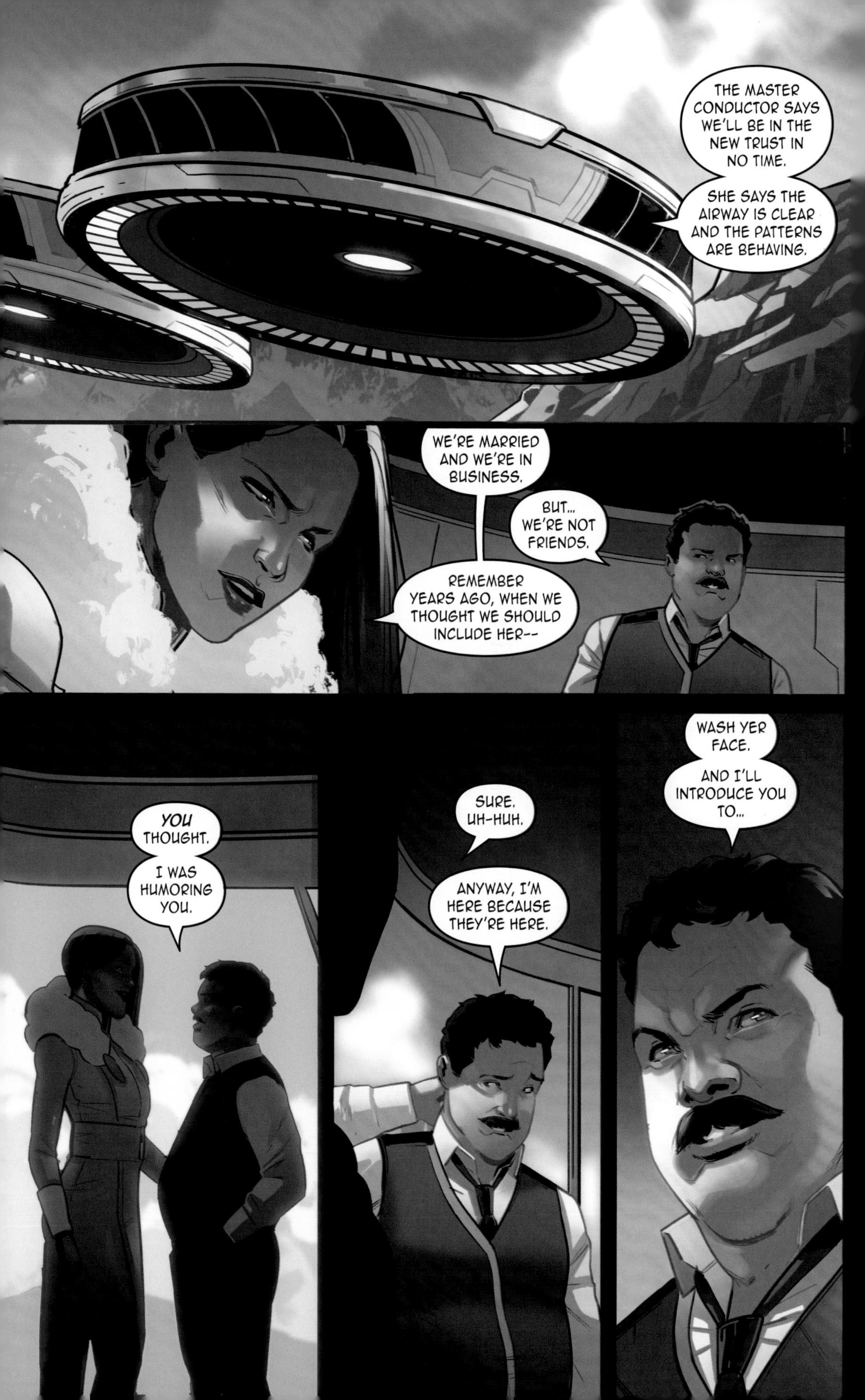
THE MASTER CONDUCTOR SAYS WE'LL BE IN THE NEW TRUST IN NO TIME.
SHE SAYS THE AIRWAY IS CLEAR AND THE PATTERNS ARE BEHAVING.
WE'RE MARRIED AND WE'RE IN BUSINESS.
BUT... WE'RE NOT FRIENDS.
REMEMBER YEARS AGO, WHEN WE THOUGHT WE SHOULD INCLUDE HER--
YOU THOUGHT.
I WAS HUMORING YOU.
SURE. UH-HUH.
ANYWAY, I'M HERE BECAUSE THEY'RE HERE.
WASH YER FACE.
AND I'LL INTRODUCE YOU TO...

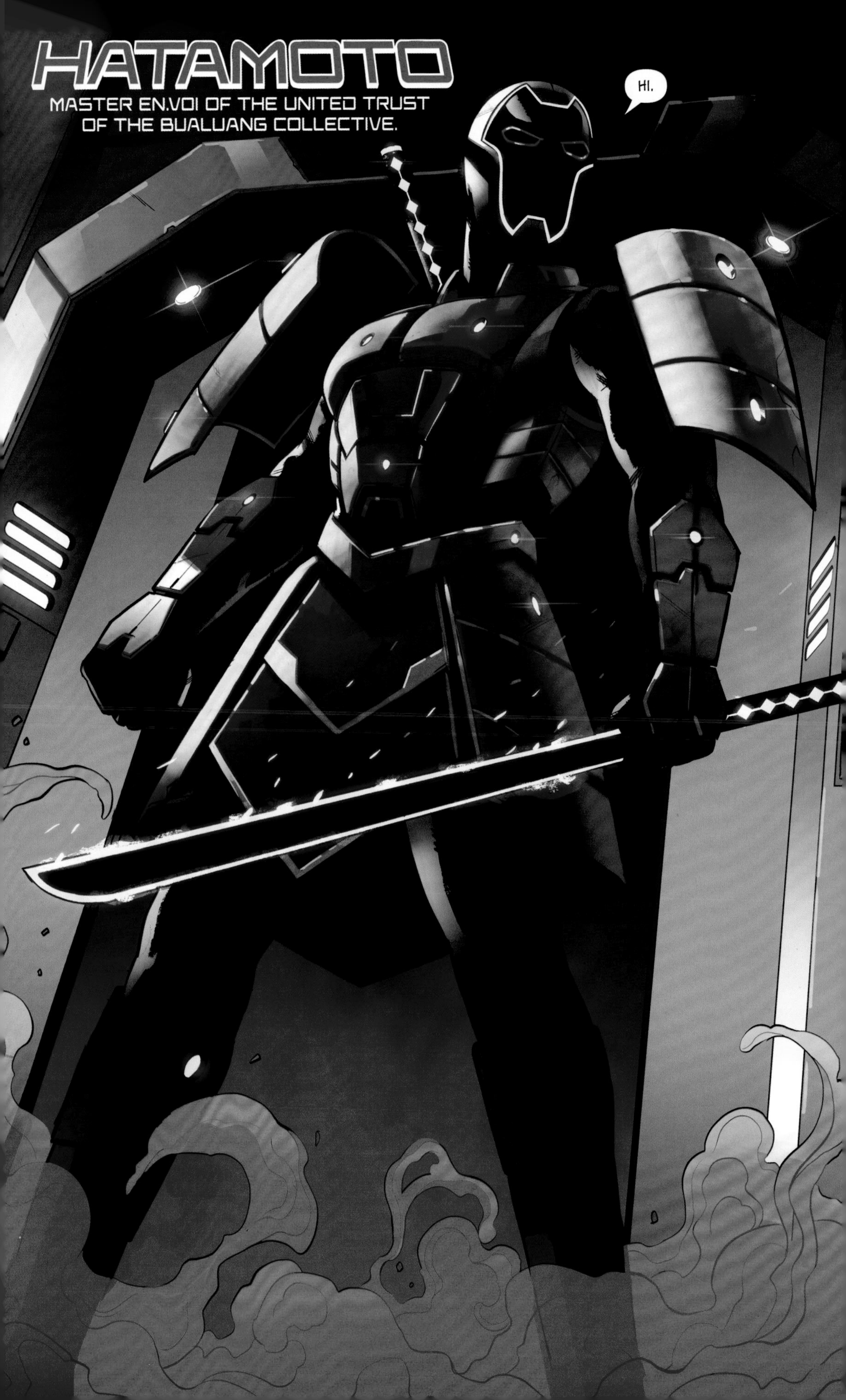
HATAMOTO
MASTER EN.VOI OF THE UNITED TRUST OF THE BUALUANG COLLECTIVE.
HI.

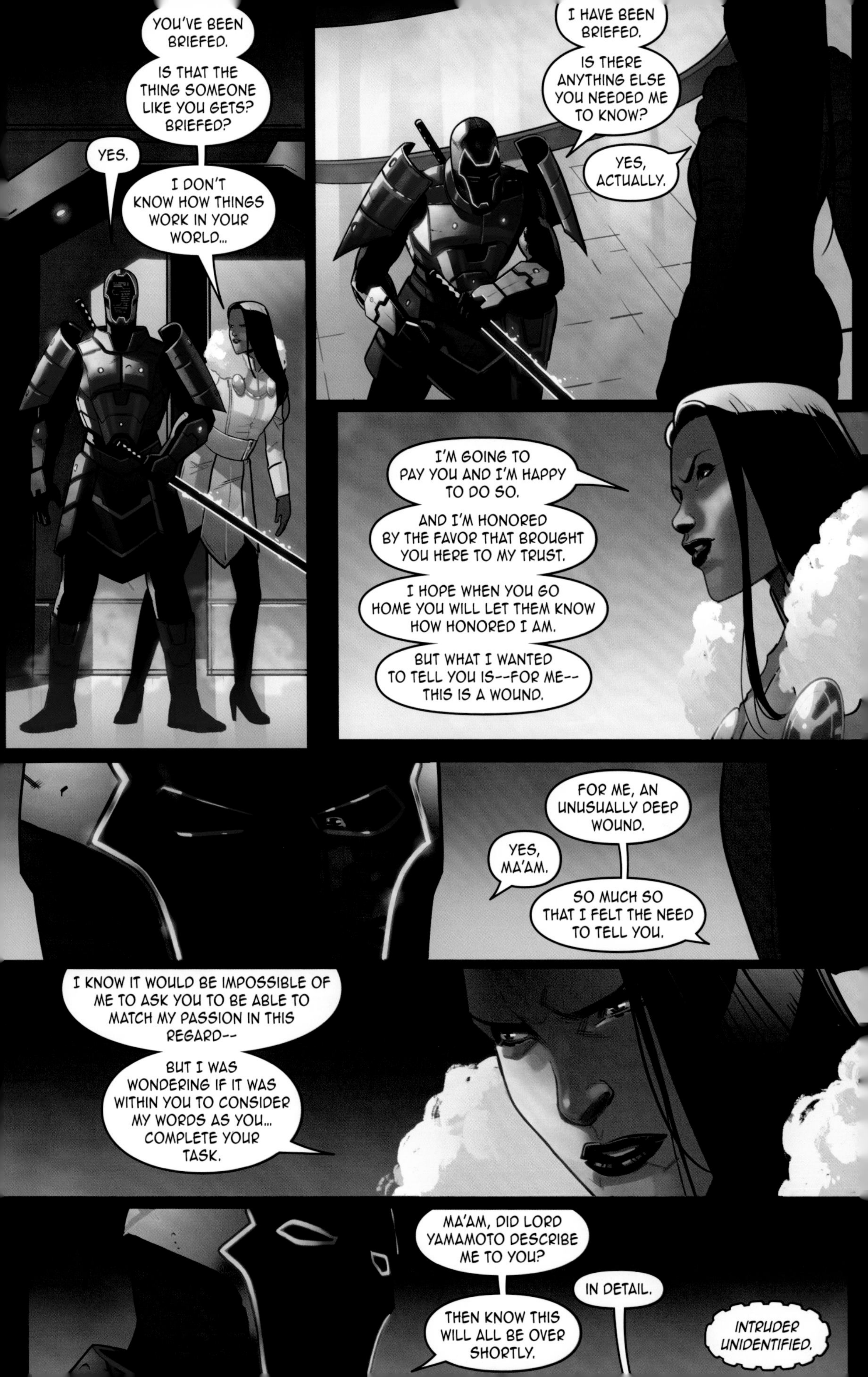
YOU'VE BEEN BRIEFED.
IS THAT THE THING SOMEONE LIKE YOU GETS? BRIEFED?
YES.
I DON'T KNOW HOW THINGS WORK IN YOUR WORLD...
I HAVE BEEN BRIEFED.
IS THERE ANYTHING ELSE YOU NEEDED ME TO KNOW?
YES, ACTUALLY.
I'M GOING TO PAY YOU AND I'M HAPPY TO DO SO.
AND I'M HONORED BY THE FAVOR THAT BROUGHT YOU HERE TO MY TRUST.
I HOPE WHEN YOU GO HOME YOU WILL LET THEM KNOW HOW HONORED I AM.
BUT WHAT I WANTED TO TELL YOU IS--FOR ME--THIS IS A WOUND.
FOR ME, AN UNUSUALLY DEEP WOUND.
YES, MA'AM.
SO MUCH SO THAT I FELT THE NEED TO TELL YOU.
I KNOW IT WOULD BE IMPOSSIBLE OF ME TO ASK YOU TO BE ABLE TO MATCH MY PASSION IN THIS REGARD--
BUT I WAS WONDERING IF IT WAS WITHIN YOU TO CONSIDER MY WORDS AS YOU... COMPLETE YOUR TASK.
MA'AM, DID LORD YAMAMOTO DESCRIBE ME TO YOU?
IN DETAIL.
THEN KNOW THIS WILL ALL BE OVER SHORTLY.
INTRUDER UNIDENTIFIED.

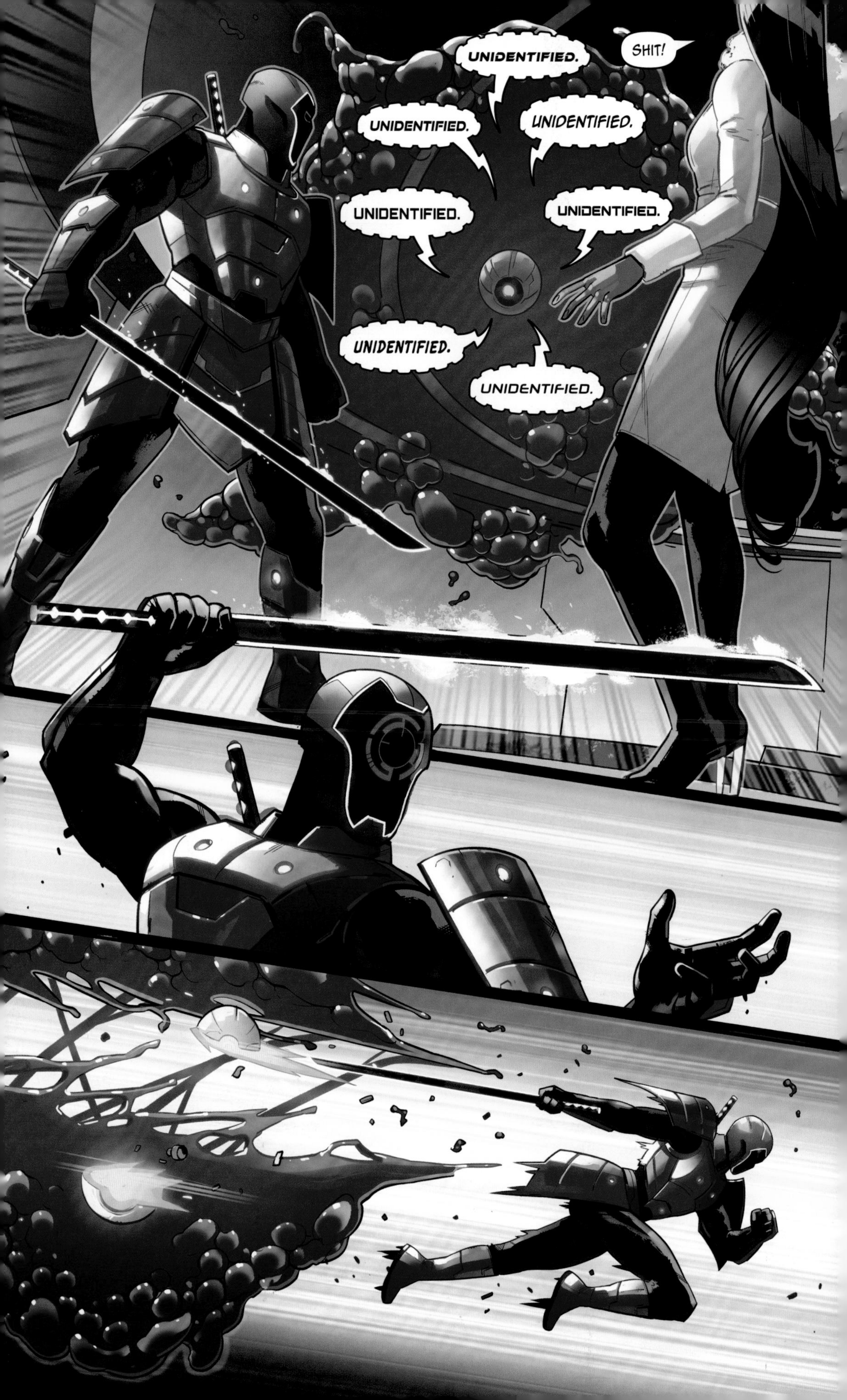
UNIDENTIFIED.
SHIT!
UNIDENTIFIED.
UNIDENTIFIED.
UNIDENTIFIED.
UNIDENTIFIED.
UNIDENTIFIED.
UNIDENTIFIED.

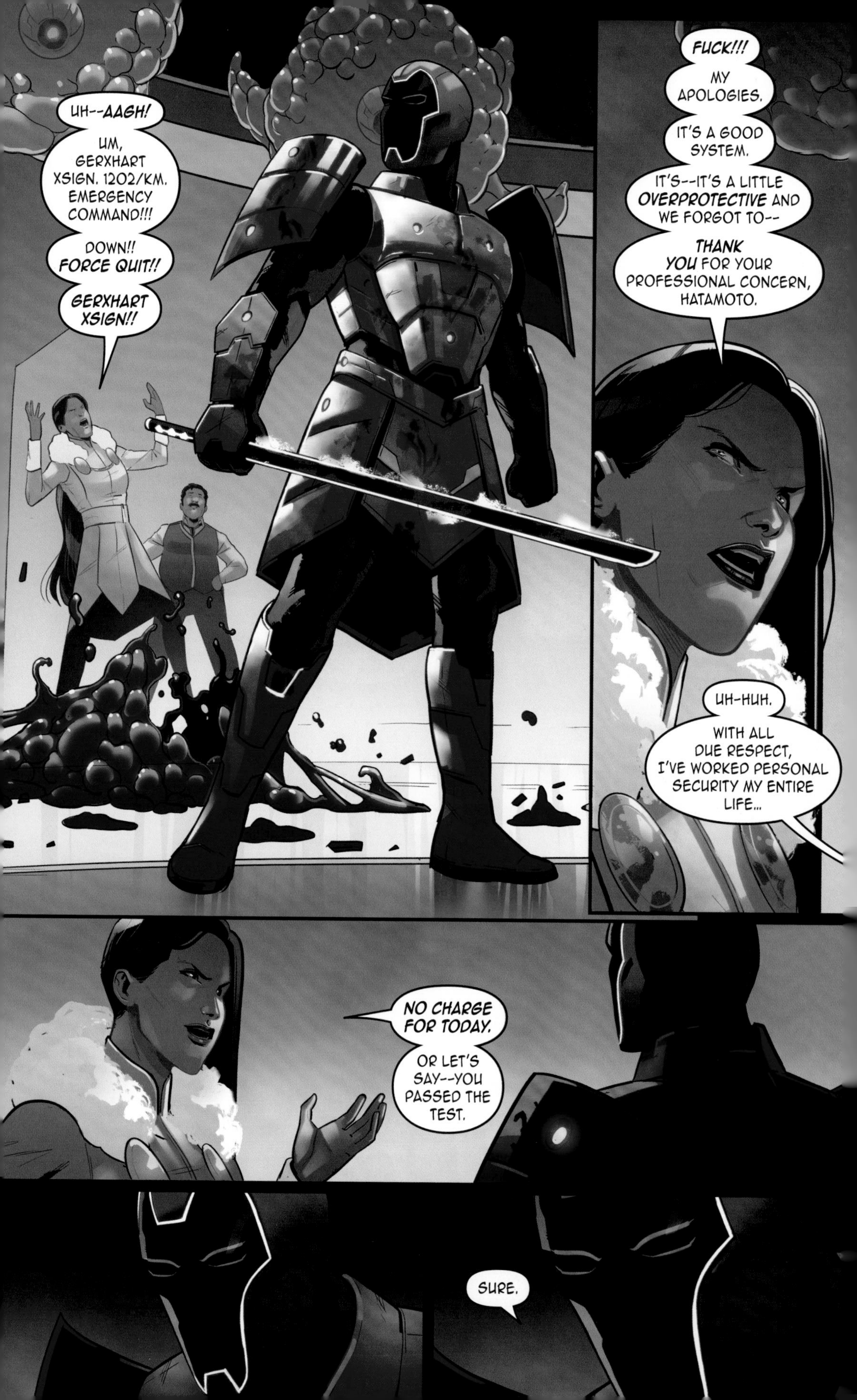
UH--AAGH!
UM, GERXHART XSIGN. 1202/KM. EMERGENCY COMMAND!!!
DOWN!! FORCE QUIT!!
GERXHART XSIGN!!
FUCK!!!
MY APOLOGIES.
IT'S A GOOD SYSTEM.
IT'S--IT'S A LITTLE OVERPROTECTIVE AND WE FORGOT TO--
THANK YOU FOR YOUR PROFESSIONAL CONCERN, HATAMOTO.
UH-HUH.
WITH ALL DUE RESPECT, I'VE WORKED PERSONAL SECURITY MY ENTIRE LIFE...
NO CHARGE FOR TODAY.
OR LET'S SAY--YOU PASSED THE TEST.
SURE.

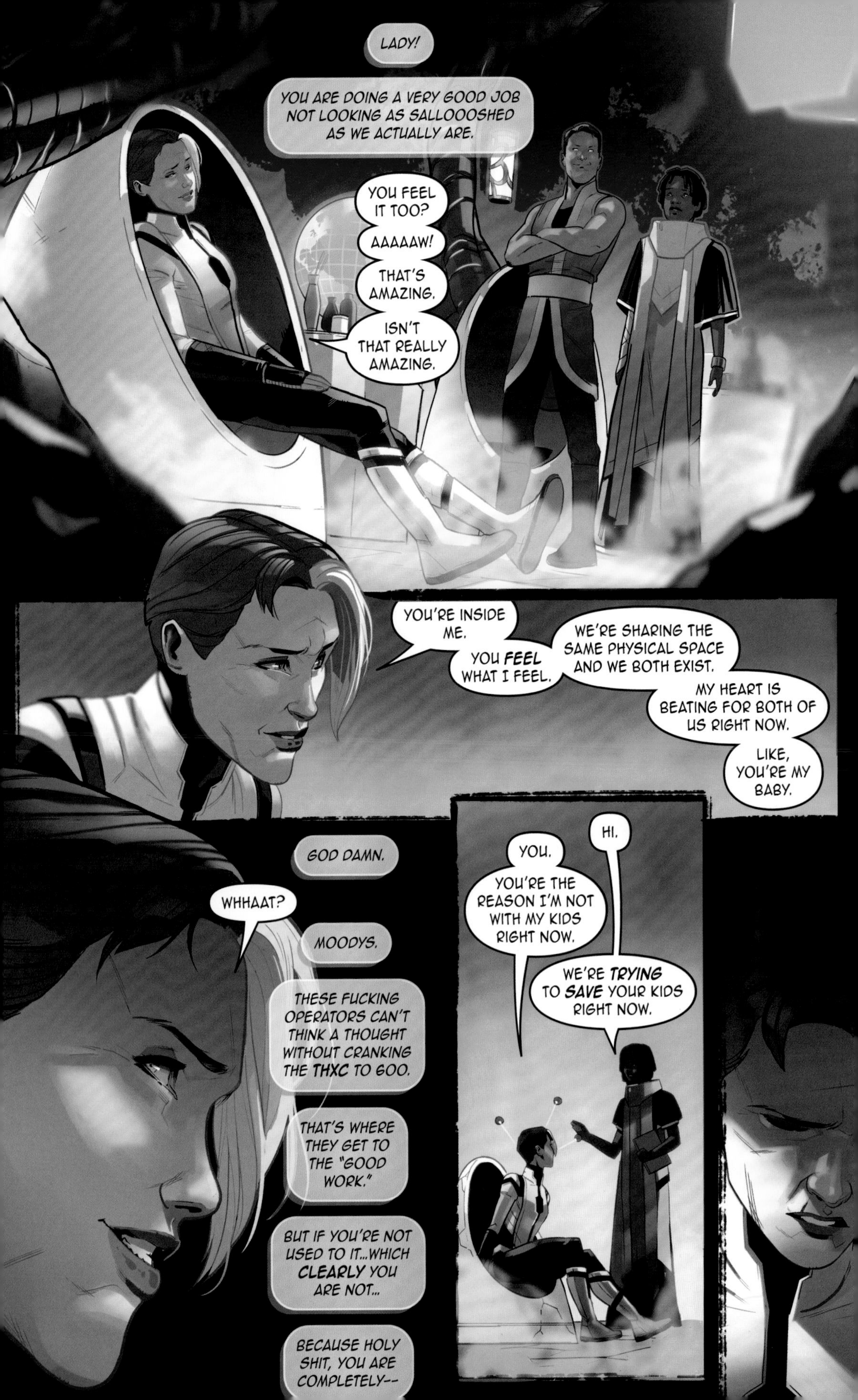
LADY!
YOU ARE DOING A VERY GOOD JOB NOT LOOKING AS SALLOOOSHED AS WE ACTUALLY ARE.
YOU FEEL IT TOO?
AAAAAW!
THAT'S AMAZING.
ISN'T THAT REALLY AMAZING.
YOU'RE INSIDE ME.
YOU **FEEL** WHAT I FEEL.
WE'RE SHARING THE SAME PHYSICAL SPACE AND WE BOTH EXIST.
MY HEART IS BEATING FOR BOTH OF US RIGHT NOW.
LIKE, YOU'RE MY BABY.
GOD DAMN.
WHHAAT?
MOODYS.
THESE FUCKING OPERATORS CAN'T THINK A THOUGHT WITHOUT CRANKING THE **THXC** TO 600.
THAT'S WHERE THEY GET TO THE "GOOD WORK."
BUT IF YOU'RE NOT USED TO IT...WHICH **CLEARLY** YOU ARE NOT...
BECAUSE HOLY SHIT, YOU ARE COMPLETELY--
HI.
YOU.
YOU'RE THE REASON I'M NOT WITH MY KIDS RIGHT NOW.
WE'RE **TRYING** TO **SAVE** YOUR KIDS RIGHT NOW.

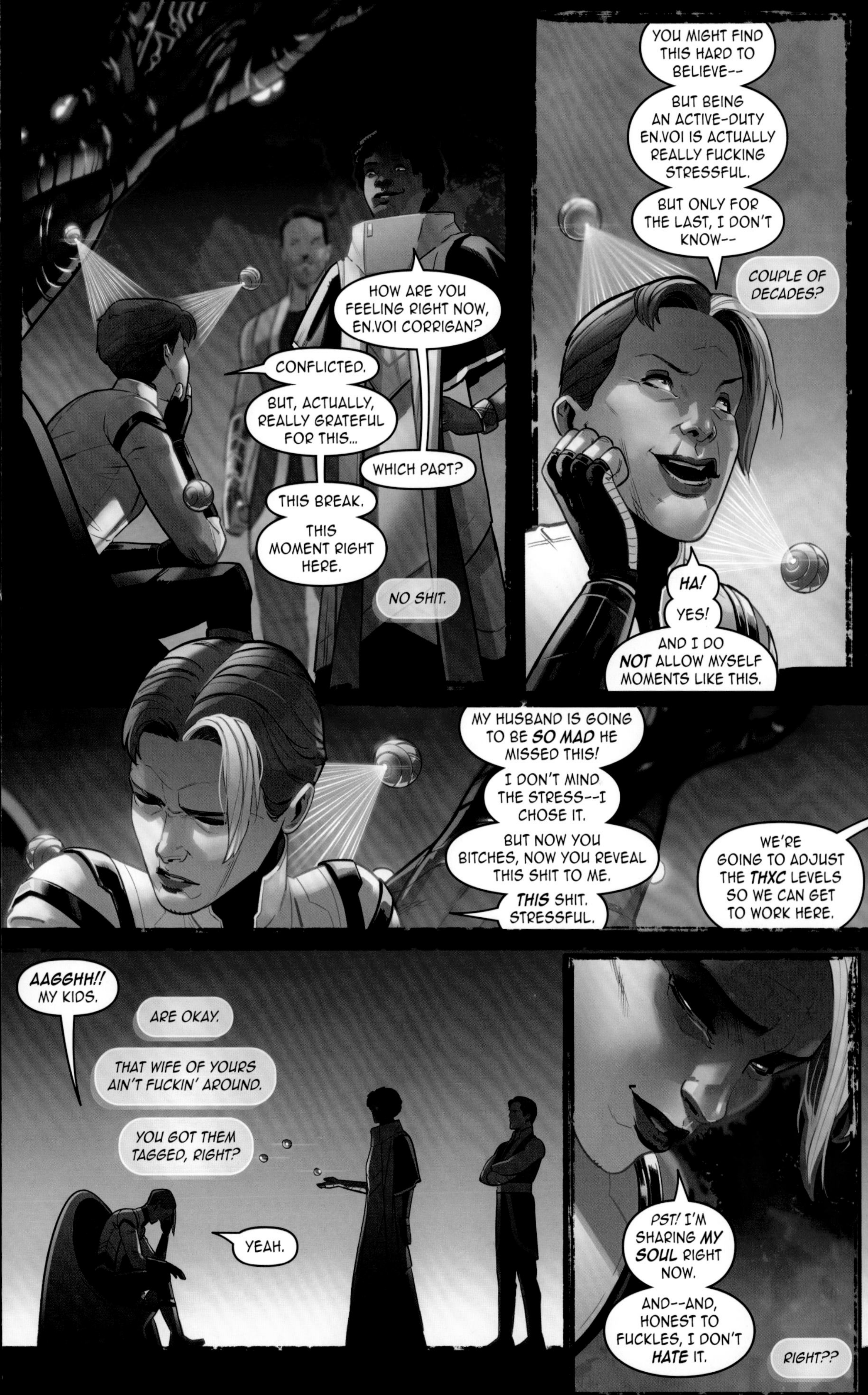
HOW ARE YOU FEELING RIGHT NOW, EN.VOI CORRIGAN?
CONFLICTED.
BUT, ACTUALLY, REALLY GRATEFUL FOR THIS...
WHICH PART?
THIS BREAK.
THIS MOMENT RIGHT HERE.
NO SHIT.
YOU MIGHT FIND THIS HARD TO BELIEVE--
BUT BEING AN ACTIVE-DUTY EN.VOI IS ACTUALLY REALLY FUCKING STRESSFUL.
BUT ONLY FOR THE LAST, I DON'T KNOW--
COUPLE OF DECADES?
HA!
YES!
AND I DO NOT ALLOW MYSELF MOMENTS LIKE THIS.
MY HUSBAND IS GOING TO BE SO MAD HE MISSED THIS!
I DON'T MIND THE STRESS--I CHOSE IT.
BUT NOW YOU BITCHES, NOW YOU REVEAL THIS SHIT TO ME.
THIS SHIT. STRESSFUL.
WE'RE GOING TO ADJUST THE THXC LEVELS SO WE CAN GET TO WORK HERE.
AAGGHH!! MY KIDS.
ARE OKAY.
THAT WIFE OF YOURS AIN'T FUCKIN' AROUND.
YOU GOT THEM TAGGED, RIGHT?
YEAH.
PST! I'M SHARING MY SOUL RIGHT NOW.
AND--AND, HONEST TO FUCKLES, I DON'T HATE IT.
RIGHT??

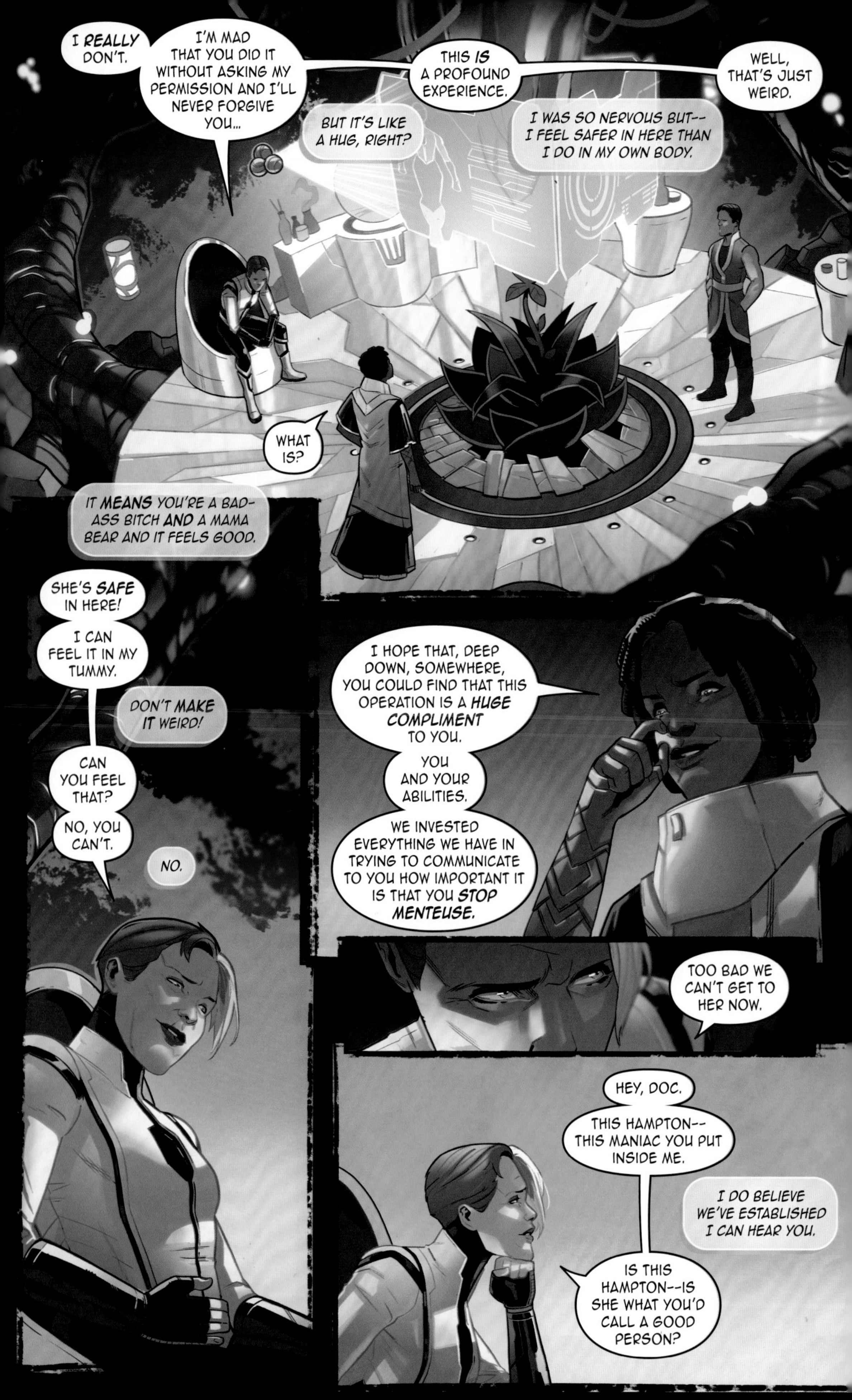

I REALLY DON'T.
I'M MAD THAT YOU DID IT WITHOUT ASKING MY PERMISSION AND I'LL NEVER FORGIVE YOU...
THIS IS A PROFOUND EXPERIENCE.
WELL, THAT'S JUST WEIRD.
BUT IT'S LIKE A HUG, RIGHT?
I WAS SO NERVOUS BUT-- I FEEL SAFER IN HERE THAN I DO IN MY OWN BODY.
WHAT IS?
IT MEANS YOU'RE A BAD-ASS BITCH AND A MAMA BEAR AND IT FEELS GOOD.
SHE'S SAFE IN HERE!
I CAN FEEL IT IN MY TUMMY.
DON'T MAKE IT WEIRD!
CAN YOU FEEL THAT?
NO, YOU CAN'T.
NO.
I HOPE THAT, DEEP DOWN, SOMEWHERE, YOU COULD FIND THAT THIS OPERATION IS A HUGE COMPLIMENT TO YOU.
YOU AND YOUR ABILITIES.
WE INVESTED EVERYTHING WE HAVE IN TRYING TO COMMUNICATE TO YOU HOW IMPORTANT IT IS THAT YOU STOP MENTEUSE.
TOO BAD WE CAN'T GET TO HER NOW.
HEY, DOC.
THIS HAMPTON-- THIS MANIAC YOU PUT INSIDE ME.
I DO BELIEVE WE'VE ESTABLISHED I CAN HEAR YOU.
IS THIS HAMPTON--IS SHE WHAT YOU'D CALL A GOOD PERSON?

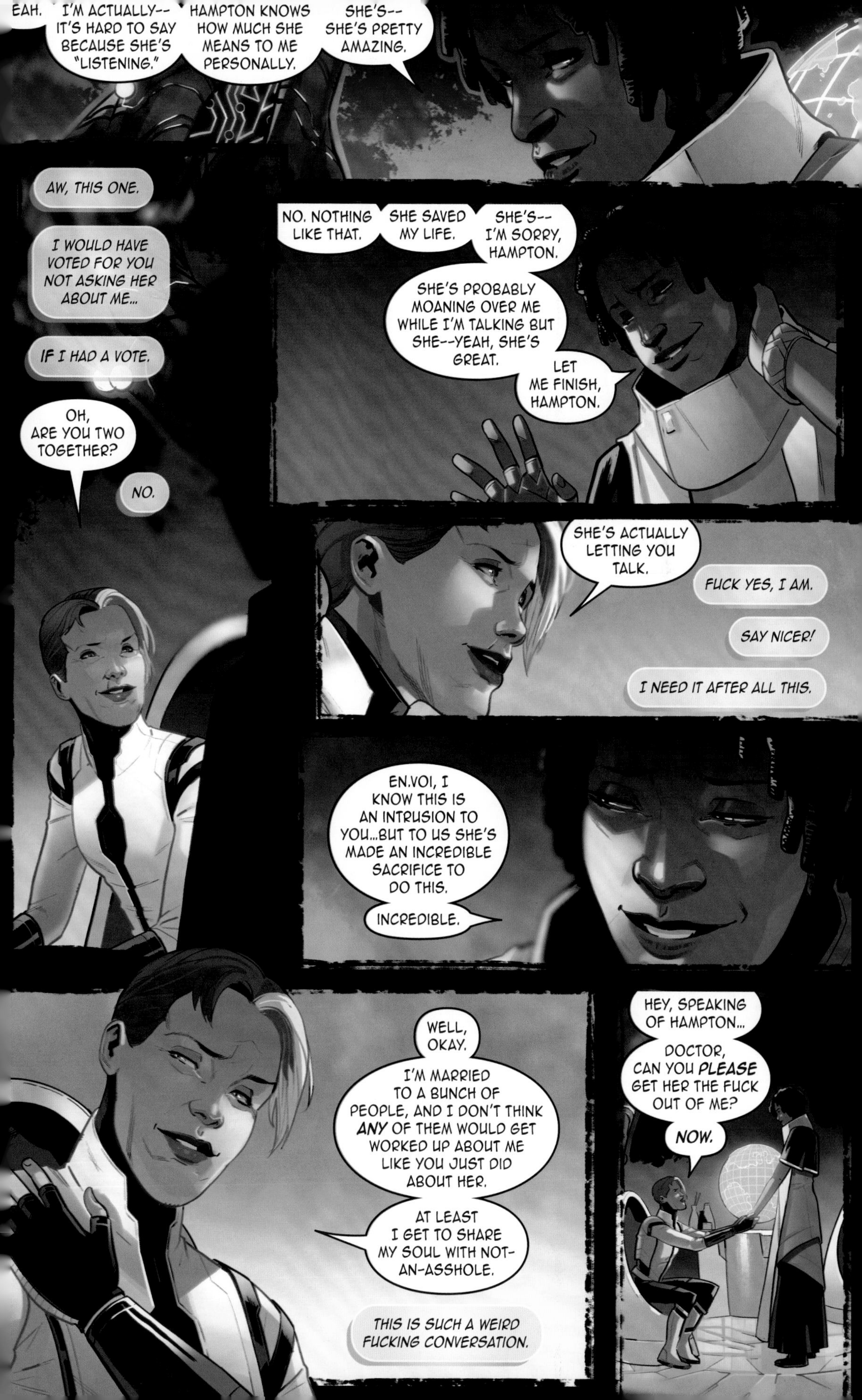
EAH.
I'M ACTUALLY-- IT'S HARD TO SAY BECAUSE SHE'S "LISTENING."
HAMPTON KNOWS HOW MUCH SHE MEANS TO ME PERSONALLY.
SHE'S-- SHE'S PRETTY AMAZING.
AW, THIS ONE.
I WOULD HAVE VOTED FOR YOU NOT ASKING HER ABOUT ME...
IF I HAD A VOTE.
OH, ARE YOU TWO TOGETHER?
NO.
NO. NOTHING LIKE THAT.
SHE SAVED MY LIFE.
SHE'S-- I'M SORRY, HAMPTON.
SHE'S PROBABLY MOANING OVER ME WHILE I'M TALKING BUT SHE--YEAH, SHE'S GREAT.
LET ME FINISH, HAMPTON.
SHE'S ACTUALLY LETTING YOU TALK.
FUCK YES, I AM.
SAY NICER!
I NEED IT AFTER ALL THIS.
EN.VOI, I KNOW THIS IS AN INTRUSION TO YOU...BUT TO US SHE'S MADE AN INCREDIBLE SACRIFICE TO DO THIS.
INCREDIBLE.
WELL, OKAY.
I'M MARRIED TO A BUNCH OF PEOPLE, AND I DON'T THINK ANY OF THEM WOULD GET WORKED UP ABOUT ME LIKE YOU JUST DID ABOUT HER.
AT LEAST I GET TO SHARE MY SOUL WITH NOT-AN-ASSHOLE.
THIS IS SUCH A WEIRD FUCKING CONVERSATION.
HEY, SPEAKING OF HAMPTON...
DOCTOR, CAN YOU PLEASE GET HER THE FUCK OUT OF ME?
NOW.

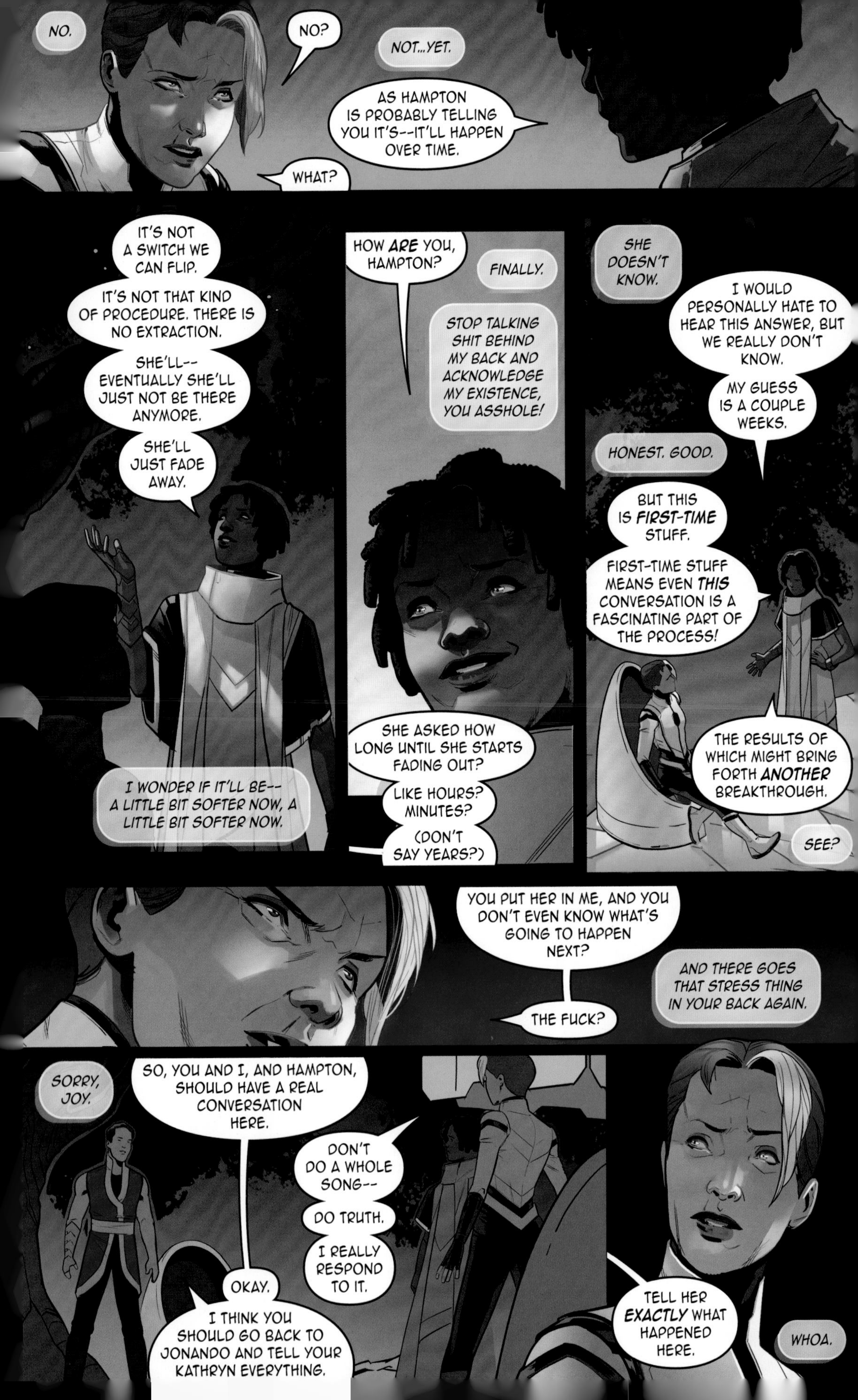
NO.
NO?
NOT...YET.
AS HAMPTON IS PROBABLY TELLING YOU IT'S--IT'LL HAPPEN OVER TIME.
WHAT?
IT'S NOT A SWITCH WE CAN FLIP.
IT'S NOT THAT KIND OF PROCEDURE. THERE IS NO EXTRACTION.
SHE'LL-- EVENTUALLY SHE'LL JUST NOT BE THERE ANYMORE.
SHE'LL JUST FADE AWAY.
I WONDER IF IT'LL BE-- A LITTLE BIT SOFTER NOW, A LITTLE BIT SOFTER NOW.
HOW ARE YOU, HAMPTON?
FINALLY.
STOP TALKING SHIT BEHIND MY BACK AND ACKNOWLEDGE MY EXISTENCE, YOU ASSHOLE!
SHE ASKED HOW LONG UNTIL SHE STARTS FADING OUT?
LIKE HOURS? MINUTES?
(DON'T SAY YEARS?)
SHE DOESN'T KNOW.
I WOULD PERSONALLY HATE TO HEAR THIS ANSWER, BUT WE REALLY DON'T KNOW.
MY GUESS IS A COUPLE WEEKS.
HONEST. GOOD.
BUT THIS IS FIRST-TIME STUFF.
FIRST-TIME STUFF MEANS EVEN THIS CONVERSATION IS A FASCINATING PART OF THE PROCESS!
THE RESULTS OF WHICH MIGHT BRING FORTH ANOTHER BREAKTHROUGH.
SEE?
YOU PUT HER IN ME, AND YOU DON'T EVEN KNOW WHAT'S GOING TO HAPPEN NEXT?
THE FUCK?
AND THERE GOES THAT STRESS THING IN YOUR BACK AGAIN.
SORRY, JOY.
SO, YOU AND I, AND HAMPTON, SHOULD HAVE A REAL CONVERSATION HERE.
OKAY.
I THINK YOU SHOULD GO BACK TO JONANDO AND TELL YOUR KATHRYN EVERYTHING.
DON'T DO A WHOLE SONG--
DO TRUTH.
I REALLY RESPOND TO IT.
TELL HER EXACTLY WHAT HAPPENED HERE.
WHOA.

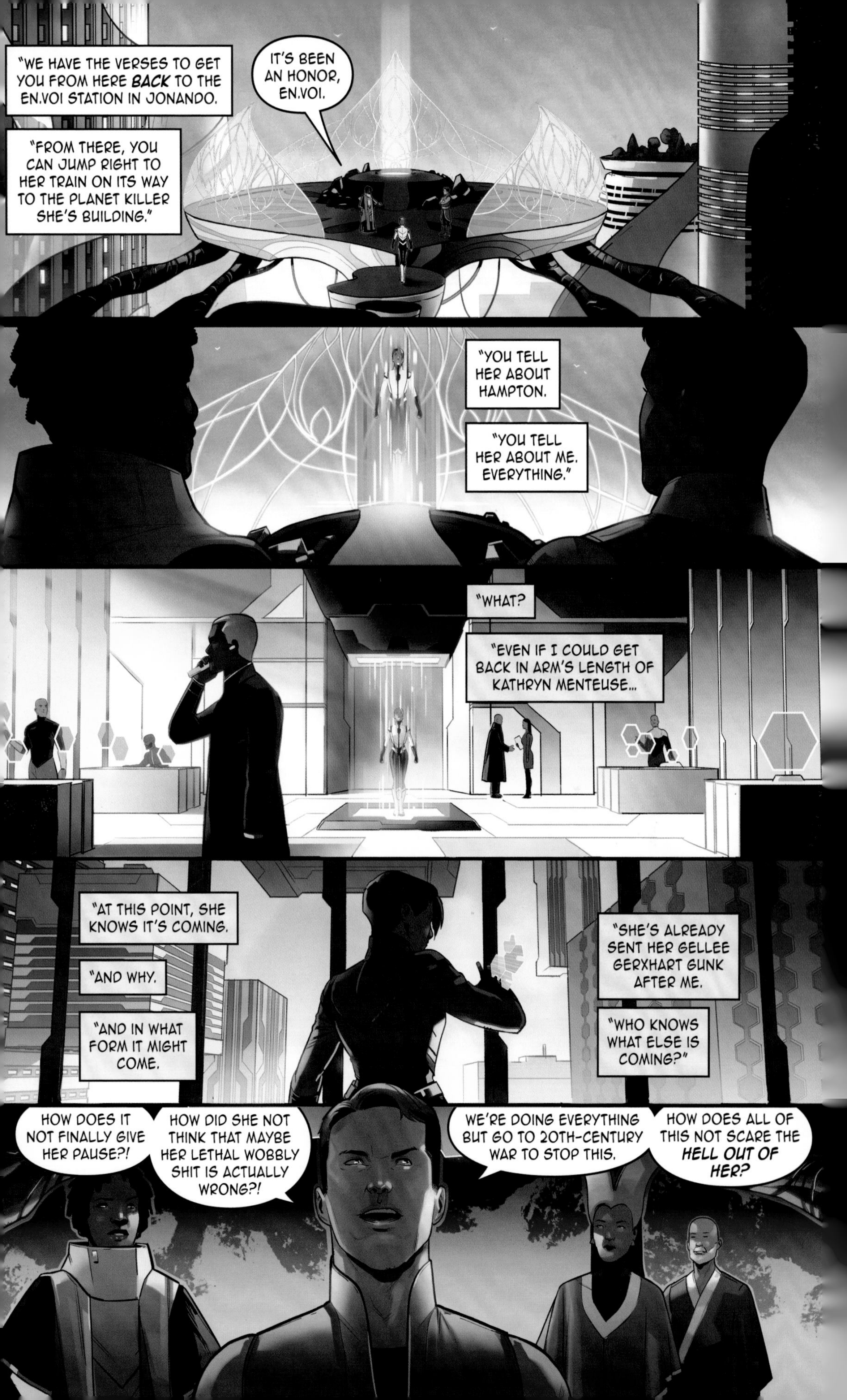
"WE HAVE THE VERSES TO GET YOU FROM HERE BACK TO THE EN.VOI STATION IN JONANDO.
"FROM THERE, YOU CAN JUMP RIGHT TO HER TRAIN ON ITS WAY TO THE PLANET KILLER SHE'S BUILDING."
IT'S BEEN AN HONOR, EN.VOI.
"YOU TELL HER ABOUT HAMPTON.
"YOU TELL HER ABOUT ME. EVERYTHING."
"WHAT?
"EVEN IF I COULD GET BACK IN ARM'S LENGTH OF KATHRYN MENTEUSE...
"AT THIS POINT, SHE KNOWS IT'S COMING.
"AND WHY.
"AND IN WHAT FORM IT MIGHT COME.
"SHE'S ALREADY SENT HER GELLEE GERXHART GUNK AFTER ME.
"WHO KNOWS WHAT ELSE IS COMING?"
HOW DOES IT NOT FINALLY GIVE HER PAUSE?!
HOW DID SHE NOT THINK THAT MAYBE HER LETHAL WOBBLY SHIT IS ACTUALLY WRONG?!
WE'RE DOING EVERYTHING BUT GO TO 20TH-CENTURY WAR TO STOP THIS.
HOW DOES ALL OF THIS NOT SCARE THE HELL OUT OF HER?

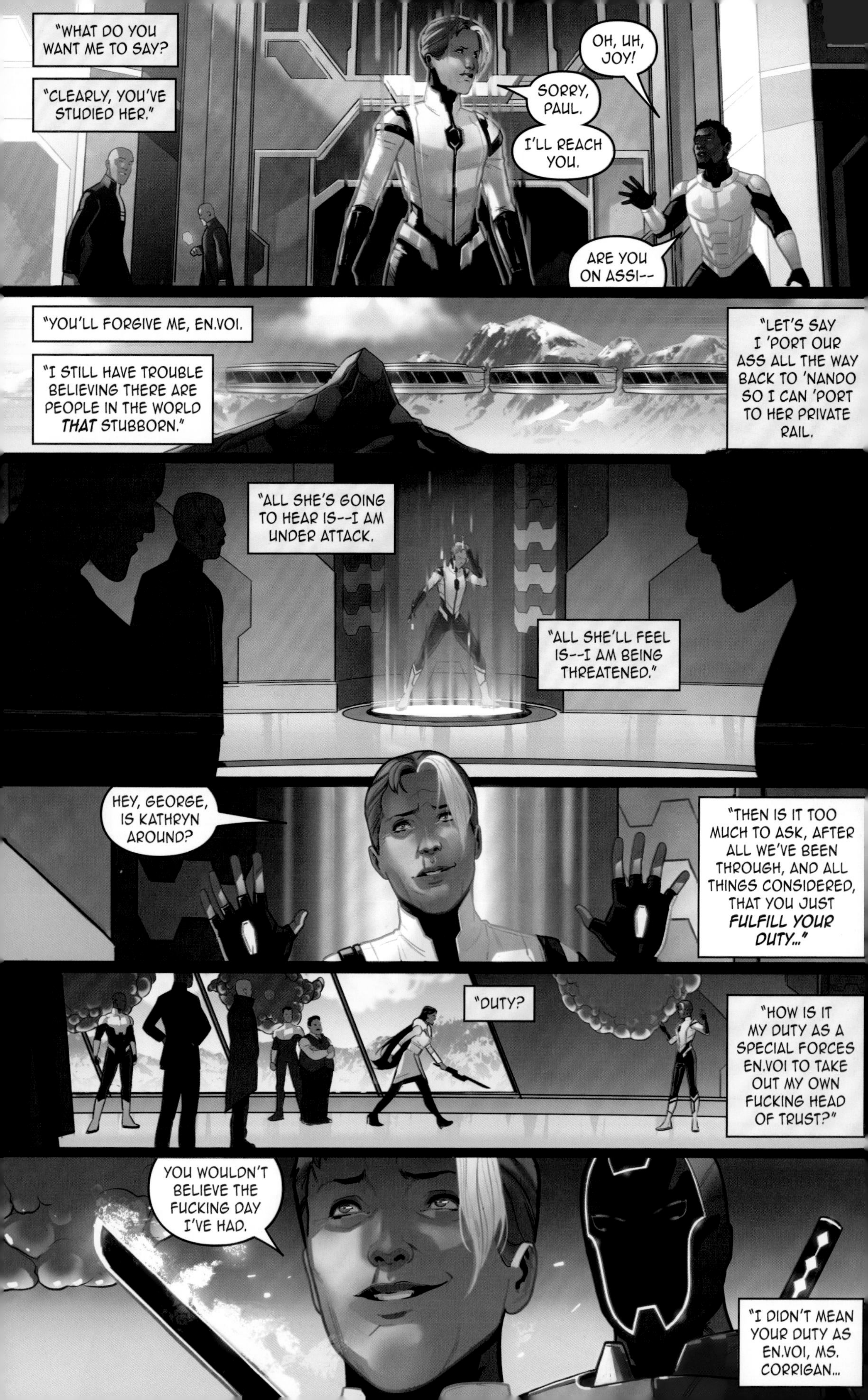
"WHAT DO YOU WANT ME TO SAY?
"CLEARLY, YOU'VE STUDIED HER."
OH, UH, JOY!
SORRY, PAUL.
I'LL REACH YOU.
ARE YOU ON ASSI--
"YOU'LL FORGIVE ME, EN.VOI.
"I STILL HAVE TROUBLE BELIEVING THERE ARE PEOPLE IN THE WORLD *THAT* STUBBORN."
"LET'S SAY I 'PORT OUR ASS ALL THE WAY BACK TO 'NANDO SO I CAN 'PORT TO HER PRIVATE RAIL.
"ALL SHE'S GOING TO HEAR IS--I AM UNDER ATTACK.
"ALL SHE'LL FEEL IS--I AM BEING THREATENED."
HEY, GEORGE, IS KATHRYN AROUND?
"THEN IS IT TOO MUCH TO ASK, AFTER ALL WE'VE BEEN THROUGH, AND ALL THINGS CONSIDERED, THAT YOU JUST ***FULFILL YOUR DUTY...***"
"DUTY?
"HOW IS IT MY DUTY AS A SPECIAL FORCES EN.VOI TO TAKE OUT MY OWN FUCKING HEAD OF TRUST?"
YOU WOULDN'T BELIEVE THE FUCKING DAY I'VE HAD.
"I DIDN'T MEAN YOUR DUTY AS EN.VOI, MS. CORRIGAN...

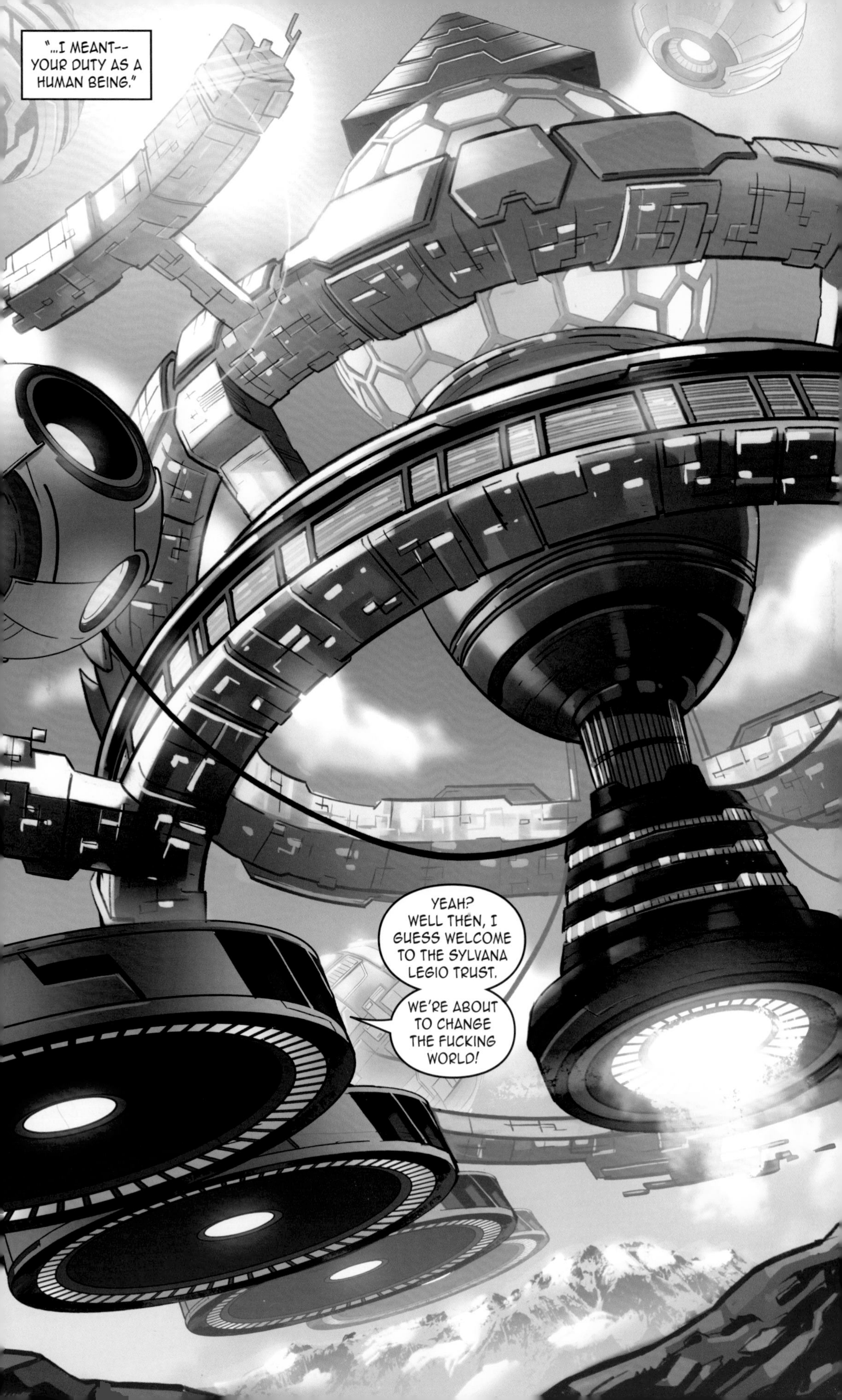
"...I MEANT--
YOUR DUTY AS A
HUMAN BEING."
YEAH? WELL THEN, I GUESS WELCOME TO THE SYLVANA LEGIO TRUST.
WE'RE ABOUT TO CHANGE THE FUCKING WORLD!

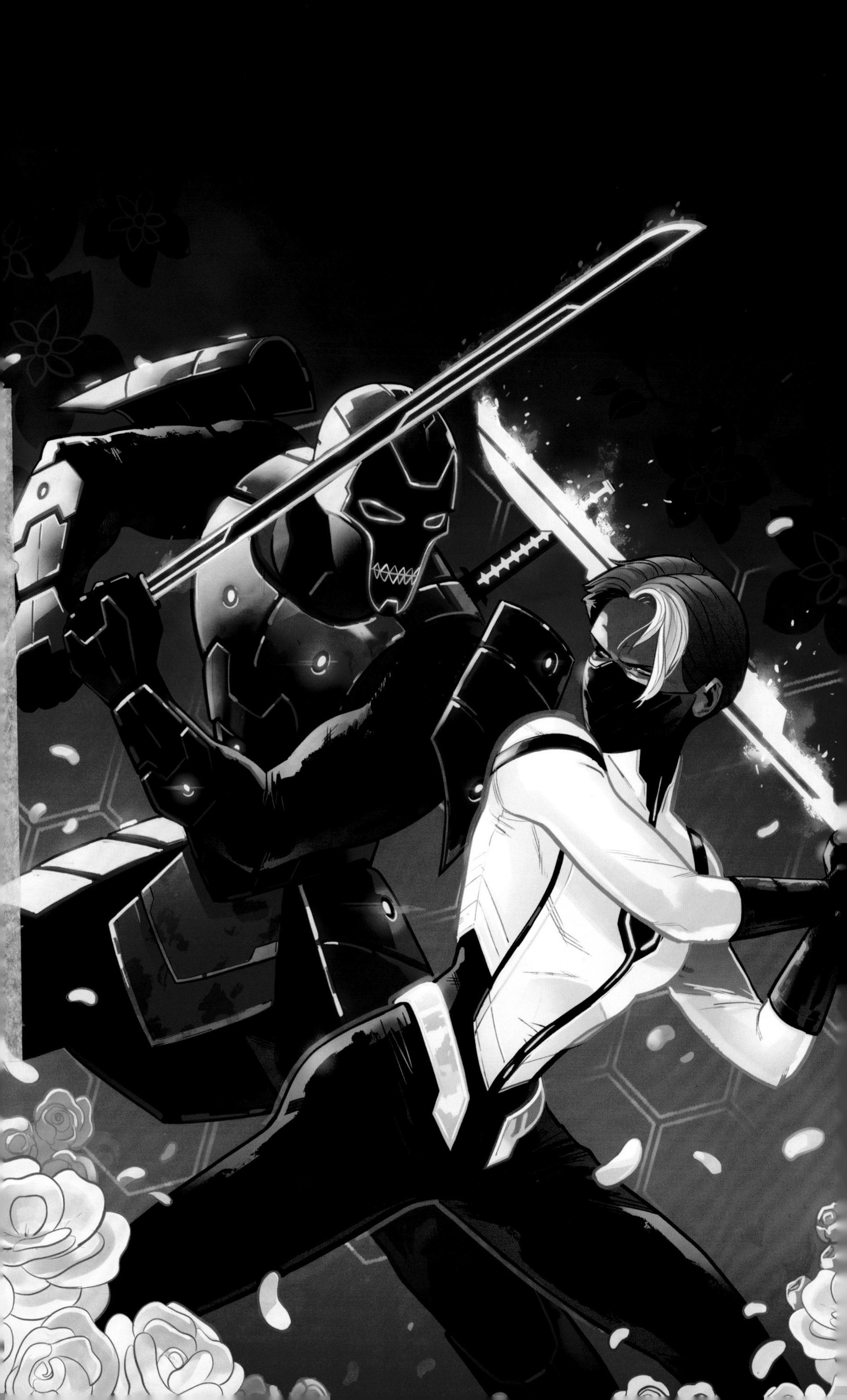

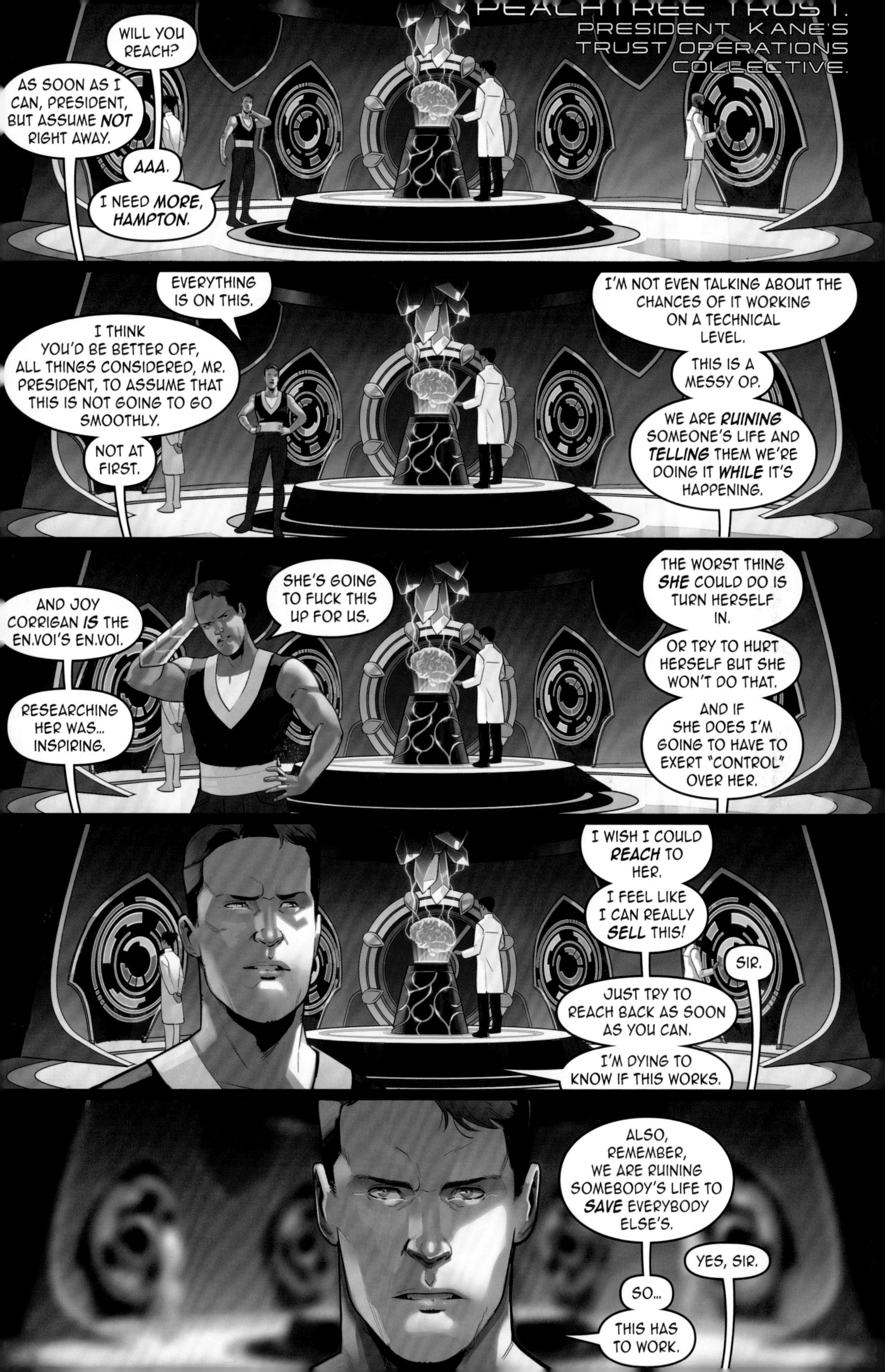
PEACHTREE TRUST.
PRESIDENT KANE'S TRUST OPERATIONS COLLECTIVE.
WILL YOU REACH?
AS SOON AS I CAN, PRESIDENT, BUT ASSUME NOT RIGHT AWAY.
AAA.
I NEED MORE, HAMPTON.
EVERYTHING IS ON THIS.
I THINK YOU'D BE BETTER OFF, ALL THINGS CONSIDERED, MR. PRESIDENT, TO ASSUME THAT THIS IS NOT GOING TO GO SMOOTHLY.
NOT AT FIRST.
I'M NOT EVEN TALKING ABOUT THE CHANCES OF IT WORKING ON A TECHNICAL LEVEL.
THIS IS A MESSY OP.
WE ARE RUINING SOMEONE'S LIFE AND TELLING THEM WE'RE DOING IT WHILE IT'S HAPPENING.
AND JOY CORRIGAN IS THE EN.VOI'S EN.VOI.
RESEARCHING HER WAS... INSPIRING.
SHE'S GOING TO FUCK THIS UP FOR US.
THE WORST THING SHE COULD DO IS TURN HERSELF IN.
OR TRY TO HURT HERSELF BUT SHE WON'T DO THAT.
AND IF SHE DOES I'M GOING TO HAVE TO EXERT "CONTROL" OVER HER.
I WISH I COULD REACH TO HER.
I FEEL LIKE I CAN REALLY SELL THIS!
SIR.
JUST TRY TO REACH BACK AS SOON AS YOU CAN.
I'M DYING TO KNOW IF THIS WORKS.
ALSO, REMEMBER, WE ARE RUINING SOMEBODY'S LIFE TO SAVE EVERYBODY ELSE'S.
SO...
THIS HAS TO WORK.
YES, SIR.

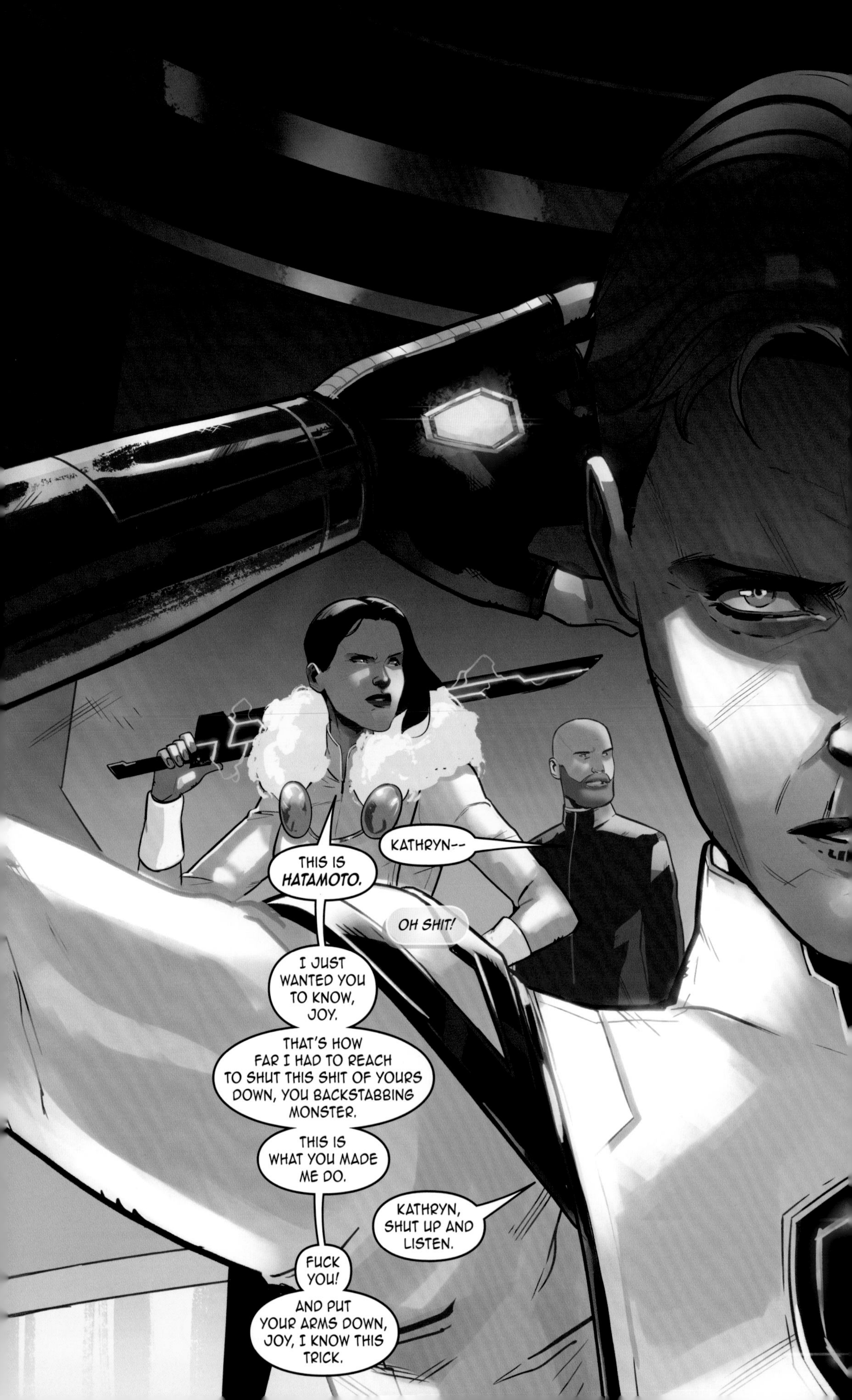
THIS IS HATAMOTO.
KATHRYN--
OH SHIT!
I JUST WANTED YOU TO KNOW, JOY.
THAT'S HOW FAR I HAD TO REACH TO SHUT THIS SHIT OF YOURS DOWN, YOU BACKSTABBING MONSTER.
THIS IS WHAT YOU MADE ME DO.
KATHRYN, SHUT UP AND LISTEN.
FUCK YOU!
AND PUT YOUR ARMS DOWN, JOY, I KNOW THIS TRICK.

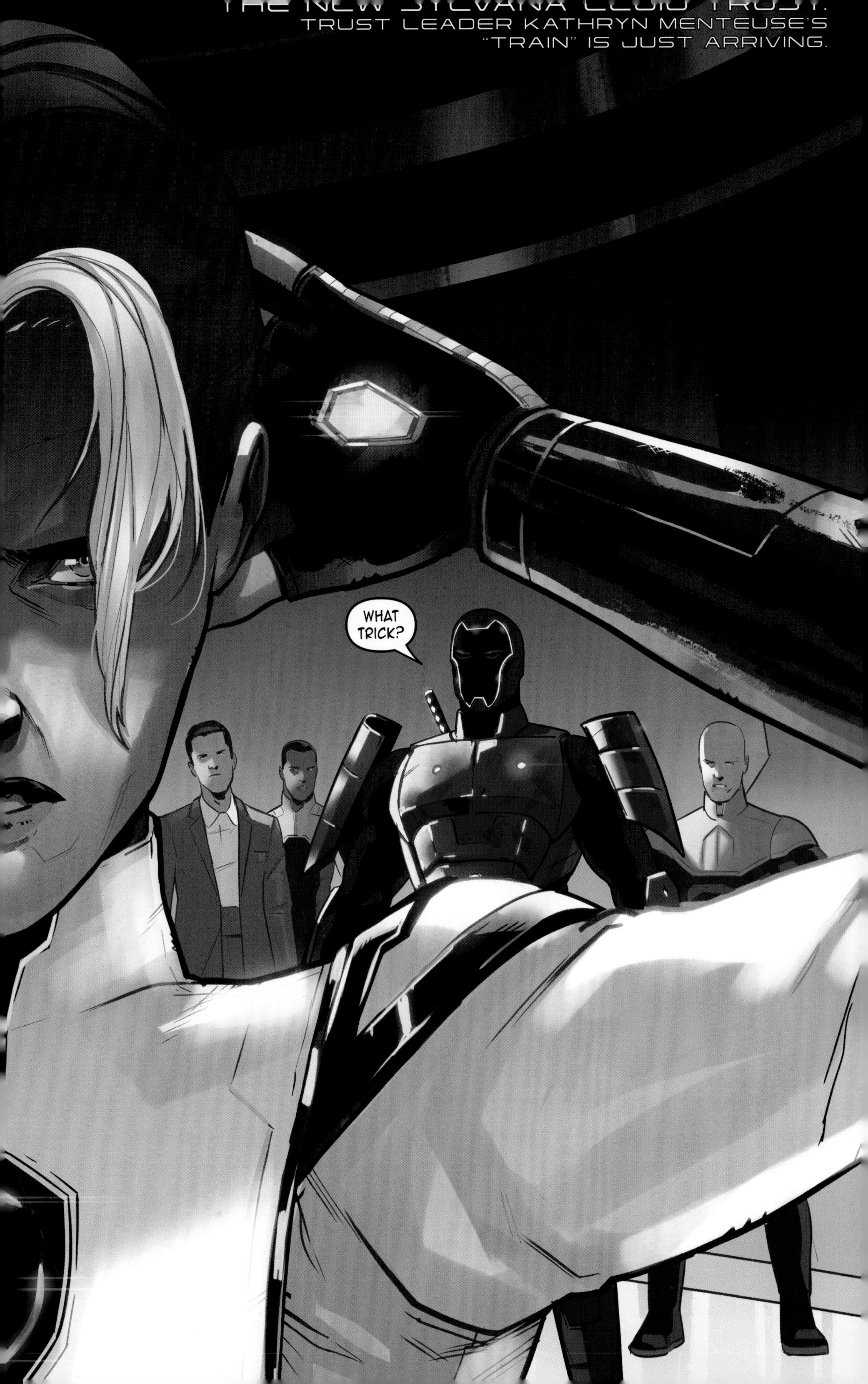

TRUST LEADER KATHRYN MENTEUSE'S "TRAIN" IS JUST ARRIVING.
WHAT TRICK?

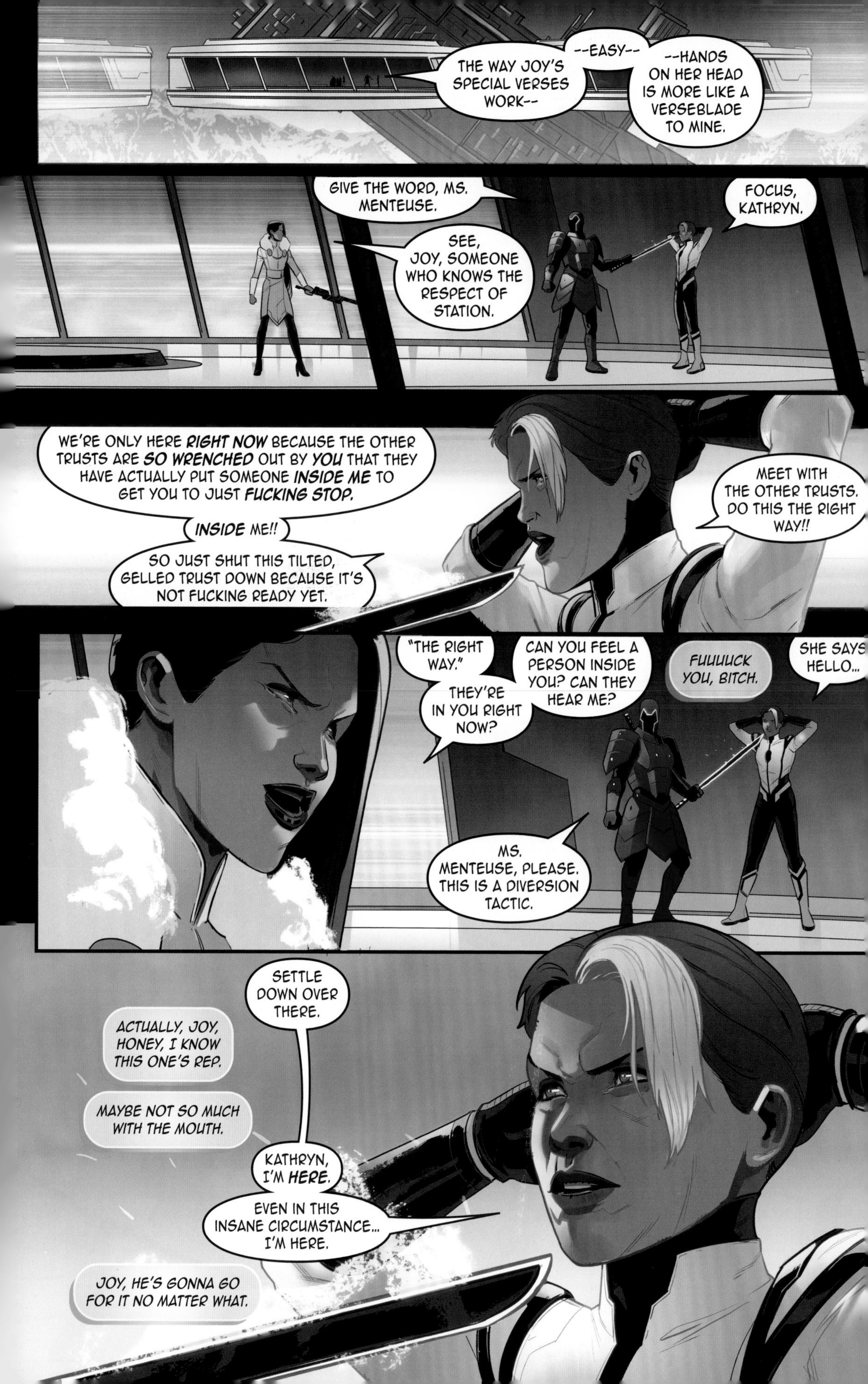
THE WAY JOY'S SPECIAL VERSES WORK--
--EASY--
--HANDS ON HER HEAD IS MORE LIKE A VERSEBLADE TO MINE.
GIVE THE WORD, MS. MENTEUSE.
SEE, JOY, SOMEONE WHO KNOWS THE RESPECT OF STATION.
FOCUS, KATHRYN.
WE'RE ONLY HERE RIGHT NOW BECAUSE THE OTHER TRUSTS ARE SO WRENCHED OUT BY YOU THAT THEY HAVE ACTUALLY PUT SOMEONE INSIDE ME TO GET YOU TO JUST FUCKING STOP.
INSIDE ME!!
SO JUST SHUT THIS TILTED, GELLED TRUST DOWN BECAUSE IT'S NOT FUCKING READY YET.
MEET WITH THE OTHER TRUSTS. DO THIS THE RIGHT WAY!!
"THE RIGHT WAY."
THEY'RE IN YOU RIGHT NOW?
CAN YOU FEEL A PERSON INSIDE YOU? CAN THEY HEAR ME?
FUUUUCK YOU, BITCH.
SHE SAYS HELLO...
MS. MENTEUSE, PLEASE. THIS IS A DIVERSION TACTIC.
SETTLE DOWN OVER THERE.
ACTUALLY, JOY, HONEY, I KNOW THIS ONE'S REP.
MAYBE NOT SO MUCH WITH THE MOUTH.
KATHRYN, I'M HERE.
EVEN IN THIS INSANE CIRCUMSTANCE... I'M HERE.
JOY, HE'S GONNA GO FOR IT NO MATTER WHAT.

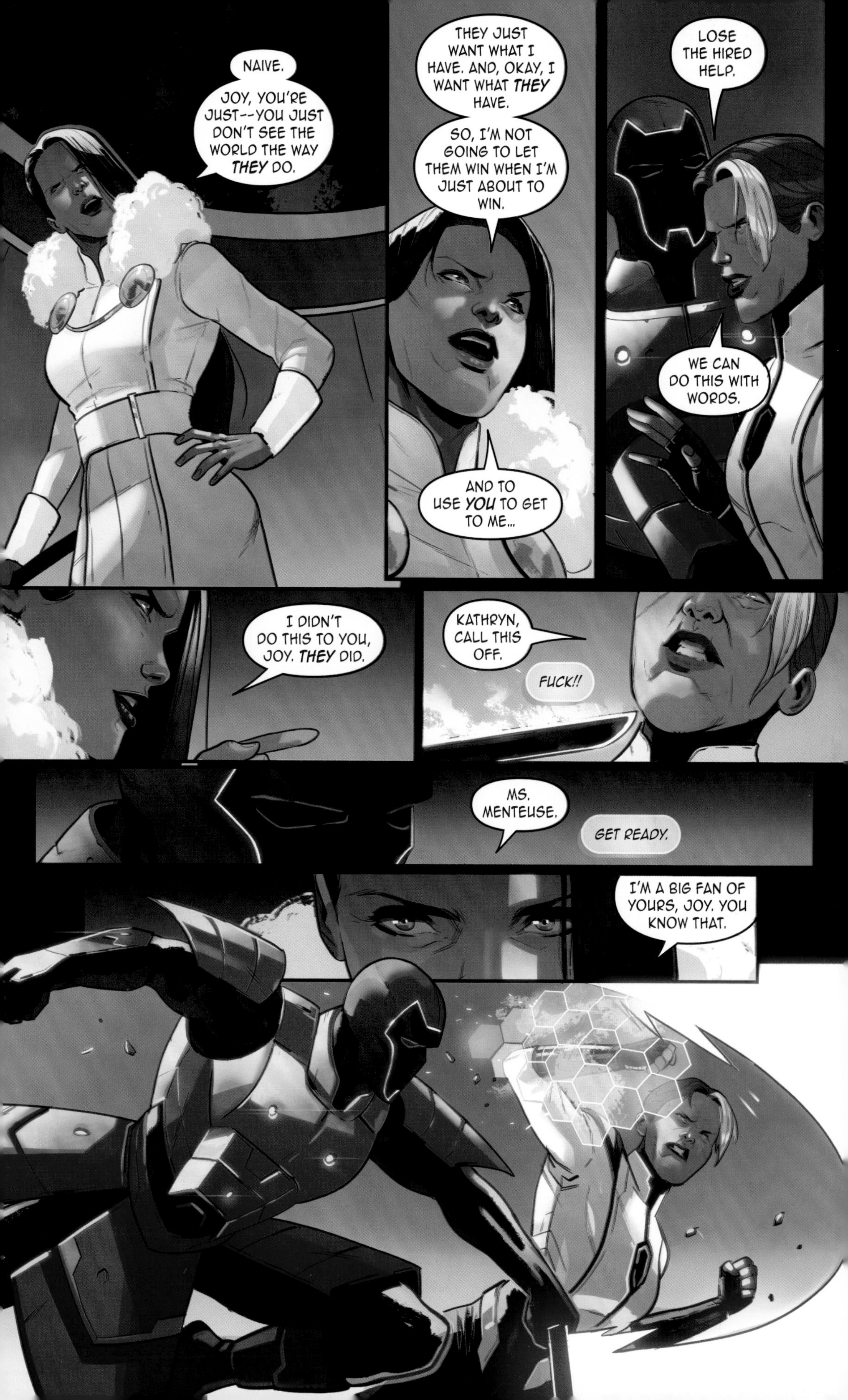
NAIVE.
JOY, YOU'RE JUST--YOU JUST DON'T SEE THE WORLD THE WAY *THEY* DO.
THEY JUST WANT WHAT I HAVE. AND, OKAY, I WANT WHAT *THEY* HAVE.
SO, I'M NOT GOING TO LET THEM WIN WHEN I'M JUST ABOUT TO WIN.
AND TO USE *YOU* TO GET TO ME...
LOSE THE HIRED HELP.
WE CAN DO THIS WITH WORDS.
I DIDN'T DO THIS TO YOU, JOY. *THEY* DID.
KATHRYN, CALL THIS OFF.
FUCK!!
MS. MENTEUSE.
GET READY.
I'M A BIG FAN OF YOURS, JOY. YOU KNOW THAT.

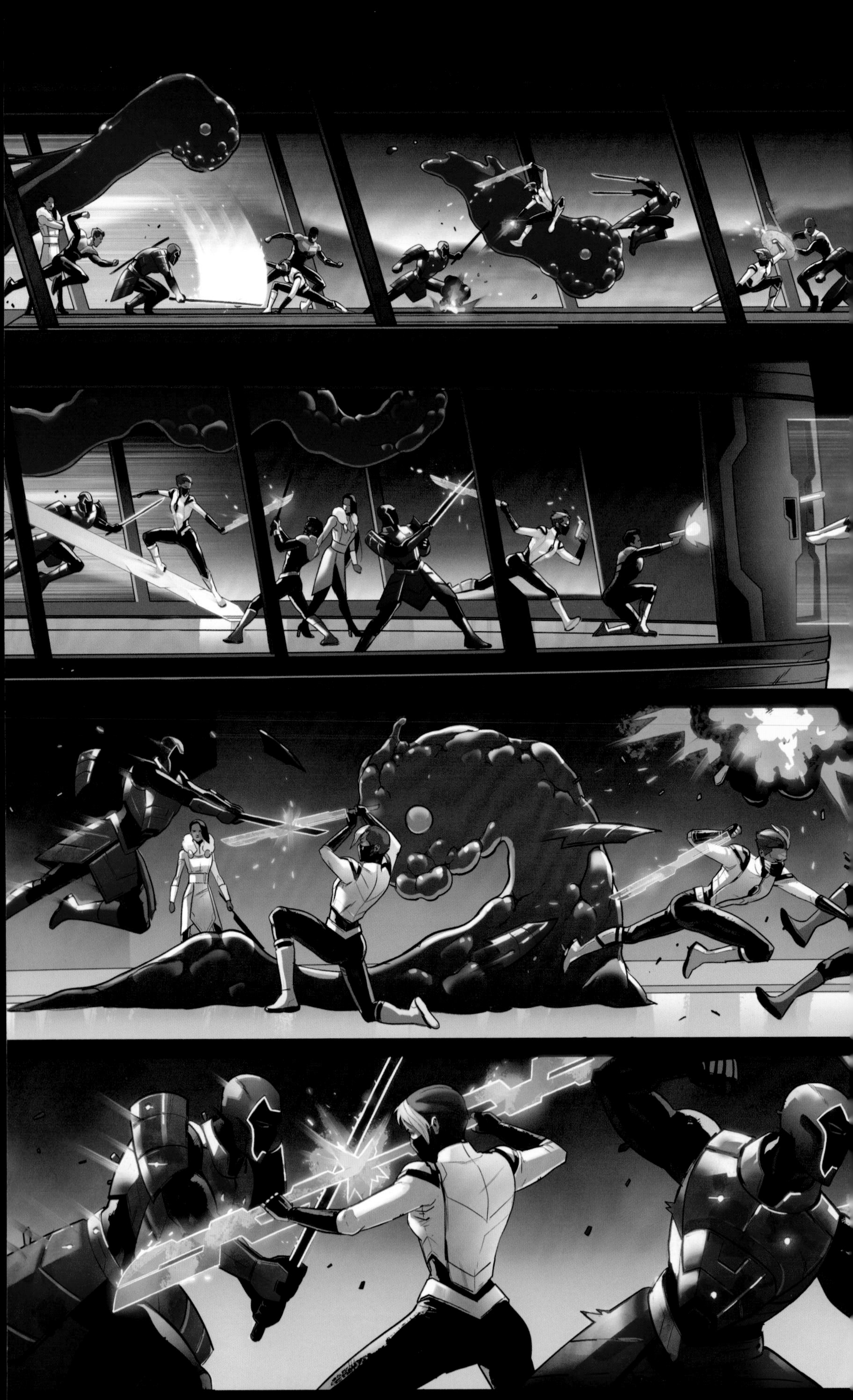

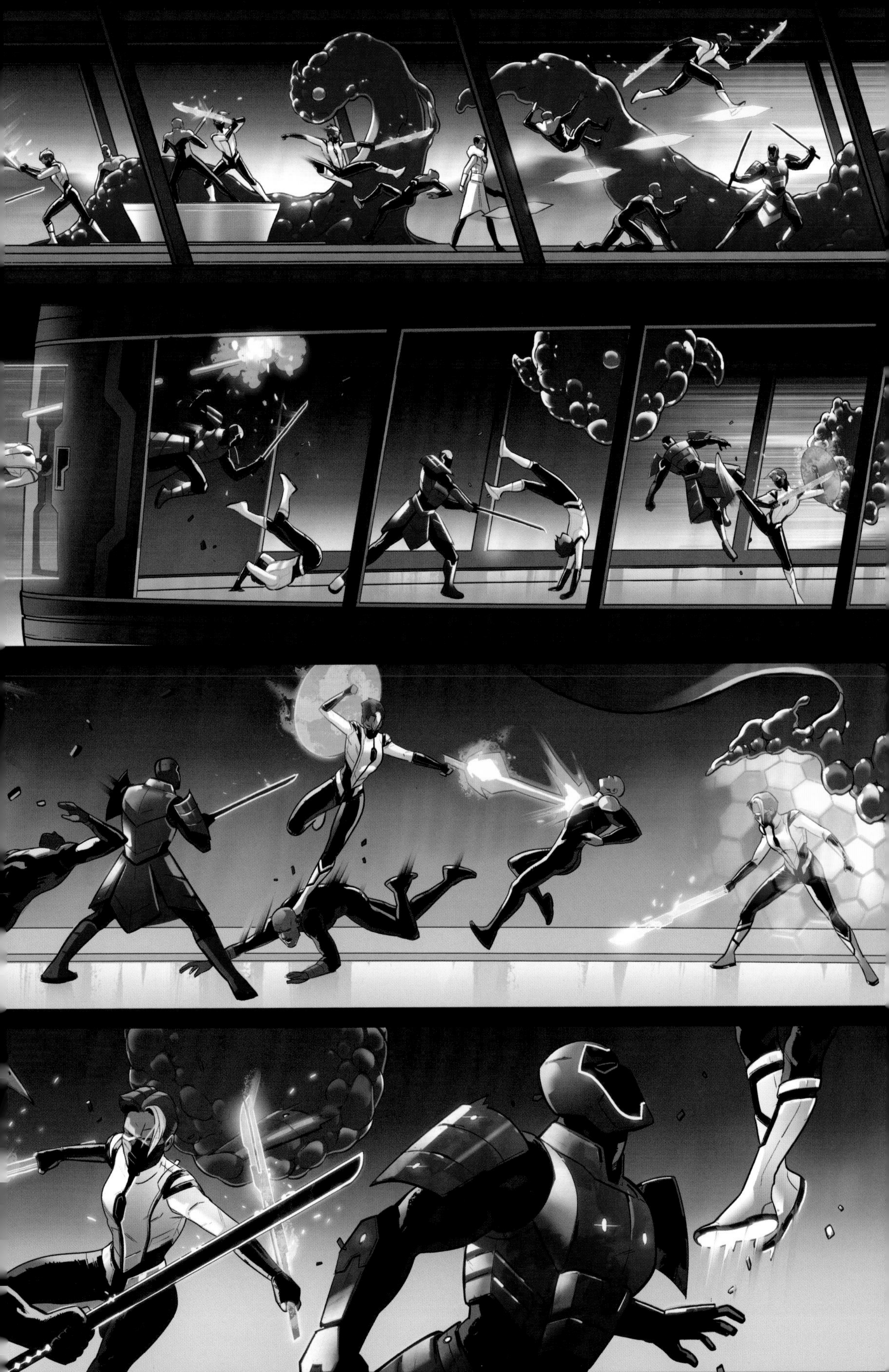

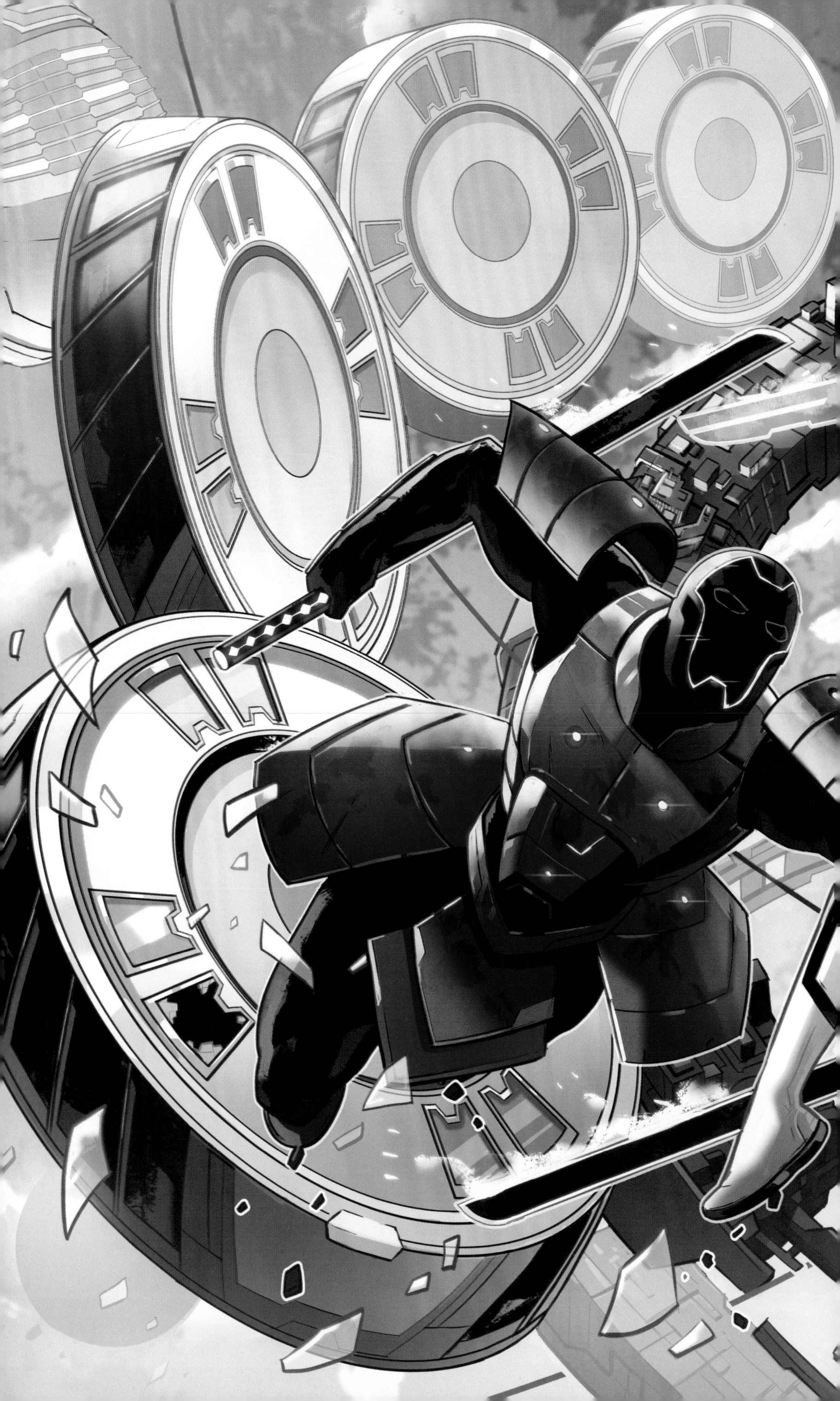

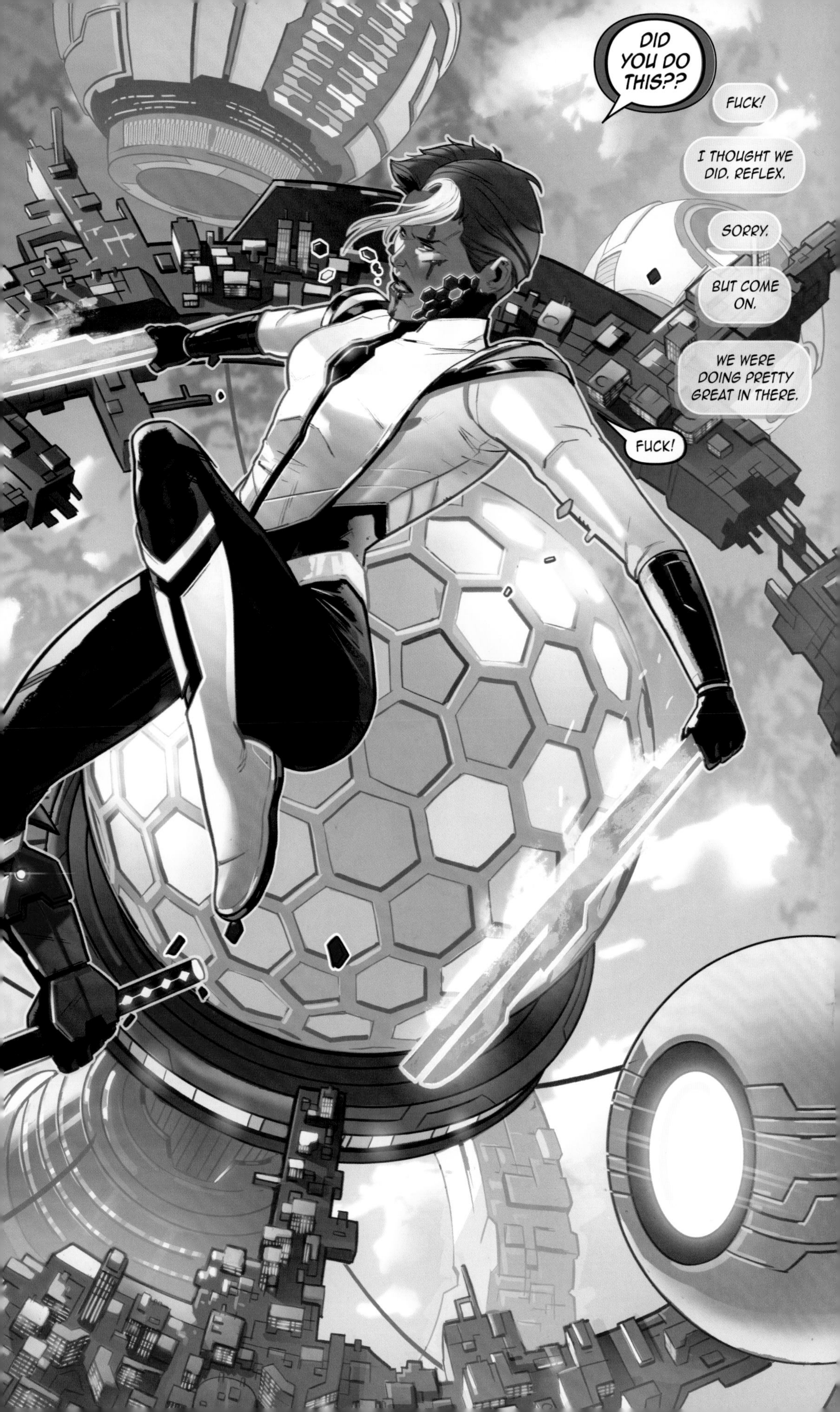
DID YOU DO THIS??
FUCK!
I THOUGHT WE DID. REFLEX.
SORRY.
BUT COME ON.
WE WERE DOING PRETTY GREAT IN THERE.
FUCK!

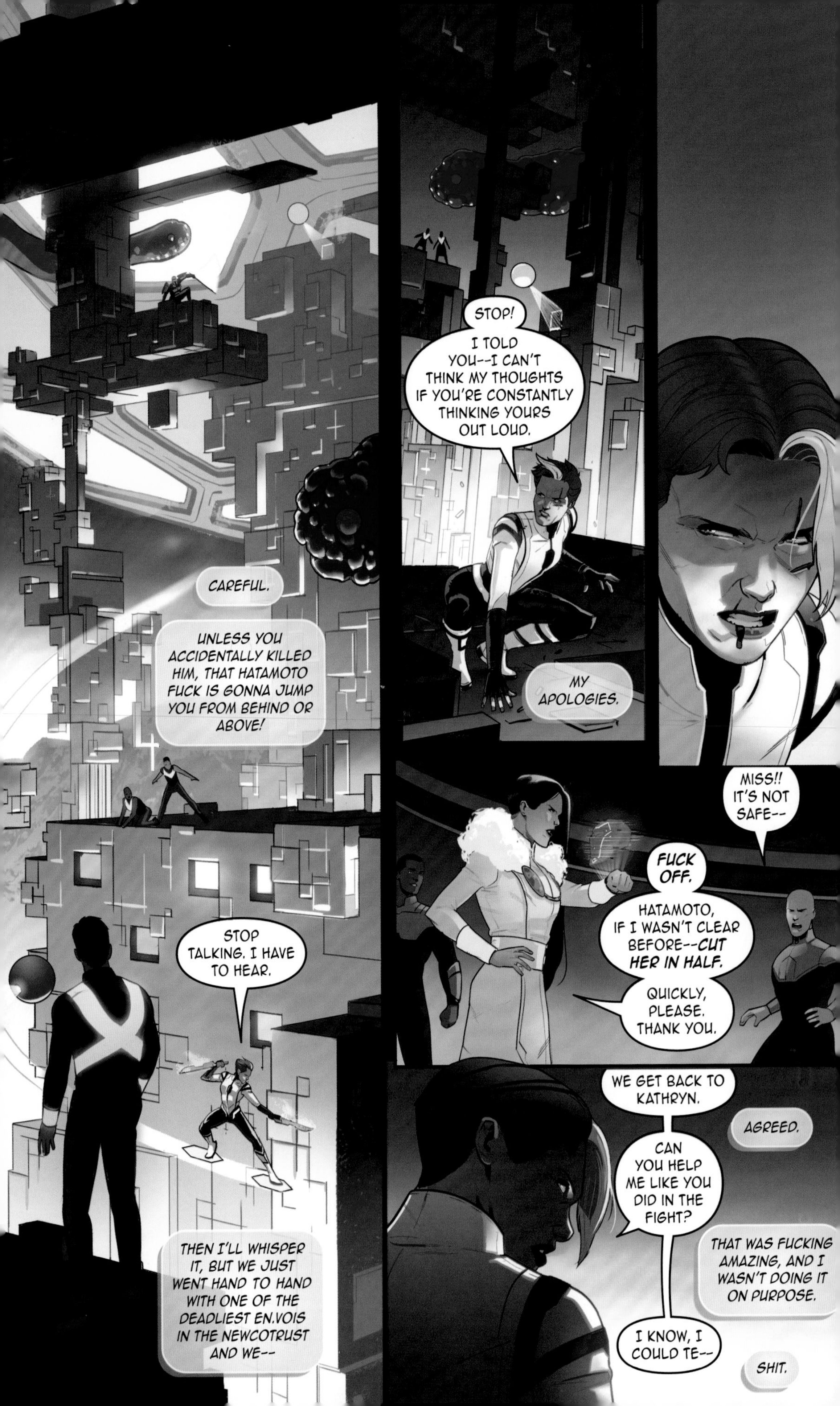
CAREFUL.
UNLESS YOU ACCIDENTALLY KILLED HIM, THAT HATAMOTO FUCK IS GONNA JUMP YOU FROM BEHIND OR ABOVE!
STOP TALKING. I HAVE TO HEAR.
THEN I'LL WHISPER IT, BUT WE JUST WENT HAND TO HAND WITH ONE OF THE DEADLIEST EN.VOIS IN THE NEWCOTRUST AND WE--
STOP!
I TOLD YOU--I CAN'T THINK MY THOUGHTS IF YOU'RE CONSTANTLY THINKING YOURS OUT LOUD.
MY APOLOGIES.
MISS!! IT'S NOT SAFE--
FUCK OFF.
HATAMOTO, IF I WASN'T CLEAR BEFORE--CUT HER IN HALF.
QUICKLY, PLEASE. THANK YOU.
WE GET BACK TO KATHRYN.
AGREED.
CAN YOU HELP ME LIKE YOU DID IN THE FIGHT?
THAT WAS FUCKING AMAZING, AND I WASN'T DOING IT ON PURPOSE.
I KNOW, I COULD TE--
SHIT.

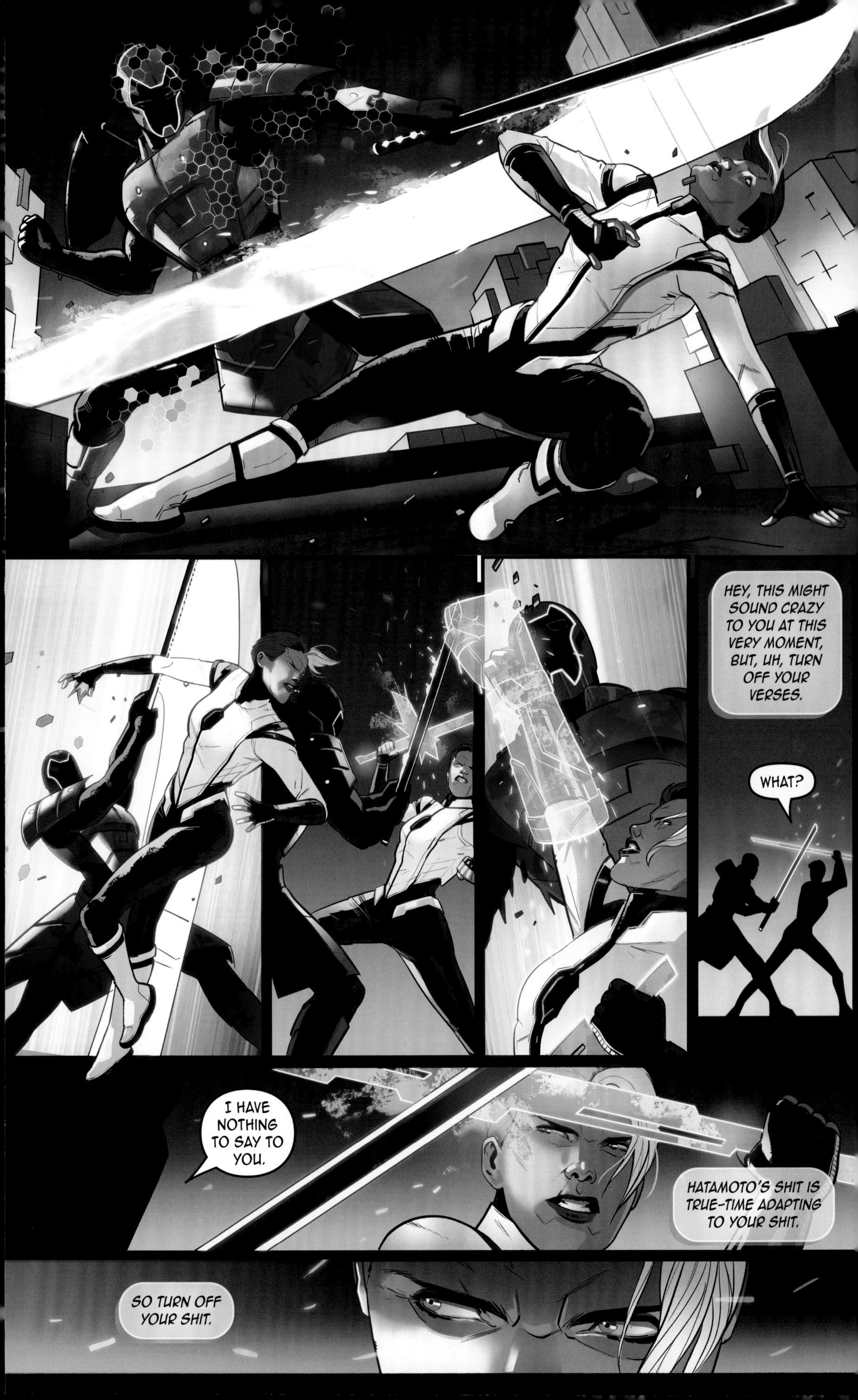
HEY, THIS MIGHT SOUND CRAZY TO YOU AT THIS VERY MOMENT, BUT, UH, TURN OFF YOUR VERSES.
WHAT?
I HAVE NOTHING TO SAY TO YOU.
HATAMOTO'S SHIT IS TRUE-TIME ADAPTING TO YOUR SHIT.
SO TURN OFF YOUR SHIT.

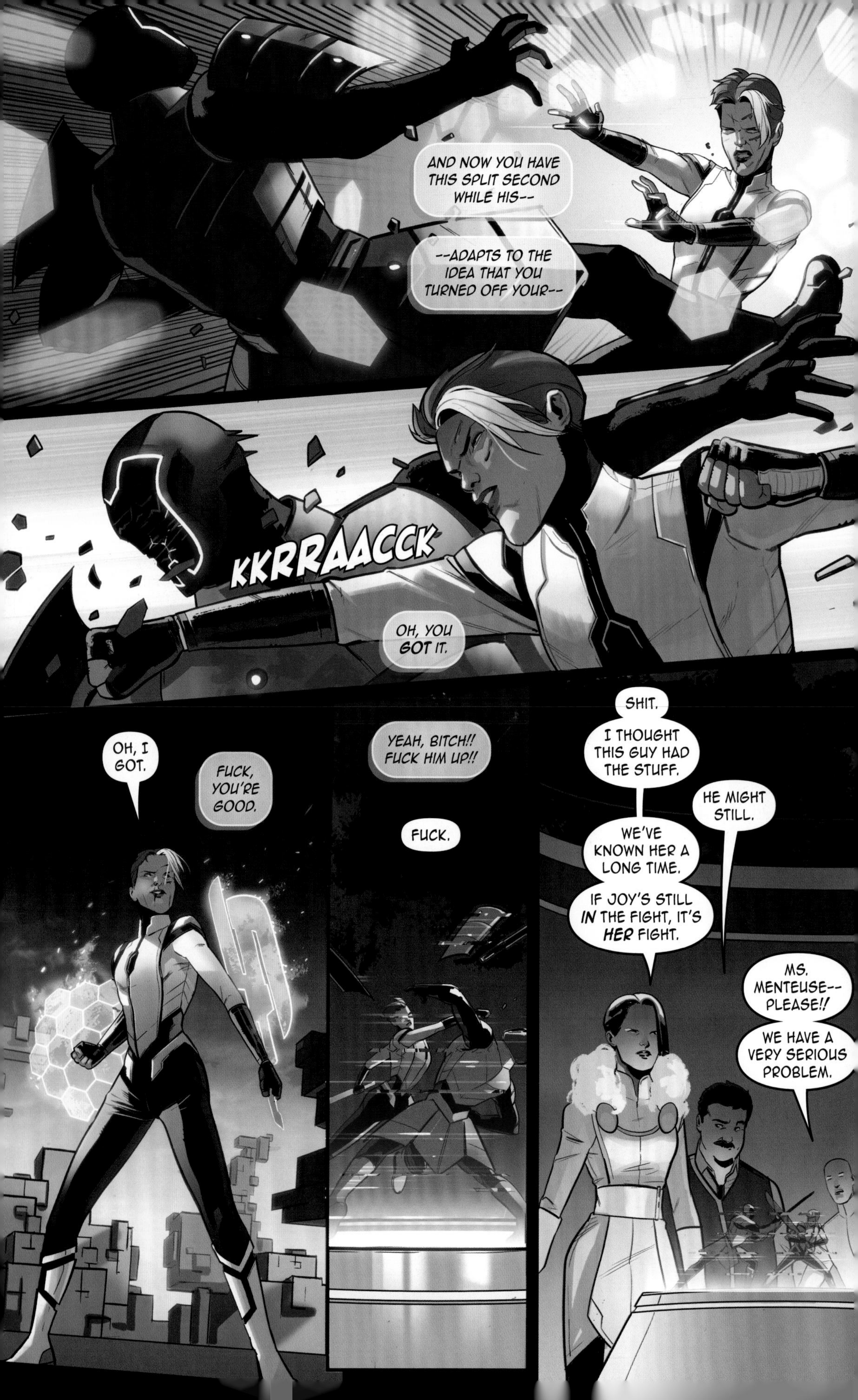
AND NOW YOU HAVE THIS SPLIT SECOND WHILE HIS--
--ADAPTS TO THE IDEA THAT YOU TURNED OFF YOUR--
KKRRAACCK
OH, YOU GOT IT.
OH, I GOT.
FUCK, YOU'RE GOOD.
YEAH, BITCH!! FUCK HIM UP!!
FUCK.
SHIT.
I THOUGHT THIS GUY HAD THE STUFF.
HE MIGHT STILL.
WE'VE KNOWN HER A LONG TIME.
IF JOY'S STILL IN THE FIGHT, IT'S HER FIGHT.
MS. MENTEUSE--PLEASE!!
WE HAVE A VERY SERIOUS PROBLEM.

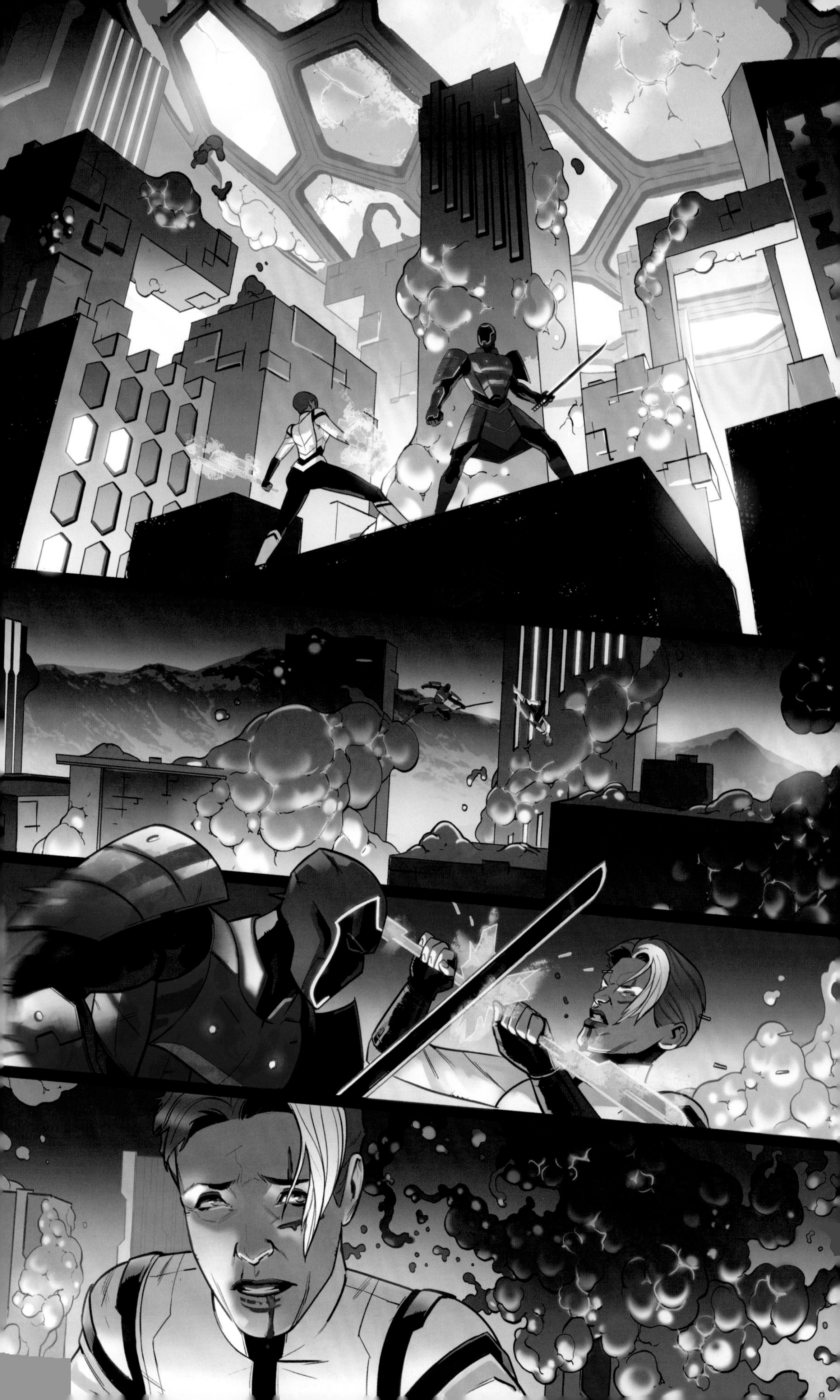

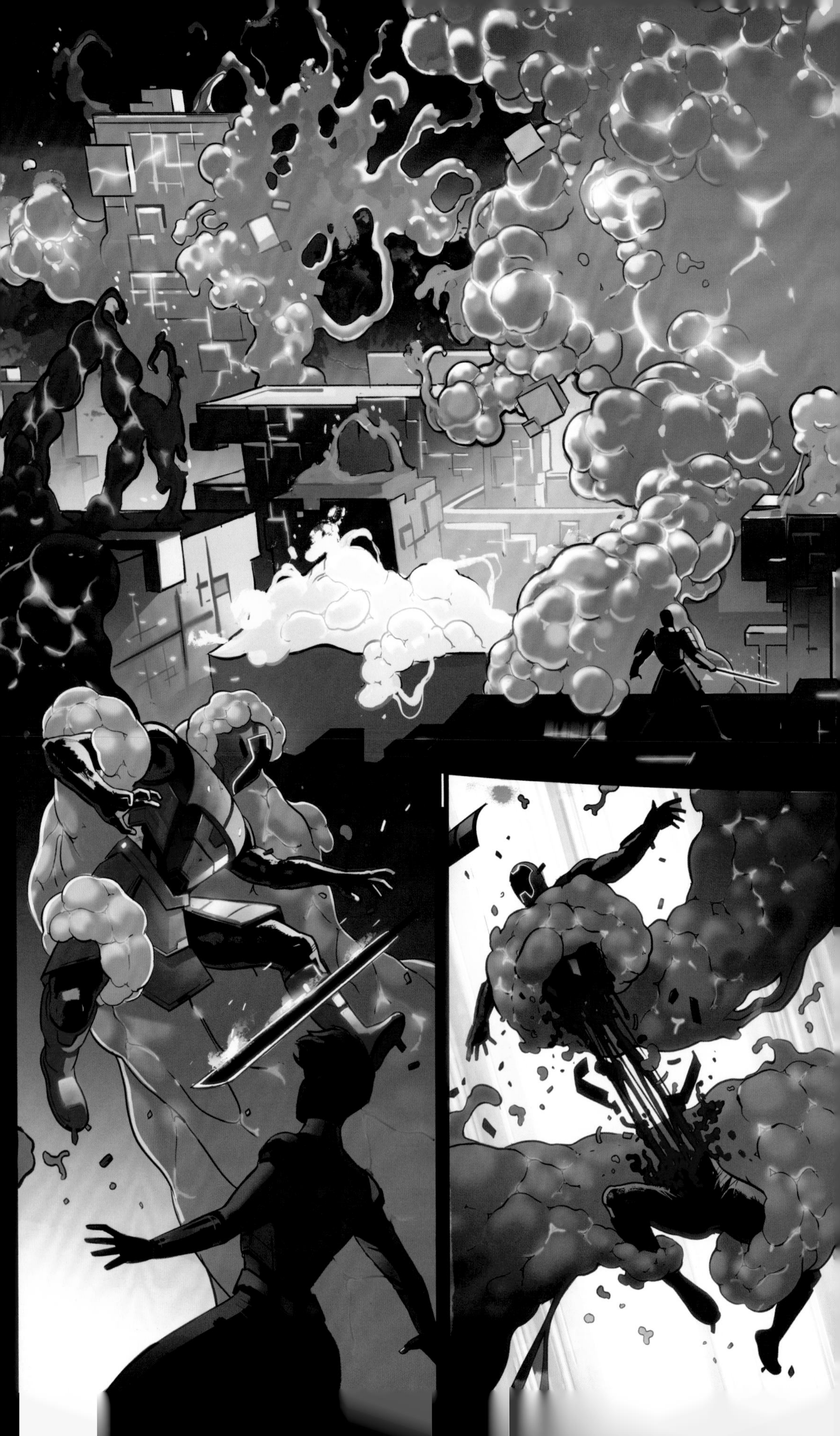

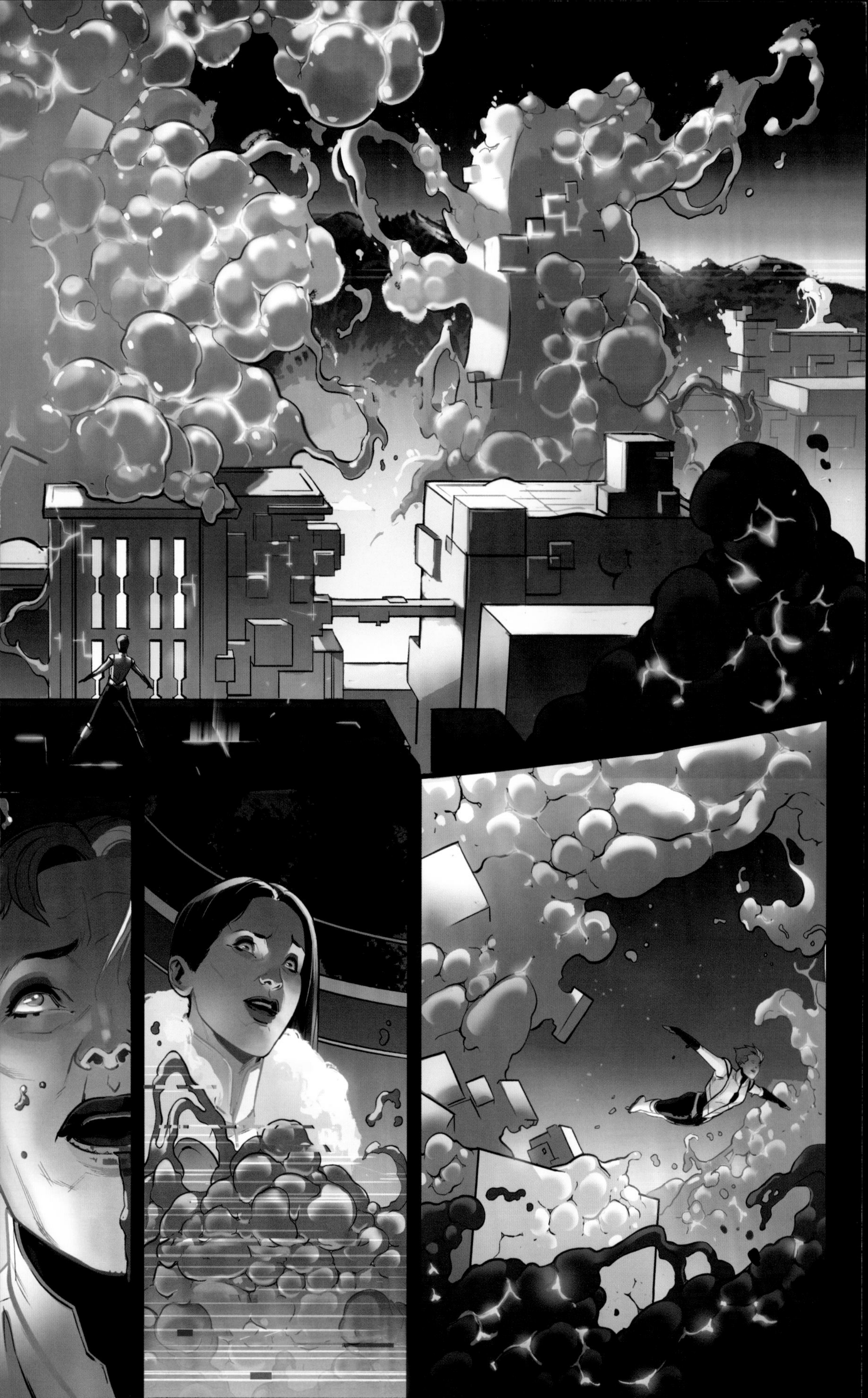

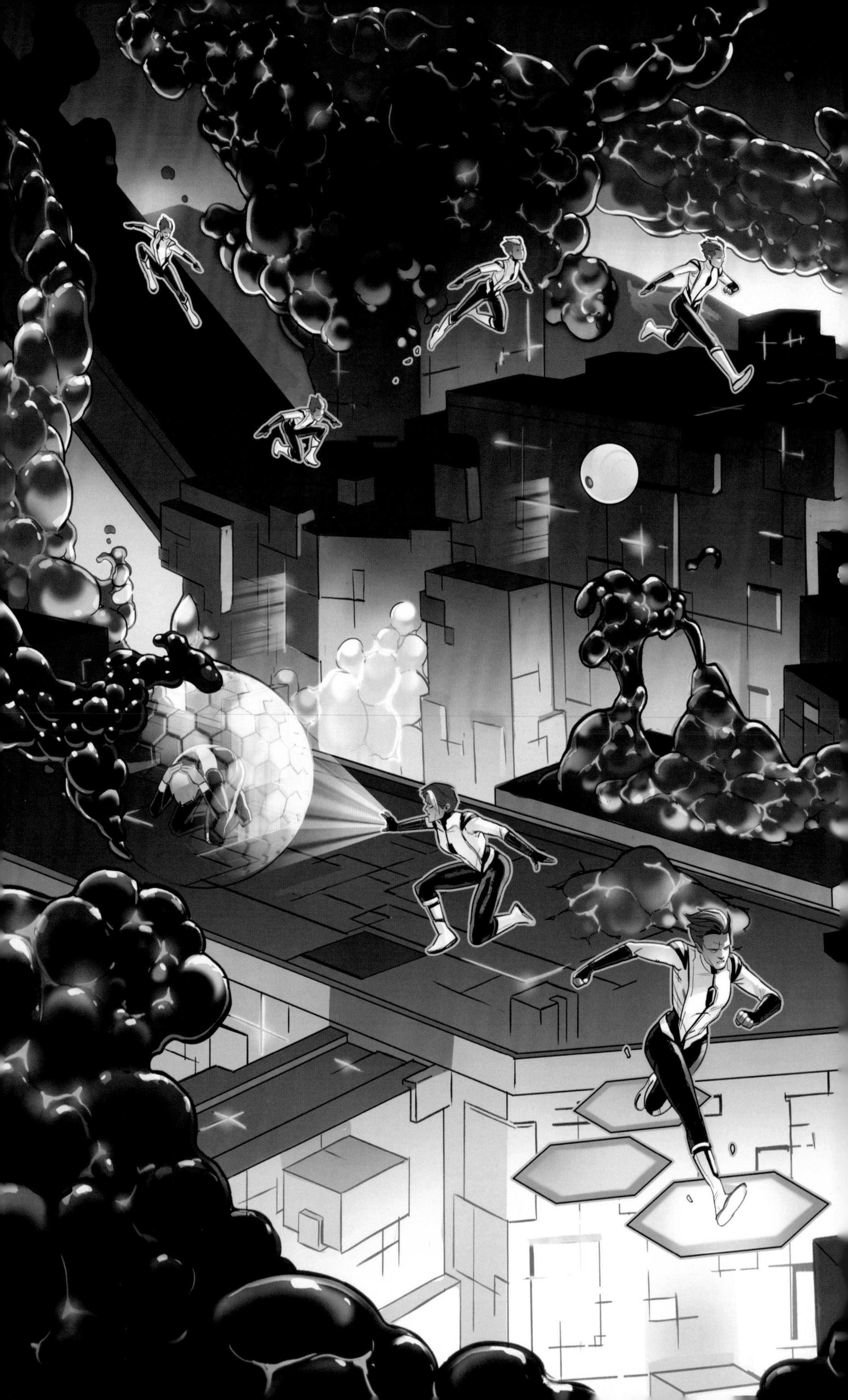

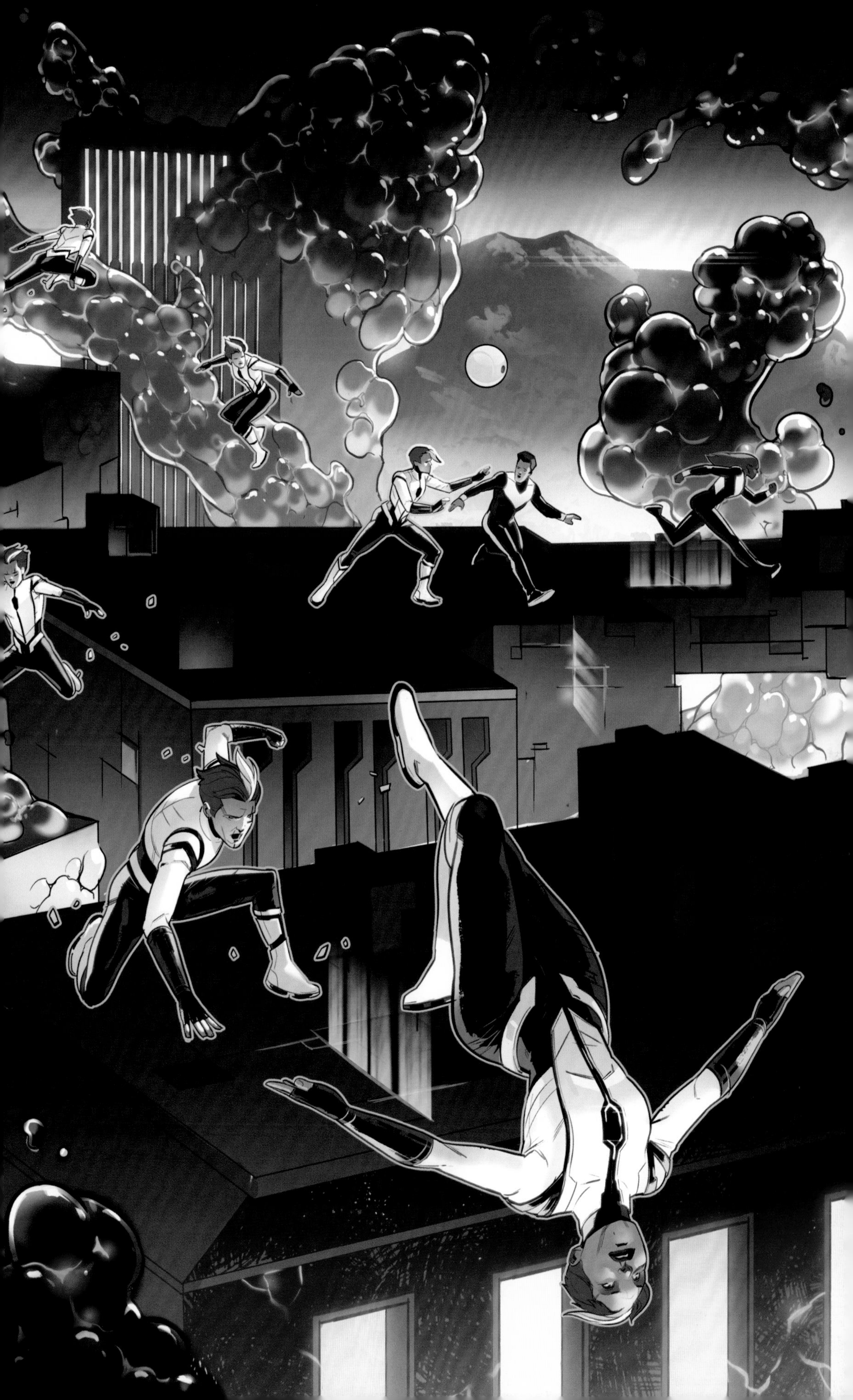

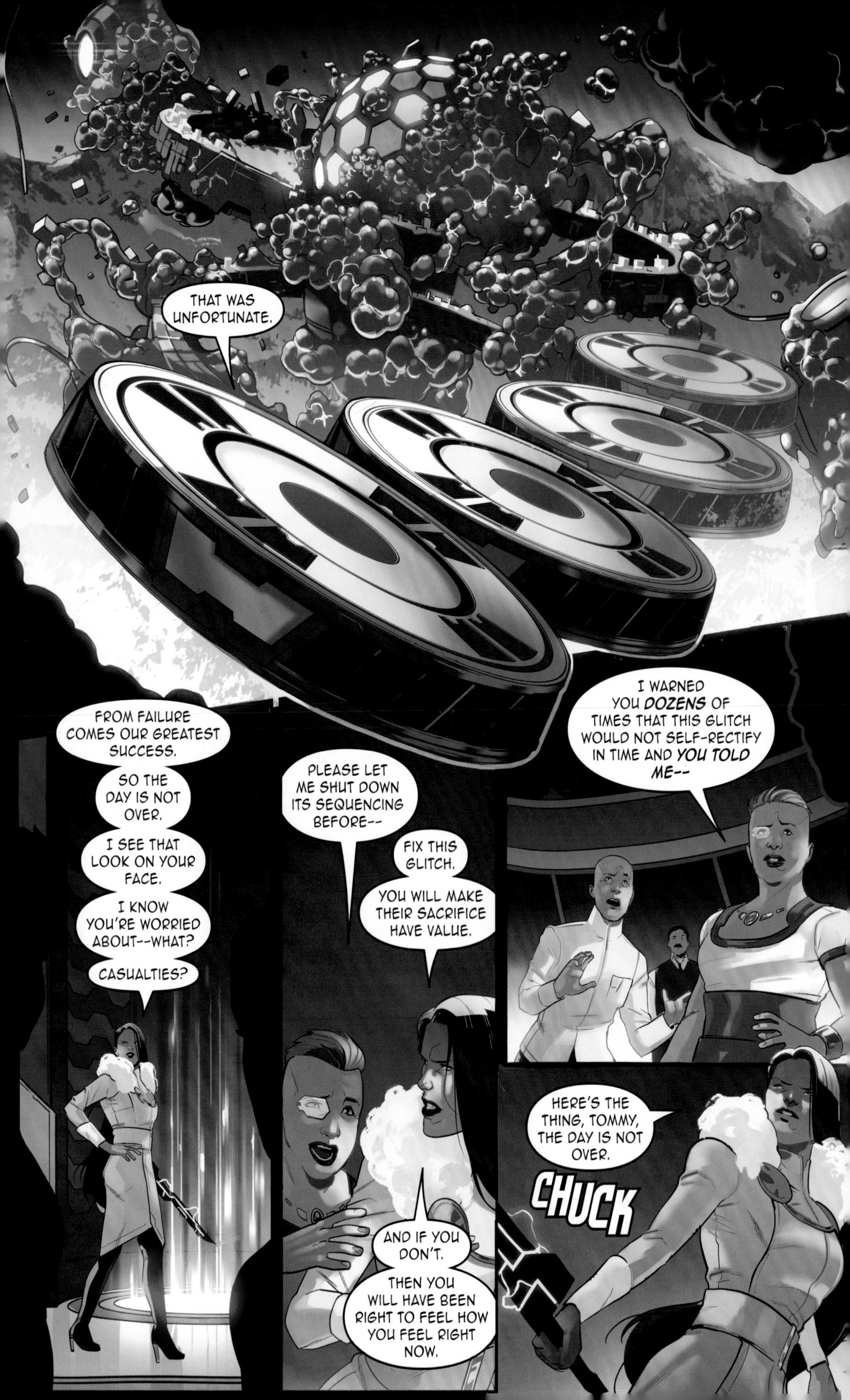
THAT WAS UNFORTUNATE.
FROM FAILURE COMES OUR GREATEST SUCCESS.
SO THE DAY IS NOT OVER.
I SEE THAT LOOK ON YOUR FACE.
I KNOW YOU'RE WORRIED ABOUT--WHAT?
CASUALTIES?
PLEASE LET ME SHUT DOWN ITS SEQUENCING BEFORE--
FIX THIS GLITCH.
YOU WILL MAKE THEIR SACRIFICE HAVE VALUE.
AND IF YOU DON'T.
THEN YOU WILL HAVE BEEN RIGHT TO FEEL HOW YOU FEEL RIGHT NOW.
I WARNED YOU *DOZENS* OF TIMES THAT THIS GLITCH WOULD NOT SELF-RECTIFY IN TIME AND *YOU TOLD ME--*
HERE'S THE THING, TOMMY, THE DAY IS NOT OVER.
CHUCK

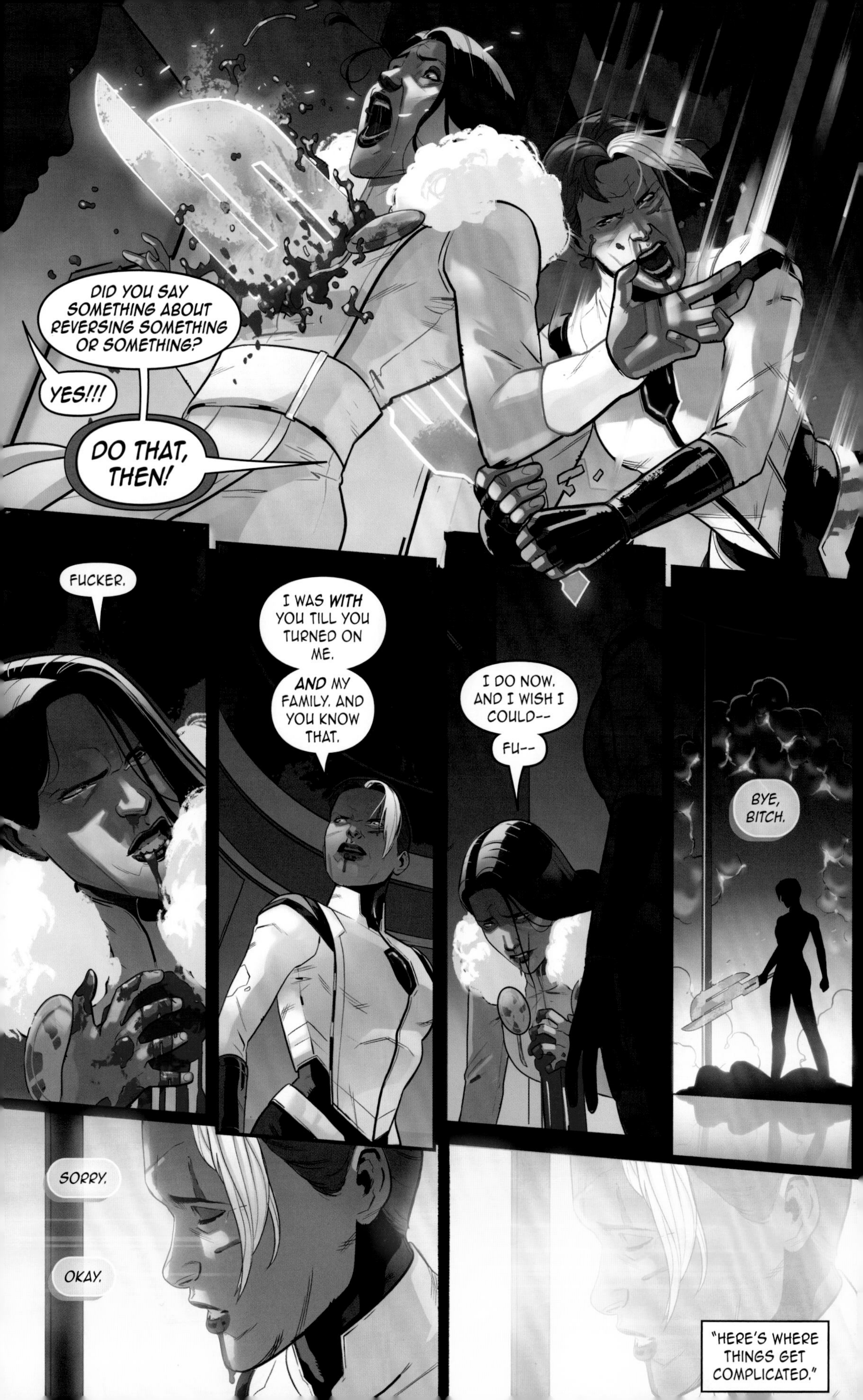
DID YOU SAY SOMETHING ABOUT REVERSING SOMETHING OR SOMETHING?
YES!!!
DO THAT, THEN!
FUCKER.
I WAS WITH YOU TILL YOU TURNED ON ME.
AND MY FAMILY. AND YOU KNOW THAT.
I DO NOW. AND I WISH I COULD--
FU--
BYE, BITCH.
SORRY.
OKAY.
"HERE'S WHERE THINGS GET COMPLICATED."

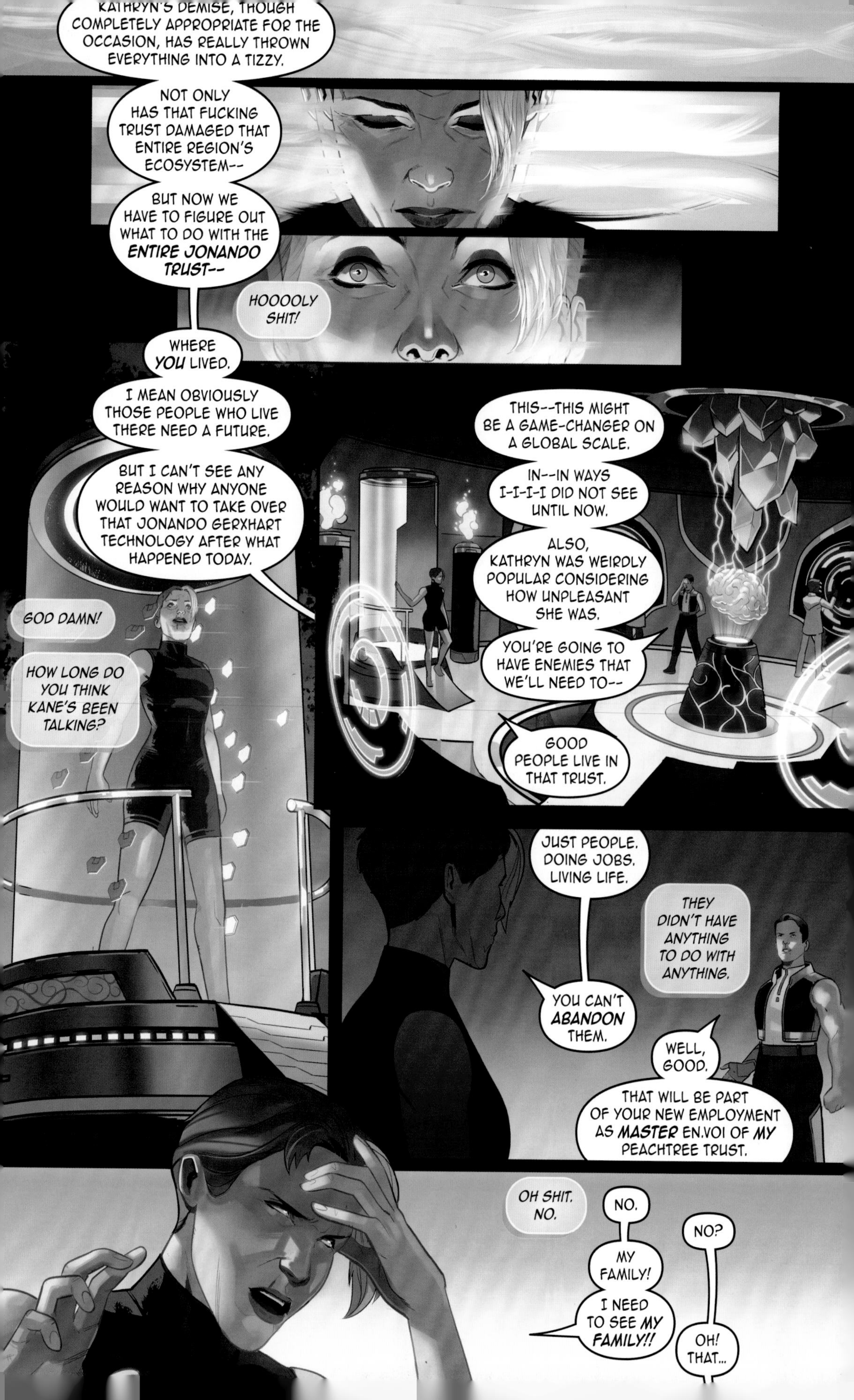

KATHRYN'S DEMISE, THOUGH COMPLETELY APPROPRIATE FOR THE OCCASION, HAS REALLY THROWN EVERYTHING INTO A TIZZY.
NOT ONLY HAS THAT FUCKING TRUST DAMAGED THAT ENTIRE REGION'S ECOSYSTEM--
BUT NOW WE HAVE TO FIGURE OUT WHAT TO DO WITH THE ENTIRE JONANDO TRUST--
HOOOOLY SHIT!
WHERE YOU LIVED.
I MEAN OBVIOUSLY THOSE PEOPLE WHO LIVE THERE NEED A FUTURE.
BUT I CAN'T SEE ANY REASON WHY ANYONE WOULD WANT TO TAKE OVER THAT JONANDO GERXHART TECHNOLOGY AFTER WHAT HAPPENED TODAY.
GOD DAMN!
HOW LONG DO YOU THINK KANE'S BEEN TALKING?
THIS--THIS MIGHT BE A GAME-CHANGER ON A GLOBAL SCALE.
IN--IN WAYS I-I-I-I DID NOT SEE UNTIL NOW.
ALSO, KATHRYN WAS WEIRDLY POPULAR CONSIDERING HOW UNPLEASANT SHE WAS.
YOU'RE GOING TO HAVE ENEMIES THAT WE'LL NEED TO--
GOOD PEOPLE LIVE IN THAT TRUST.
JUST PEOPLE. DOING JOBS. LIVING LIFE.
THEY DIDN'T HAVE ANYTHING TO DO WITH ANYTHING.
YOU CAN'T ABANDON THEM.
WELL, GOOD.
THAT WILL BE PART OF YOUR NEW EMPLOYMENT AS MASTER EN.VOI OF MY PEACHTREE TRUST.
OH SHIT. NO.
NO.
MY FAMILY!
I NEED TO SEE MY FAMILY!!
NO?
OH! THAT...

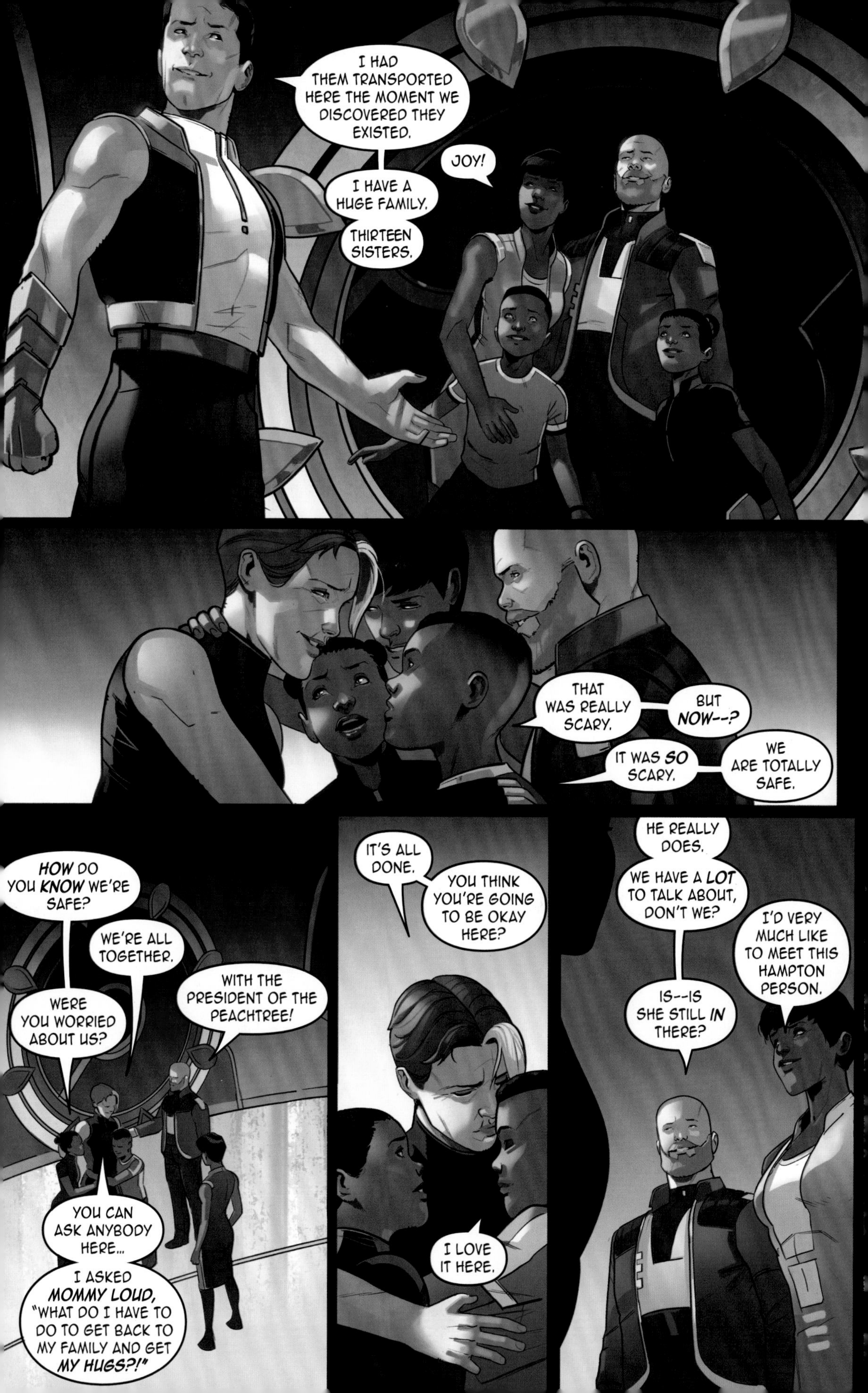

I HAD THEM TRANSPORTED HERE THE MOMENT WE DISCOVERED THEY EXISTED.
I HAVE A HUGE FAMILY.
THIRTEEN SISTERS.
JOY!
THAT WAS REALLY SCARY.
BUT NOW--?
IT WAS SO SCARY.
WE ARE TOTALLY SAFE.
HOW DO YOU KNOW WE'RE SAFE?
WE'RE ALL TOGETHER.
WERE YOU WORRIED ABOUT US?
WITH THE PRESIDENT OF THE PEACHTREE!
YOU CAN ASK ANYBODY HERE...
I ASKED MOMMY LOUD, "WHAT DO I HAVE TO DO TO GET BACK TO MY FAMILY AND GET MY HUGS?!"
IT'S ALL DONE.
YOU THINK YOU'RE GOING TO BE OKAY HERE?
I LOVE IT HERE.
HE REALLY DOES.
WE HAVE A LOT TO TALK ABOUT, DON'T WE?
IS--IS SHE STILL IN THERE?
I'D VERY MUCH LIKE TO MEET THIS HAMPTON PERSON.

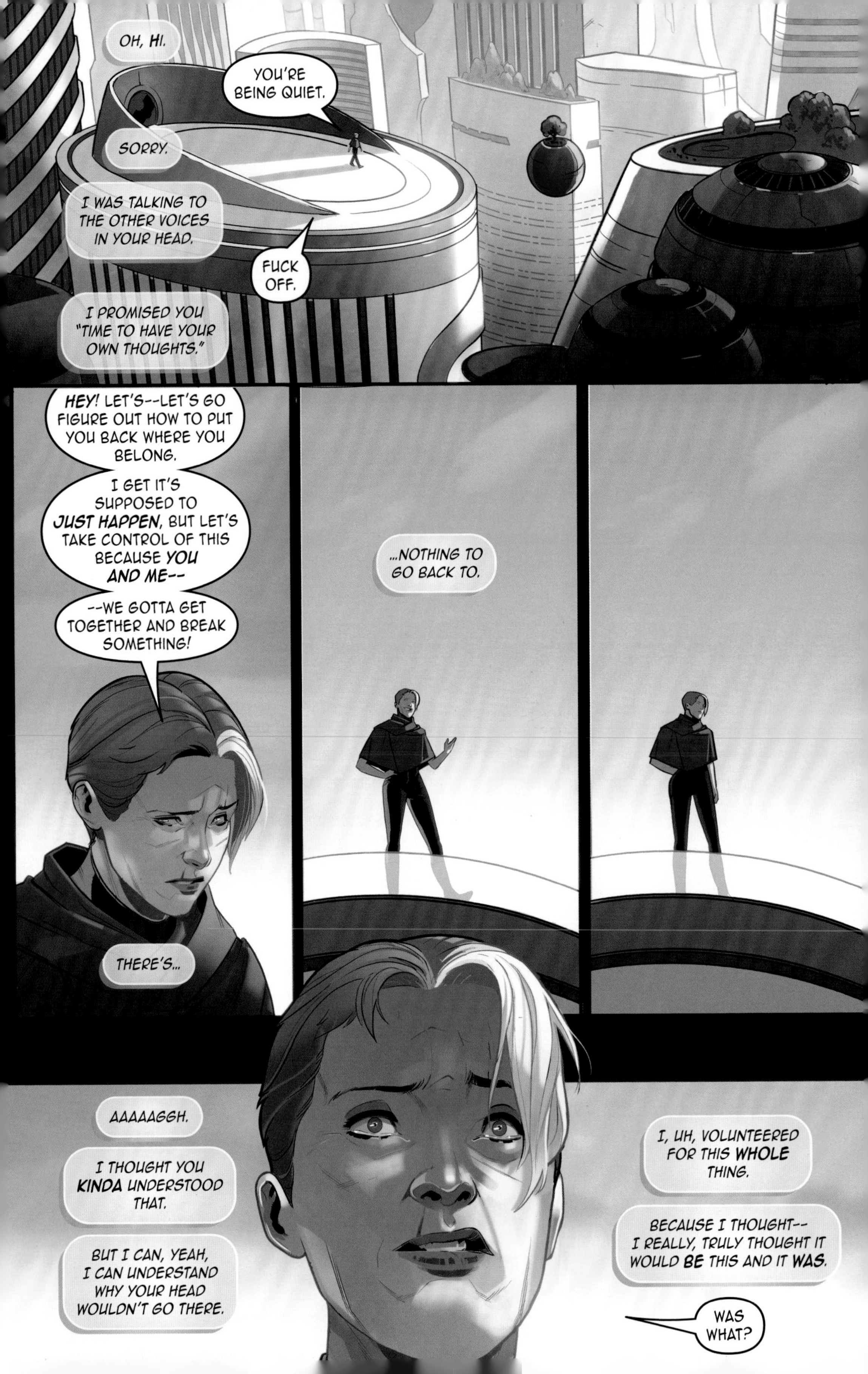
OH, HI.
YOU'RE BEING QUIET.
SORRY.
I WAS TALKING TO THE OTHER VOICES IN YOUR HEAD.
FUCK OFF.
I PROMISED YOU "TIME TO HAVE YOUR OWN THOUGHTS."
HEY! LET'S--LET'S GO FIGURE OUT HOW TO PUT YOU BACK WHERE YOU BELONG.
I GET IT'S SUPPOSED TO JUST HAPPEN, BUT LET'S TAKE CONTROL OF THIS BECAUSE YOU AND ME--
--WE GOTTA GET TOGETHER AND BREAK SOMETHING!
THERE'S...
...NOTHING TO GO BACK TO.
AAAAAGGH.
I THOUGHT YOU KINDA UNDERSTOOD THAT.
BUT I CAN, YEAH, I CAN UNDERSTAND WHY YOUR HEAD WOULDN'T GO THERE.
I, UH, VOLUNTEERED FOR THIS WHOLE THING.
BECAUSE I THOUGHT-- I REALLY, TRULY THOUGHT IT WOULD BE THIS AND IT WAS.
WAS WHAT?

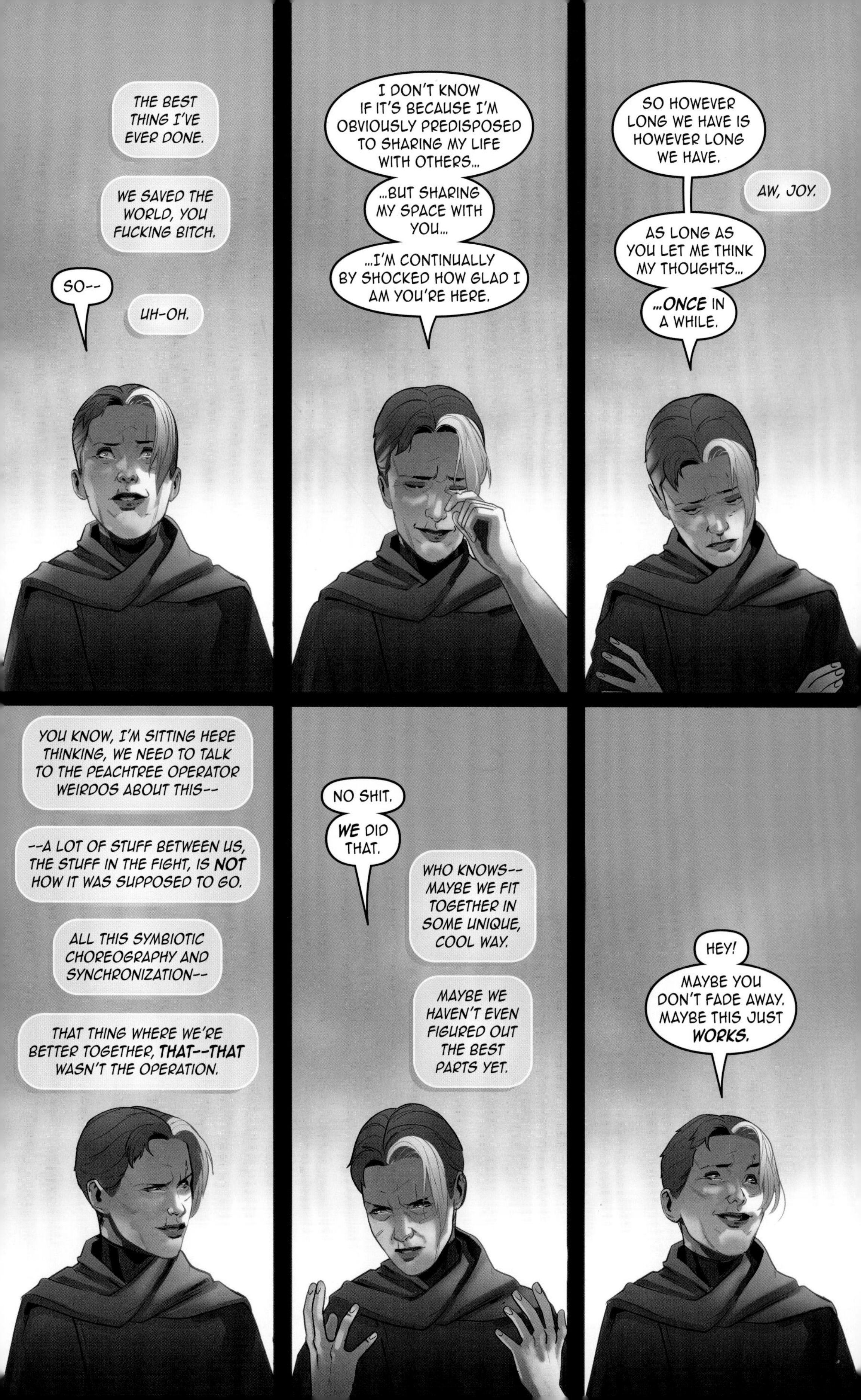
THE BEST THING I'VE EVER DONE.
WE SAVED THE WORLD, YOU FUCKING BITCH.
SO--
UH-OH.
I DON'T KNOW IF IT'S BECAUSE I'M OBVIOUSLY PREDISPOSED TO SHARING MY LIFE WITH OTHERS...
...BUT SHARING MY SPACE WITH YOU...
...I'M CONTINUALLY BY SHOCKED HOW GLAD I AM YOU'RE HERE.
SO HOWEVER LONG WE HAVE IS HOWEVER LONG WE HAVE.
AW, JOY.
AS LONG AS YOU LET ME THINK MY THOUGHTS...
...**ONCE** IN A WHILE.
YOU KNOW, I'M SITTING HERE THINKING, WE NEED TO TALK TO THE PEACHTREE OPERATOR WEIRDOS ABOUT THIS--
--A LOT OF STUFF BETWEEN US, THE STUFF IN THE FIGHT, IS **NOT** HOW IT WAS SUPPOSED TO GO.
ALL THIS SYMBIOTIC CHOREOGRAPHY AND SYNCHRONIZATION--
THAT THING WHERE WE'RE BETTER TOGETHER, **THAT--THAT** WASN'T THE OPERATION.
NO SHIT.
WE DID THAT.
WHO KNOWS-- MAYBE WE FIT TOGETHER IN SOME UNIQUE, COOL WAY.
MAYBE WE HAVEN'T EVEN FIGURED OUT THE BEST PARTS YET.
HEY!
MAYBE YOU DON'T FADE AWAY. MAYBE THIS JUST **WORKS.**

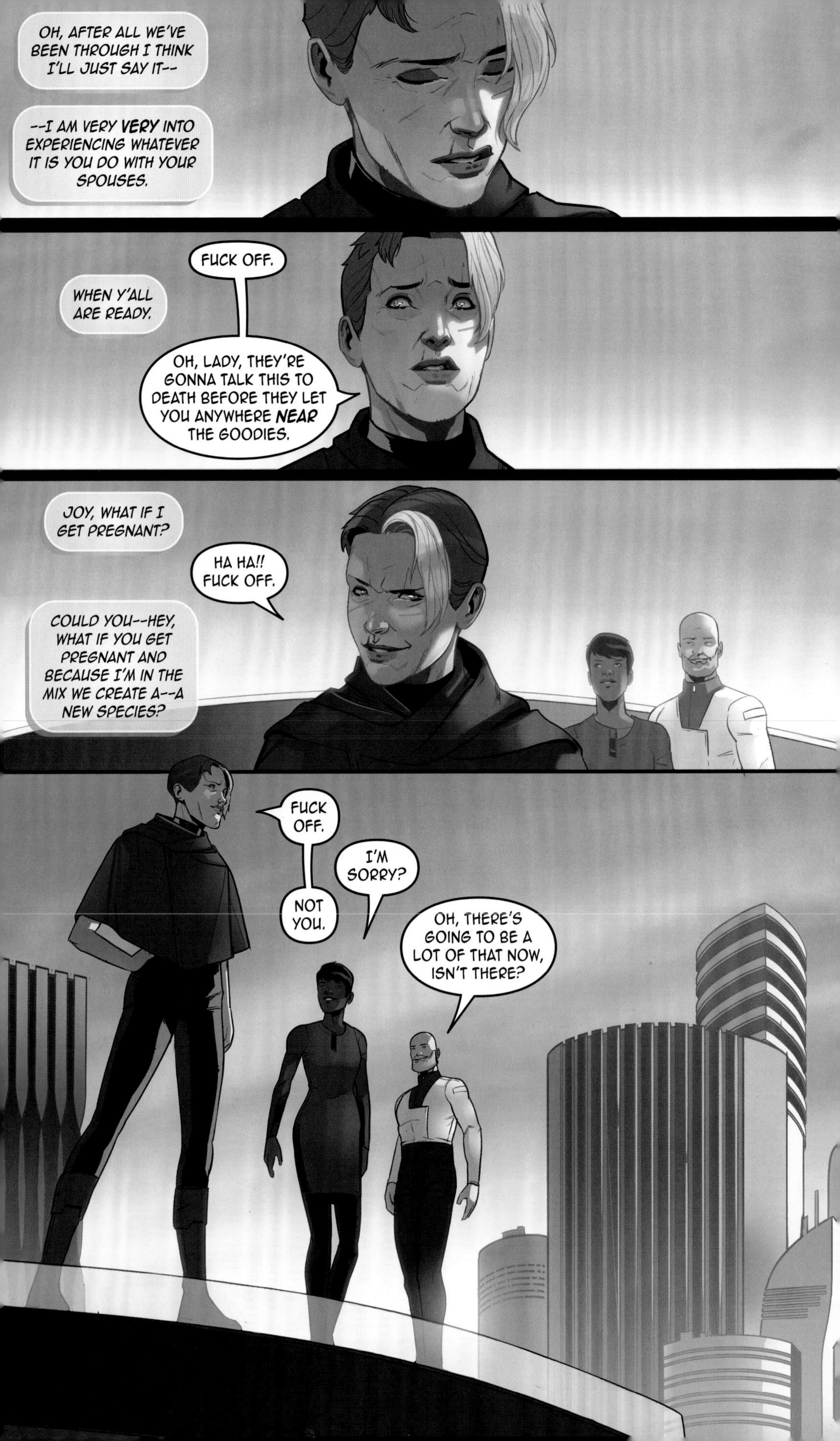
OH, AFTER ALL WE'VE BEEN THROUGH I THINK I'LL JUST SAY IT--
--I AM VERY **VERY** INTO EXPERIENCING WHATEVER IT IS YOU DO WITH YOUR SPOUSES.
WHEN Y'ALL ARE READY.
FUCK OFF.
OH, LADY, THEY'RE GONNA TALK THIS TO DEATH BEFORE THEY LET YOU ANYWHERE **NEAR** THE GOODIES.
JOY, WHAT IF I GET PREGNANT?
HA HA!! FUCK OFF.
COULD YOU--HEY, WHAT IF YOU GET PREGNANT AND BECAUSE I'M IN THE MIX WE CREATE A--A NEW SPECIES?
FUCK OFF.
NOT YOU.
I'M SORRY?
OH, THERE'S GOING TO BE A LOT OF THAT NOW, ISN'T THERE?

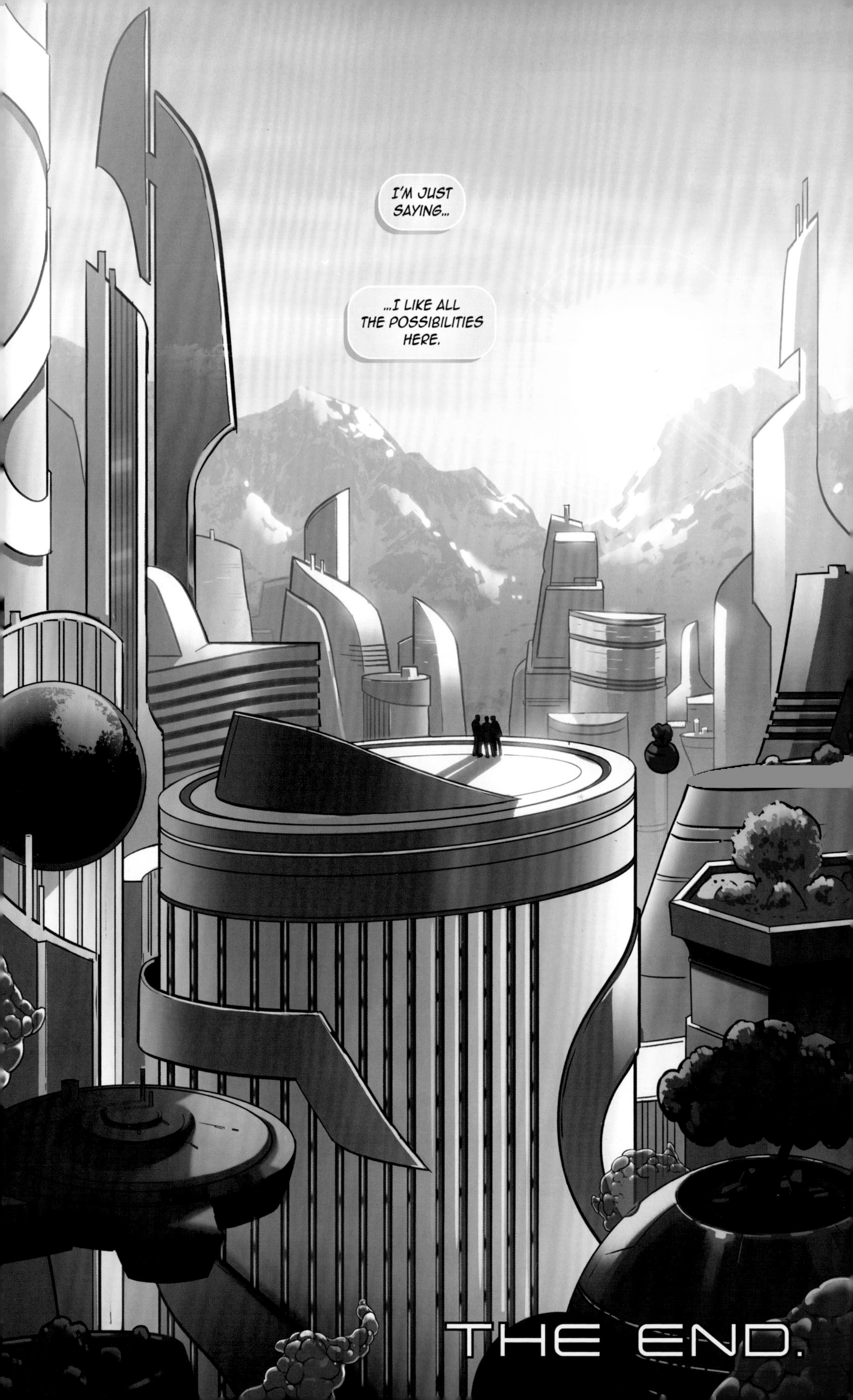
I'M JUST SAYING...
...I LIKE ALL THE POSSIBILITIES HERE.
THE END.

Joy Operations #1 Cover B by David Mack

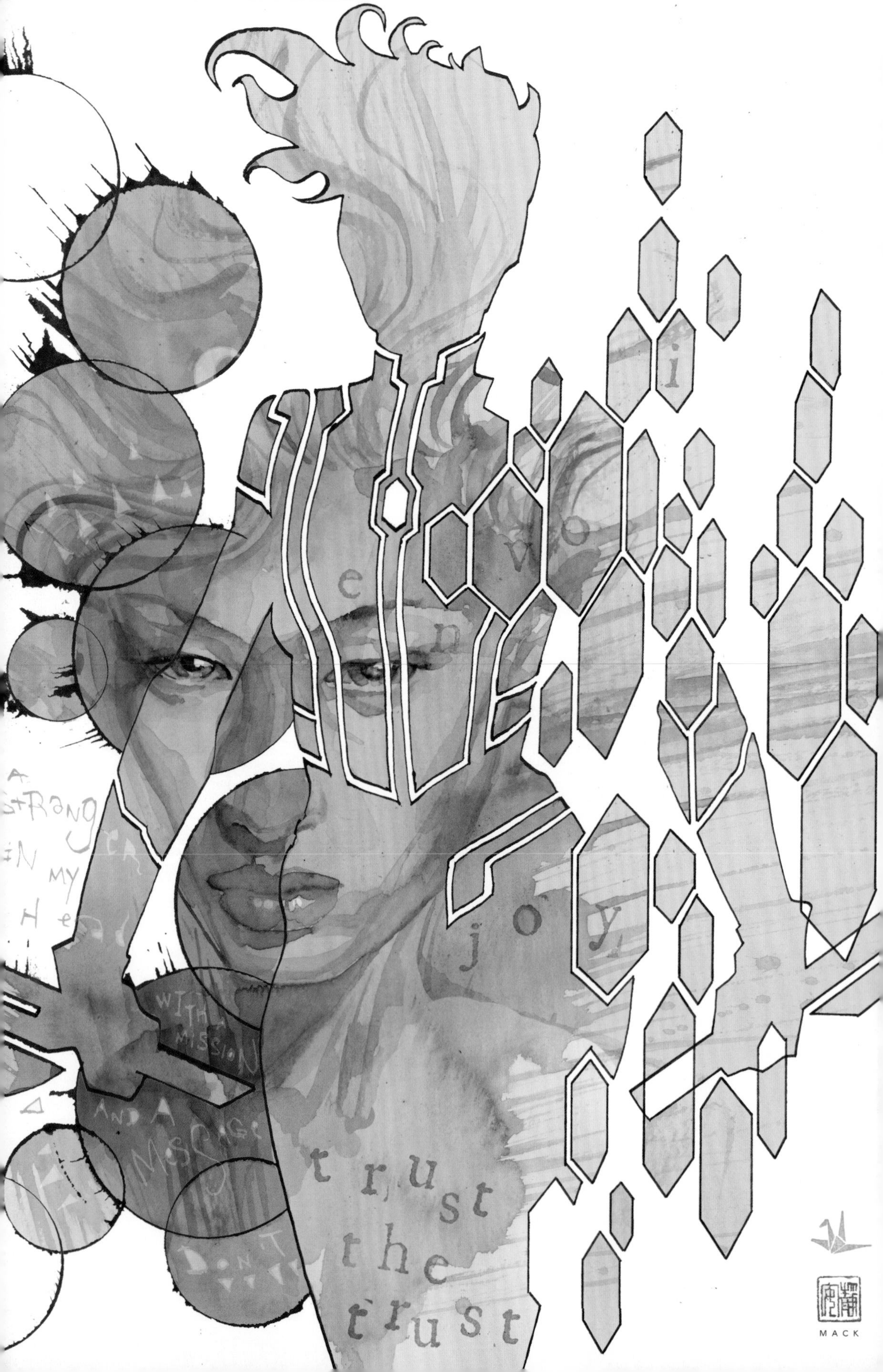

i
o
v
e
n
A
stRangER
IN MY
Head
WITH A
MISSION
AND A
MESSAGE
DON'T
joy
trust
the
trust
MACK

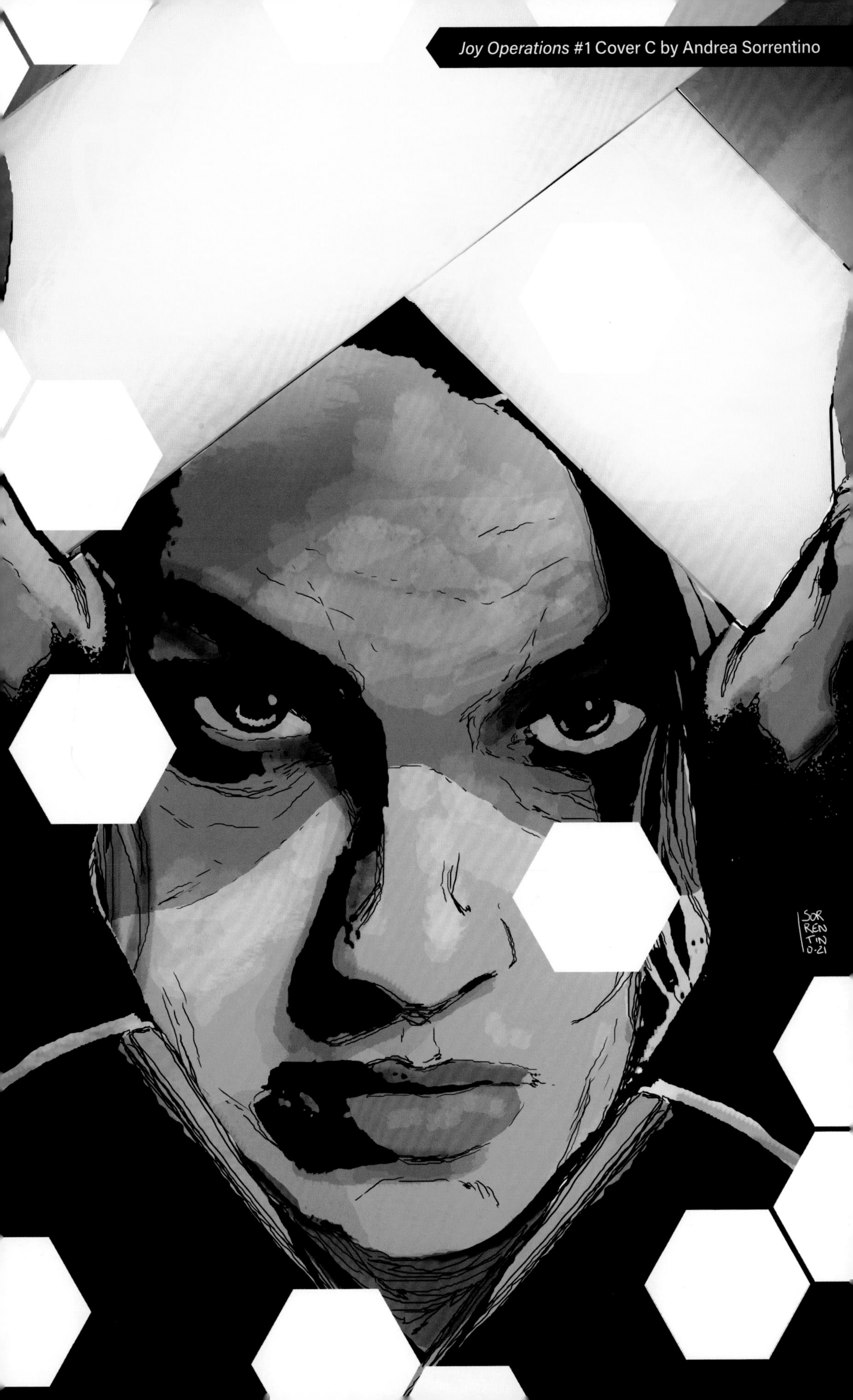
SOR
REN
TIN
O·21

Joy Operations #1 Cover C by Andrea Sorrentino

Joy Operations #1 Cover D by Christian Ward

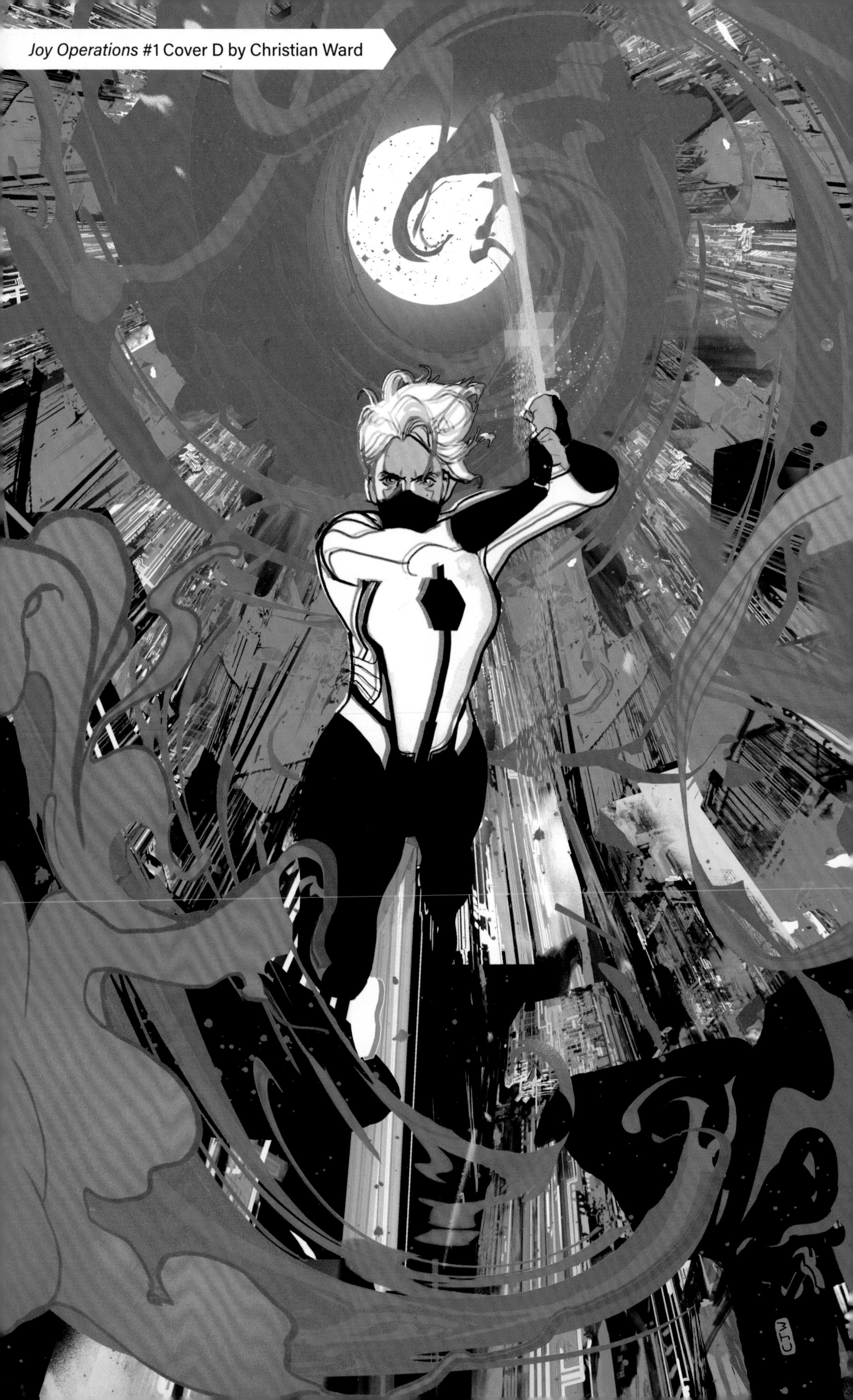

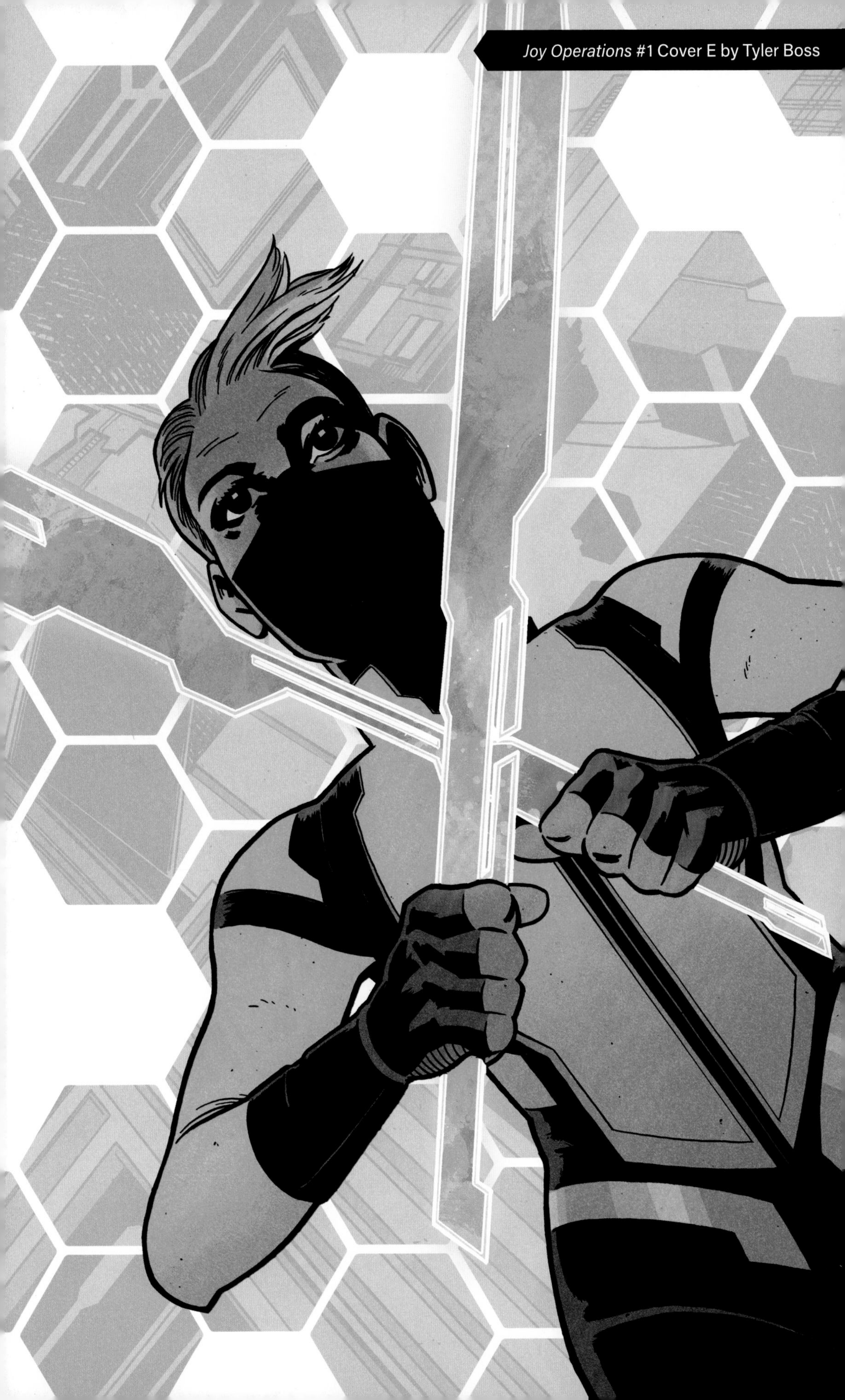

Joy Operations #1 Cover E by Tyler Boss

Joy Operations #2 Cover B by Michael Avon Oeming

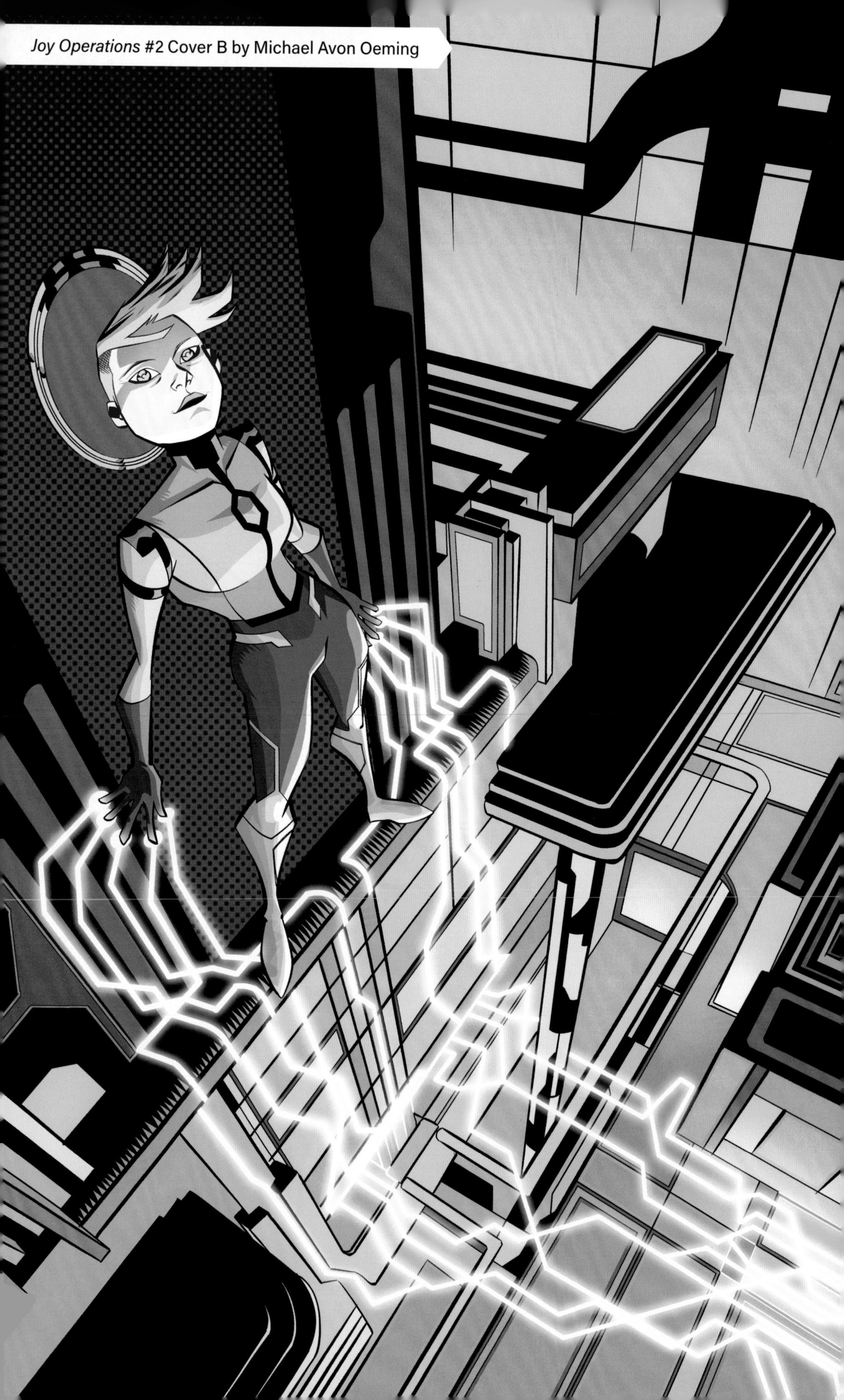

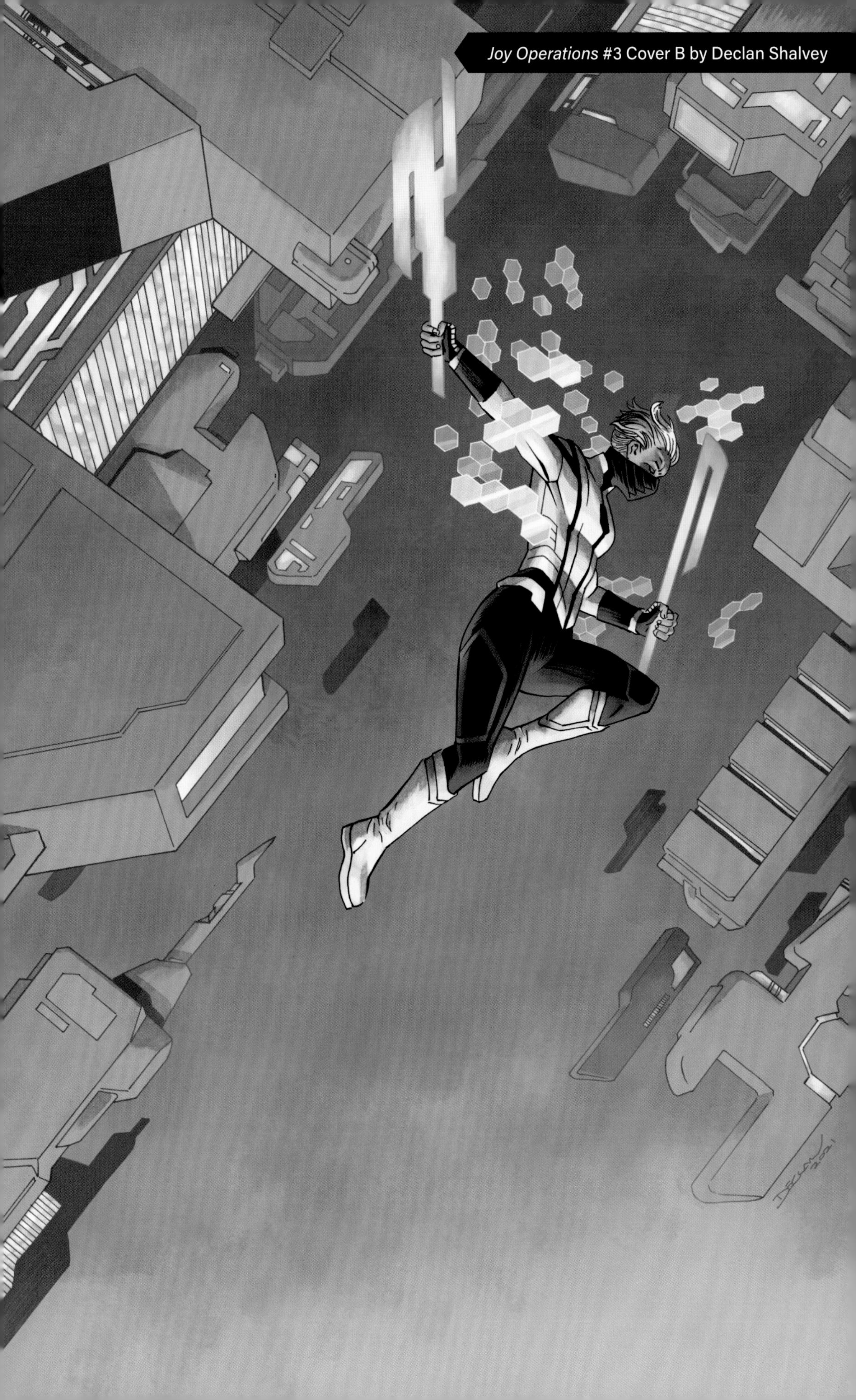

Joy Operations #3 Cover B by Declan Shalvey

Joy Operations #4 Cover B by David Marquez

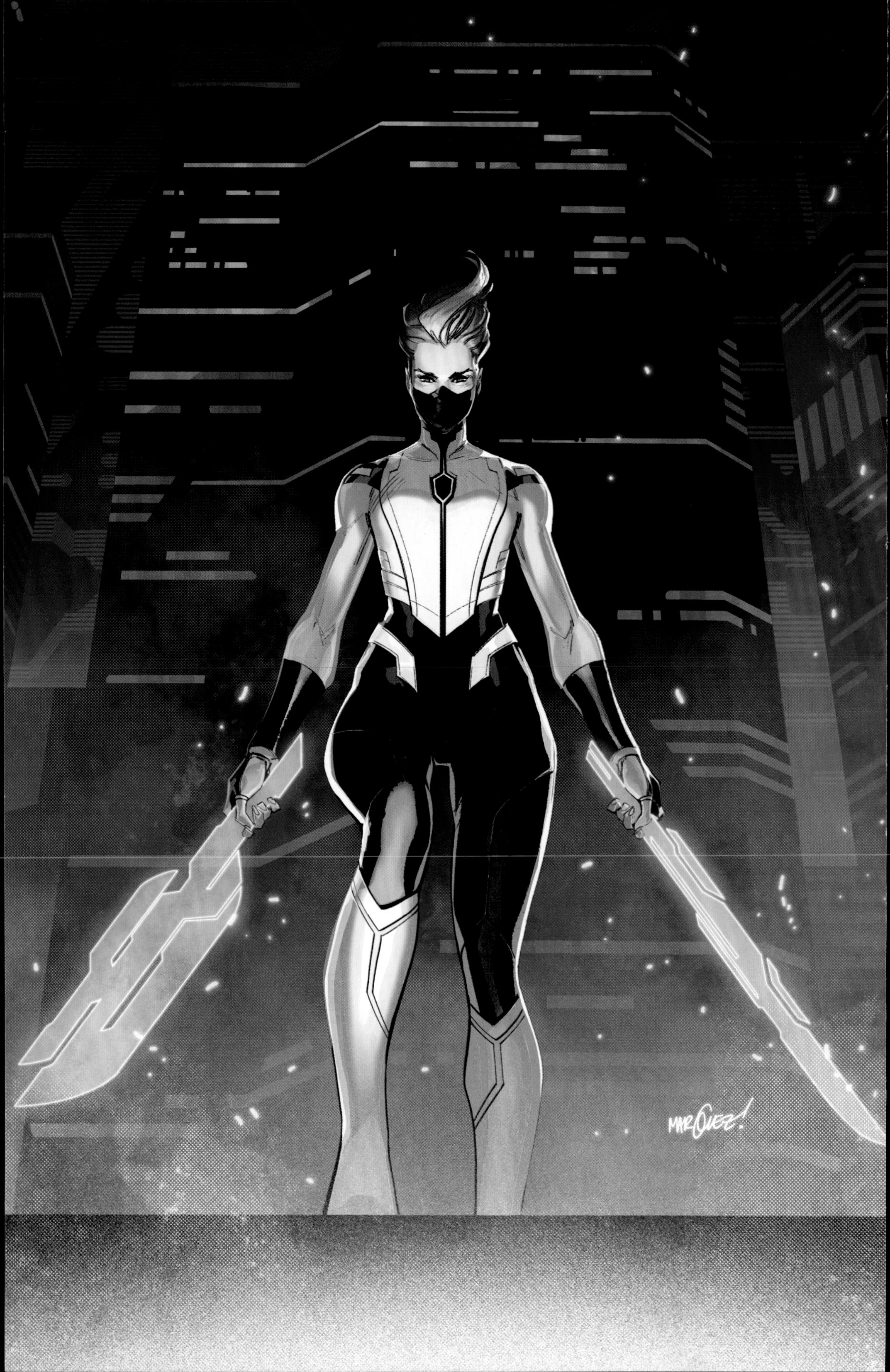

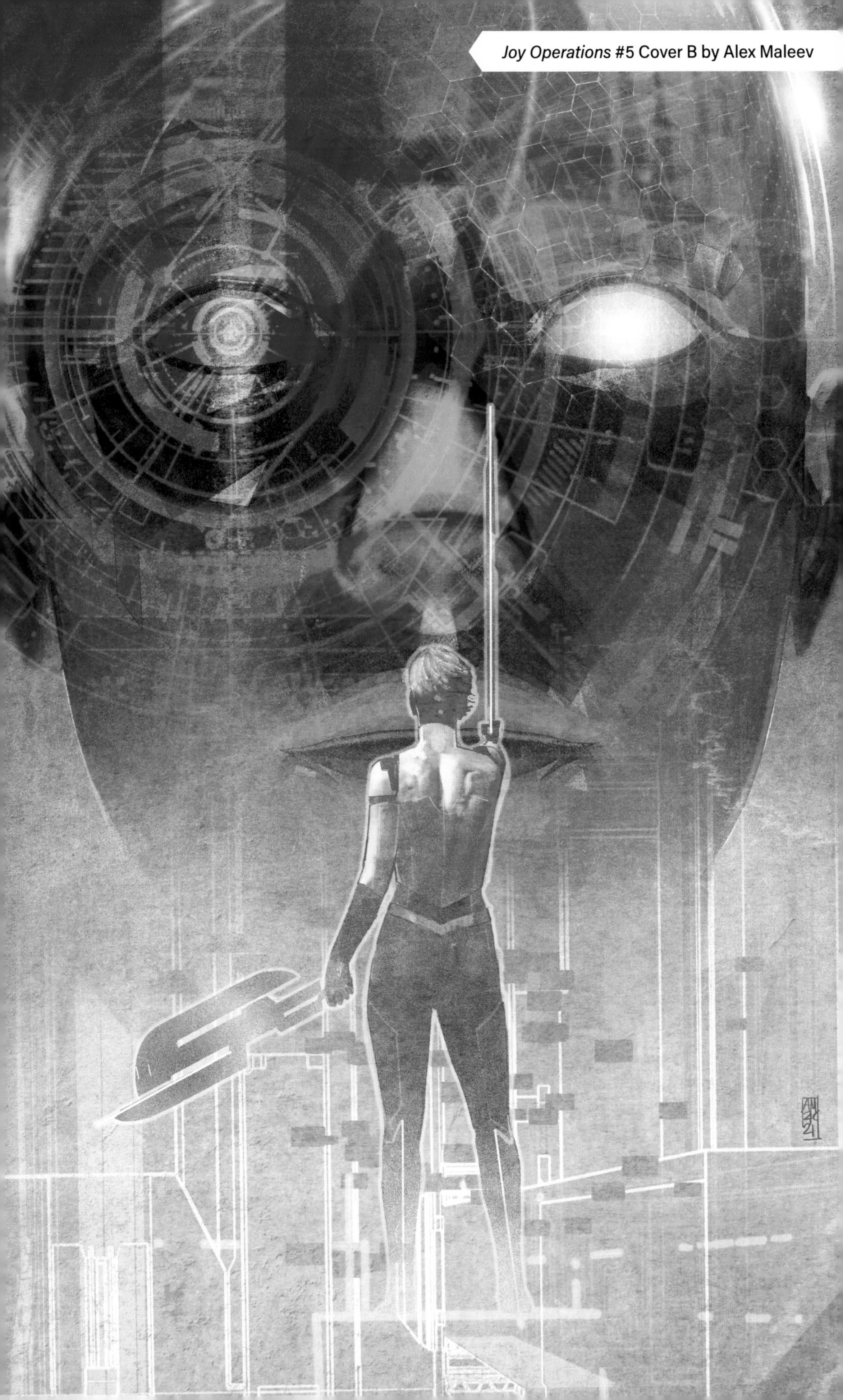

Joy Operations #5 Cover B by Alex Maleev

JOY OPERATIONS™

SKETCHBOOK

Notes by Stephen Byrne

I was experimenting here with overlapping-weave design elements in the neck, belt, and boots but ultimately decided that this type of look was too busy and unnecessarily complicated.

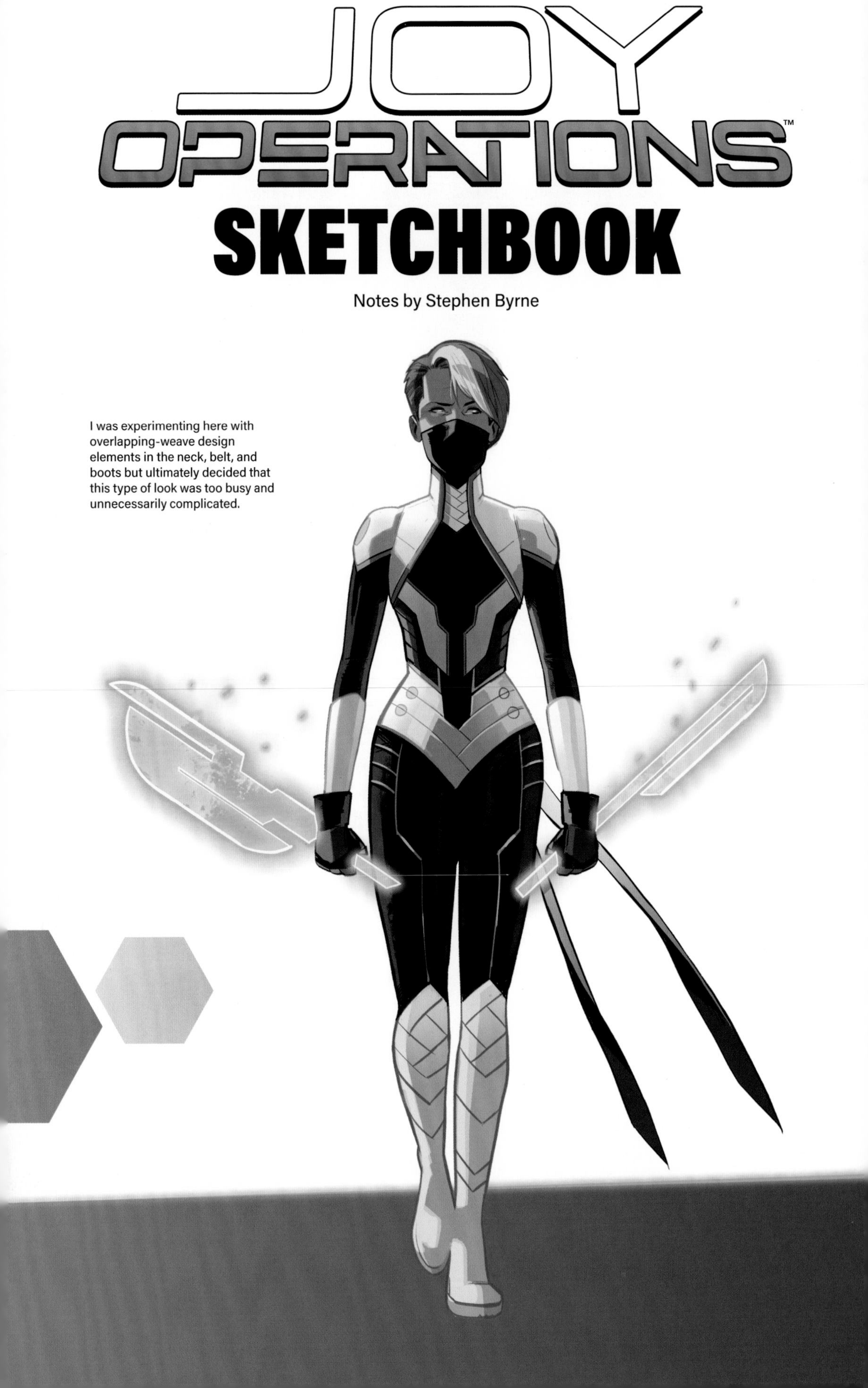

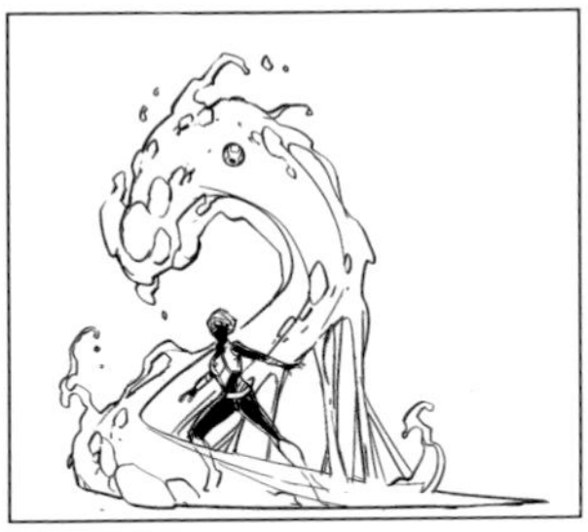

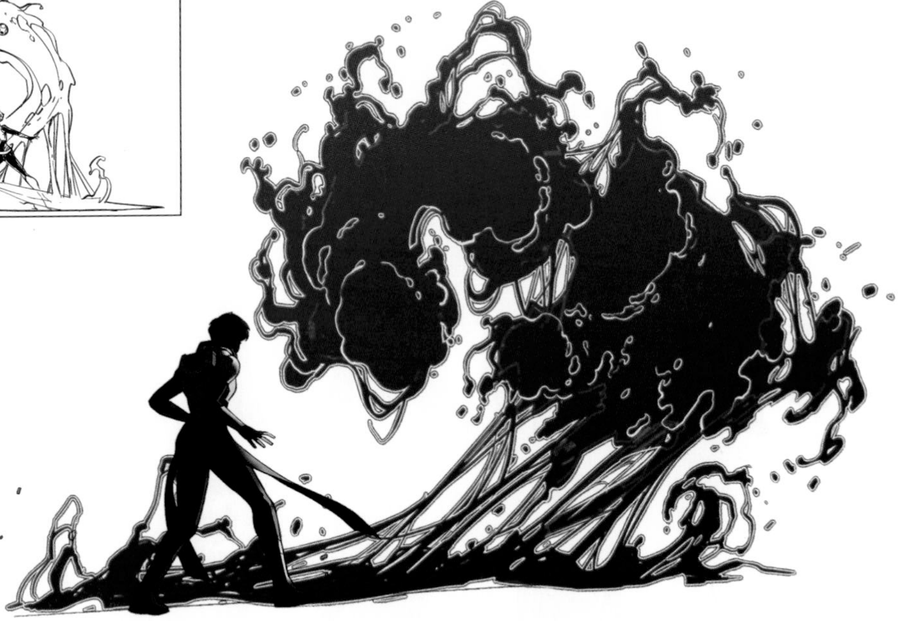

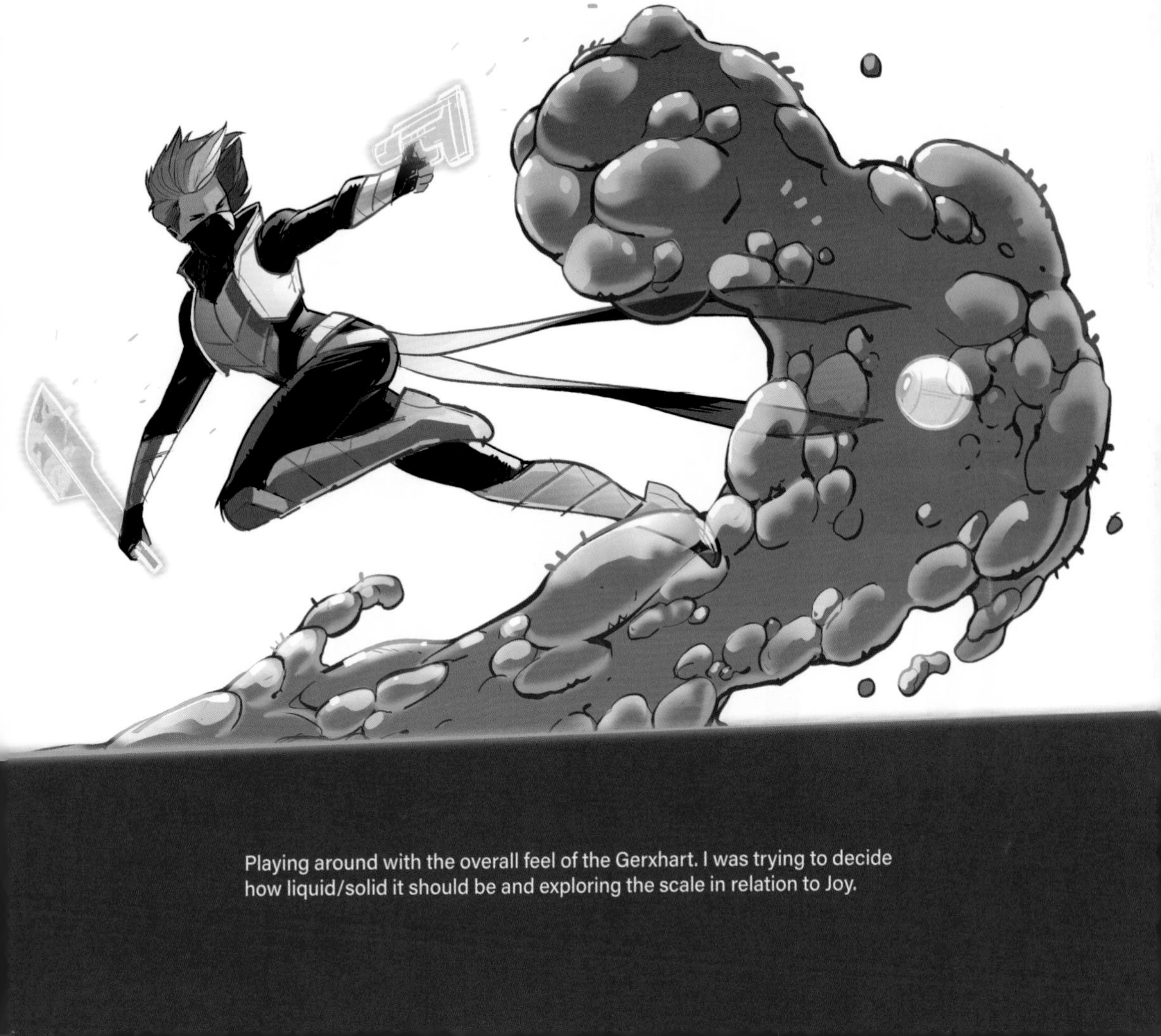

Playing around with the overall feel of the Gerxhart. I was trying to decide how liquid/solid it should be and exploring the scale in relation to Joy.

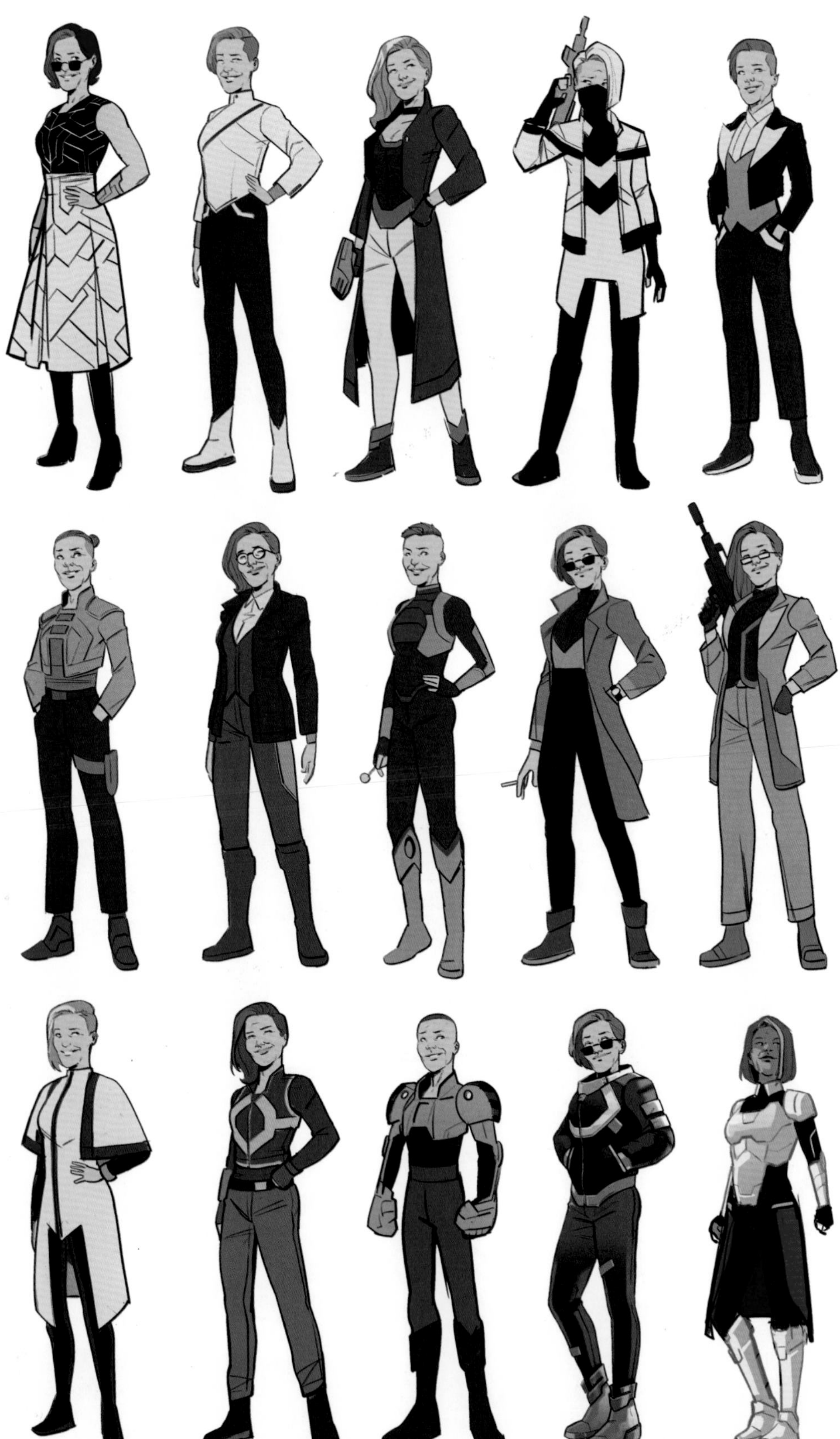

This was one of the earliest stages of designing Joy, based on initial conversations with Brian. I was throwing different stuff out there to see what we responded to. There are a lot of aesthetics and personalities here. It helped us to narrow our focus.

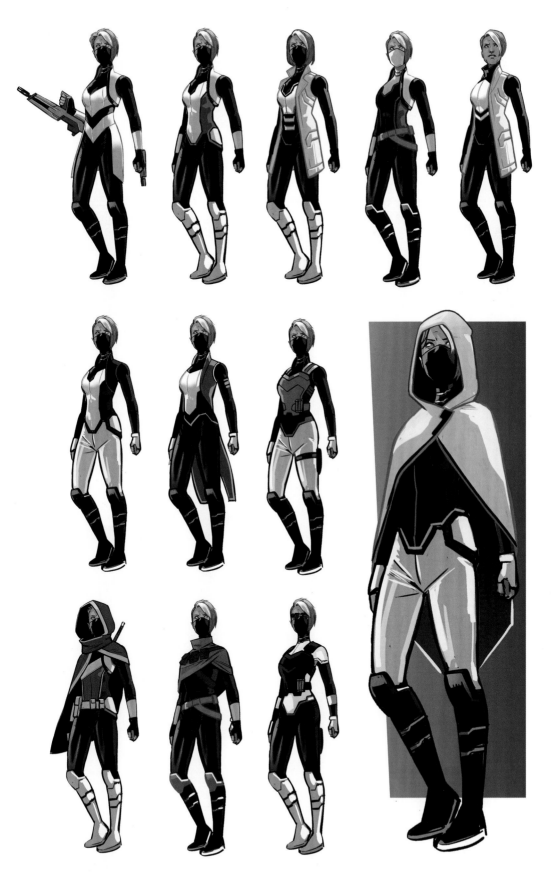

We liked the sleek black-and-white tech look as an aesthetic for Joy and her trust. I was playing around with different options within that framework. I think a lot of these looks are too complicated, but going through this process helped me to realize the benefits of simplification.

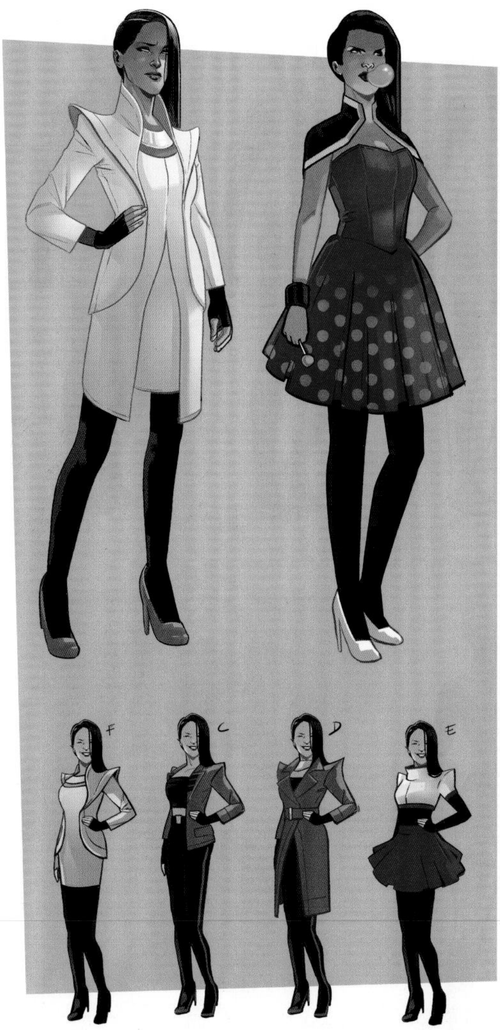
F
C
D
E

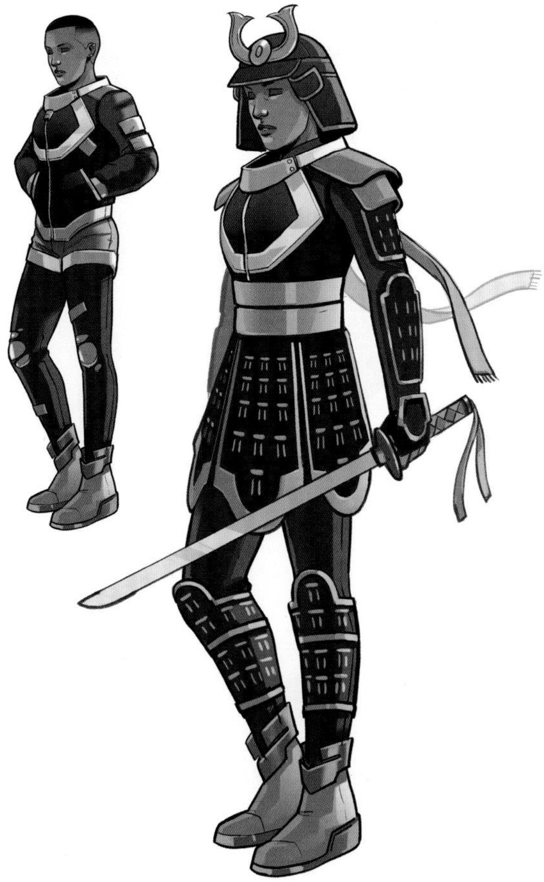

These were some early explorations of Kathryn's aesthetic. I was playing with the idea of a younger version of the character, so some of these designs reflect a more spoiled rich-teenager vibe.

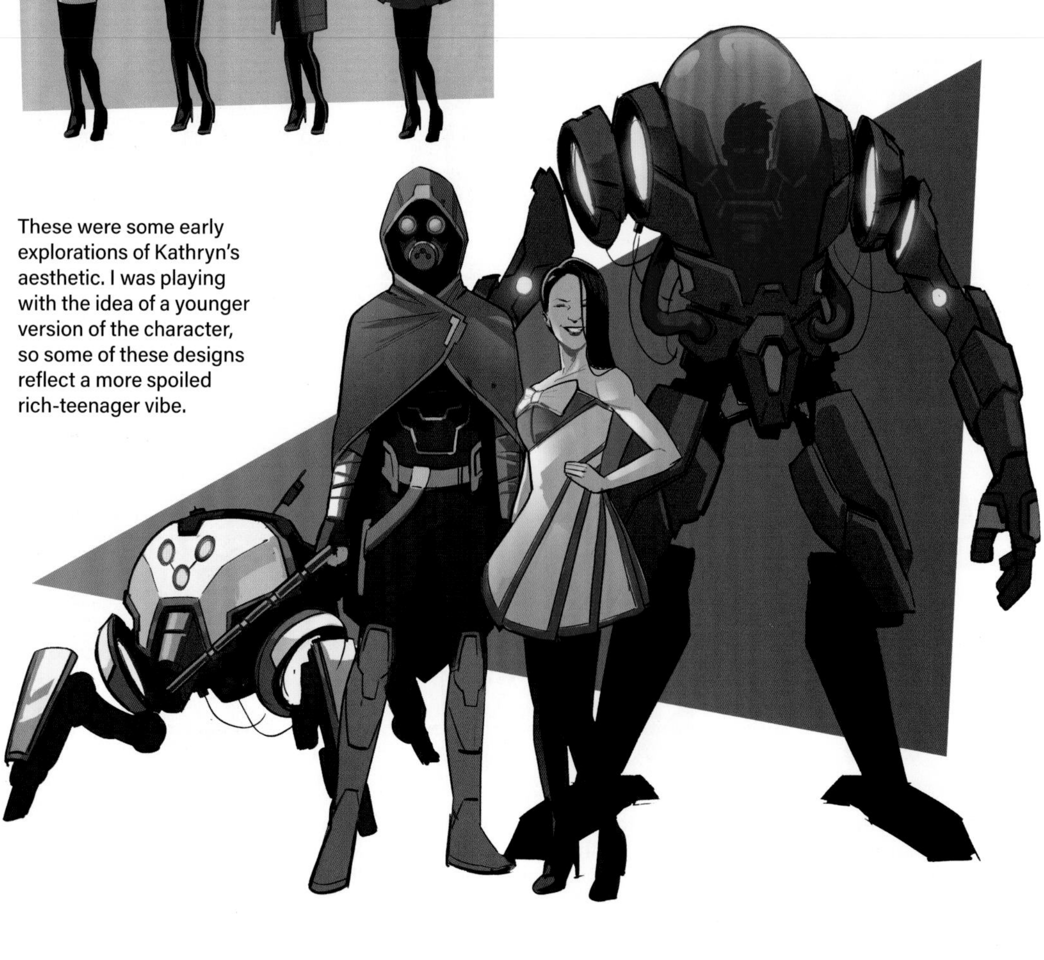

Brian and I discussed the cultures of the different trusts. These designs were my early thoughts about characters that could embody the visual feel of the people from different trusts.

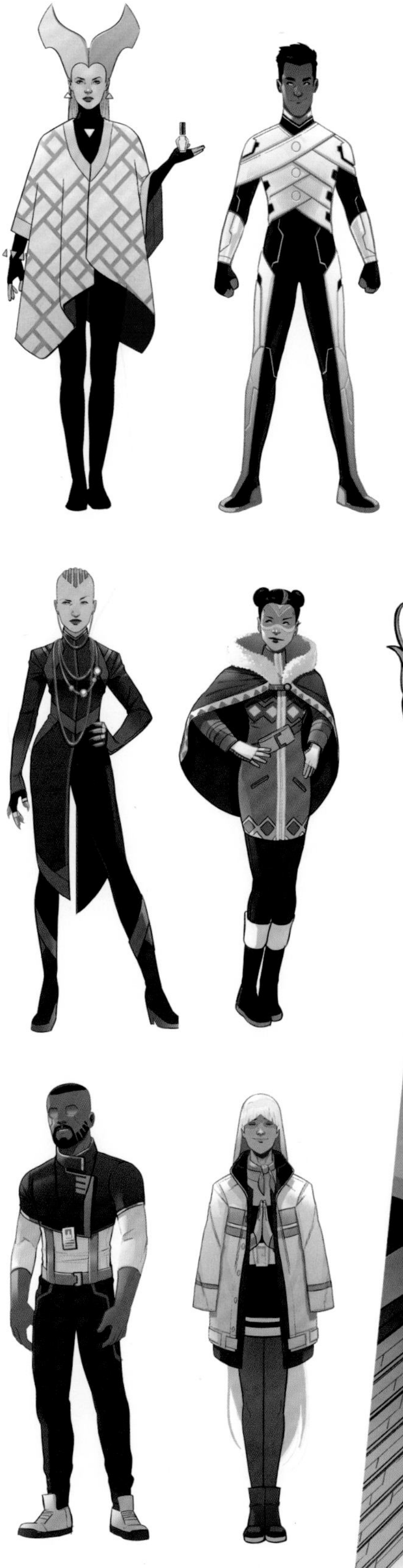

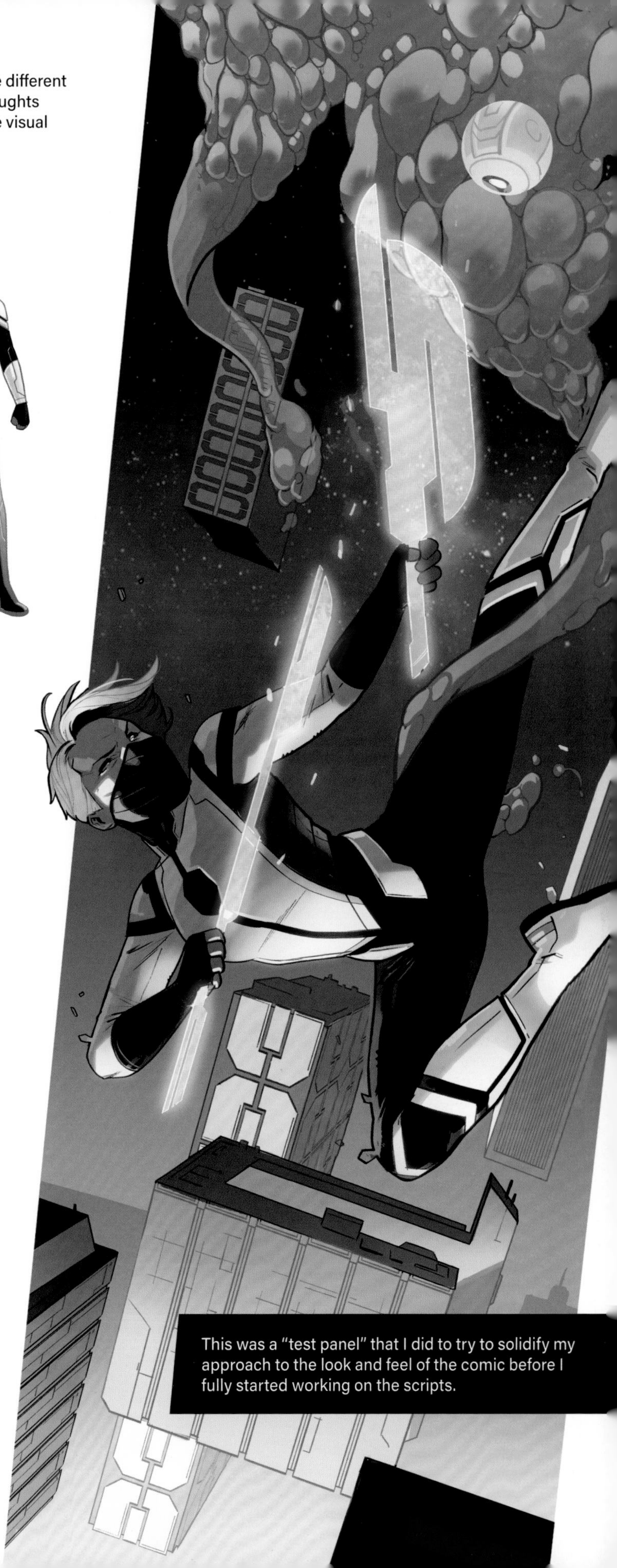

This was a "test panel" that I did to try to solidify my approach to the look and feel of the comic before I fully started working on the scripts.

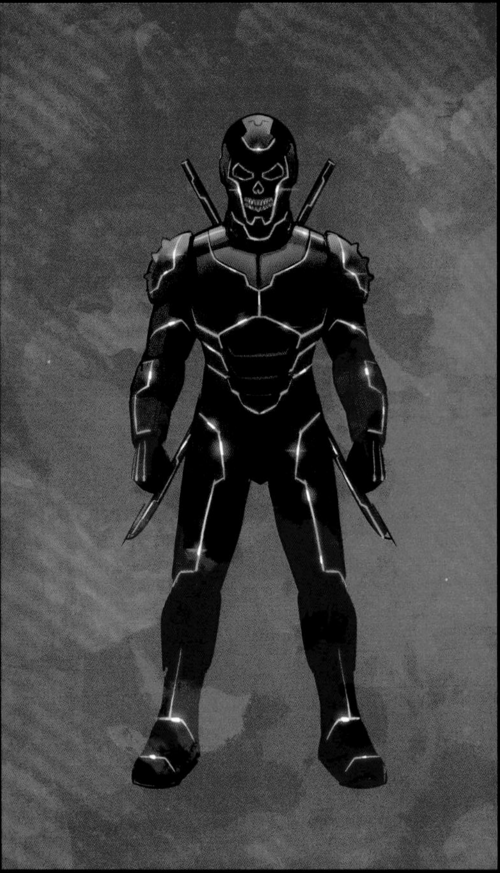
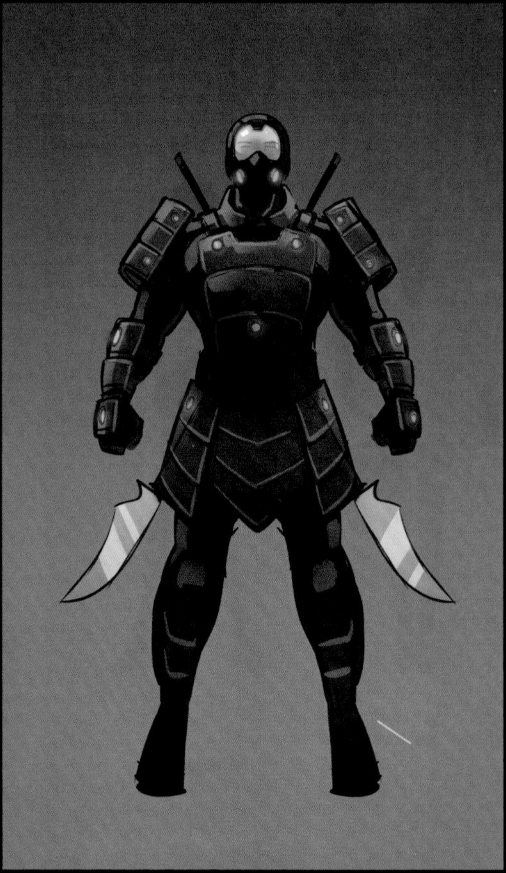
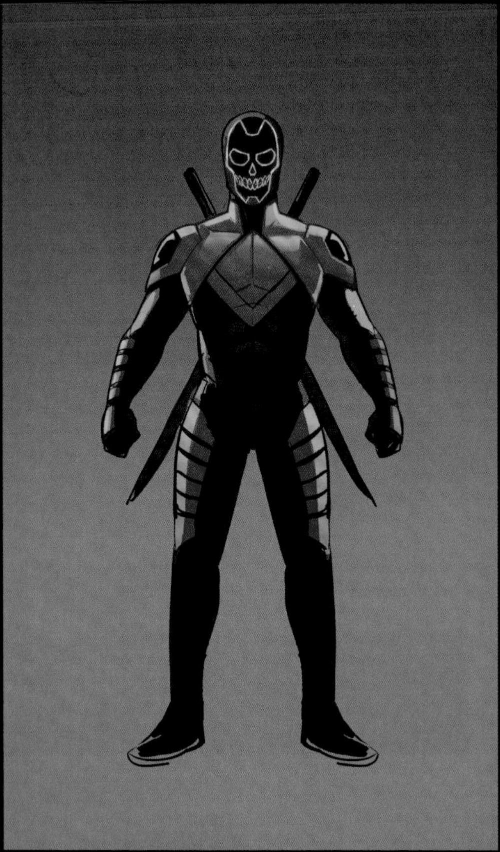
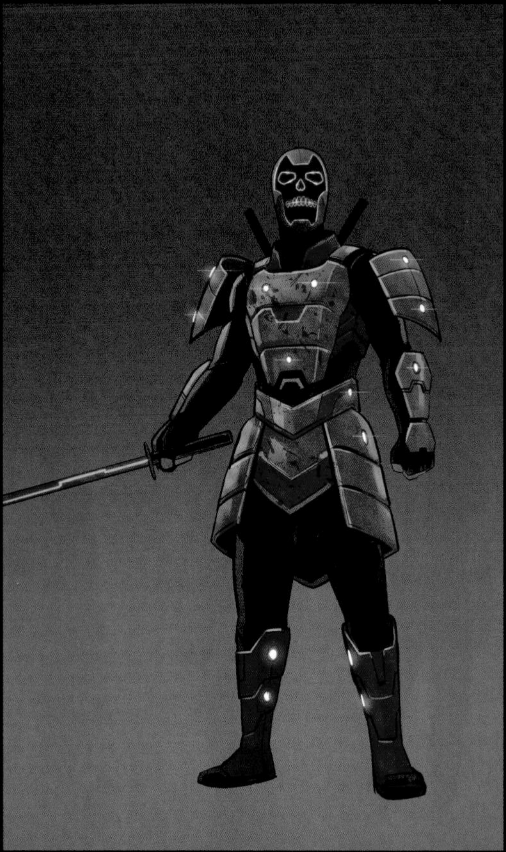

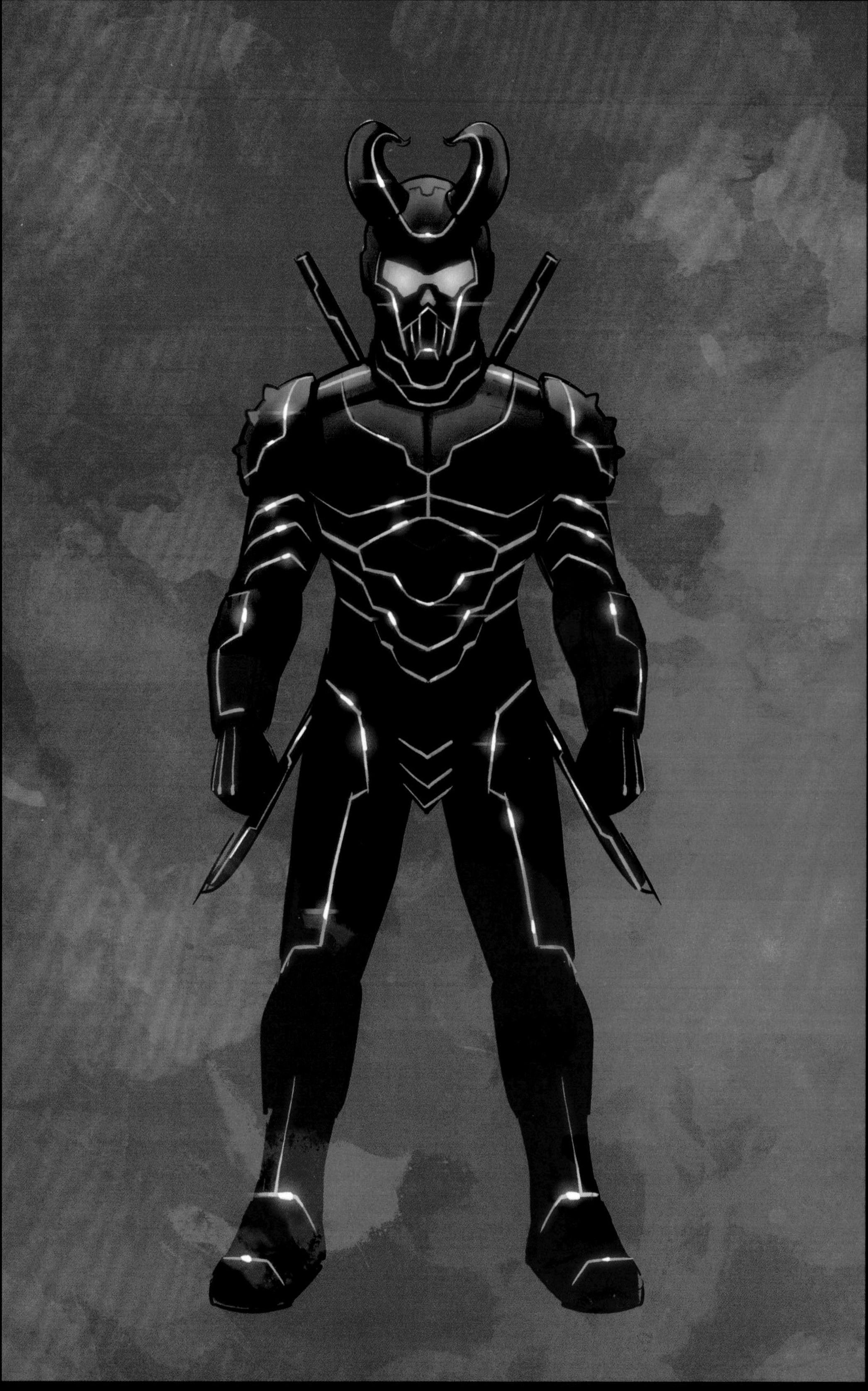

Concepts for Hatamoto. I liked the black-and-red color scheme as a contrast to the cool blues and whites that we had seen for most of the book up until his arrival. I was excited by the idea of a "digital skull" face and explored some different options for armor. Brian was particularly drawn to the sci-fi samurai vibe.

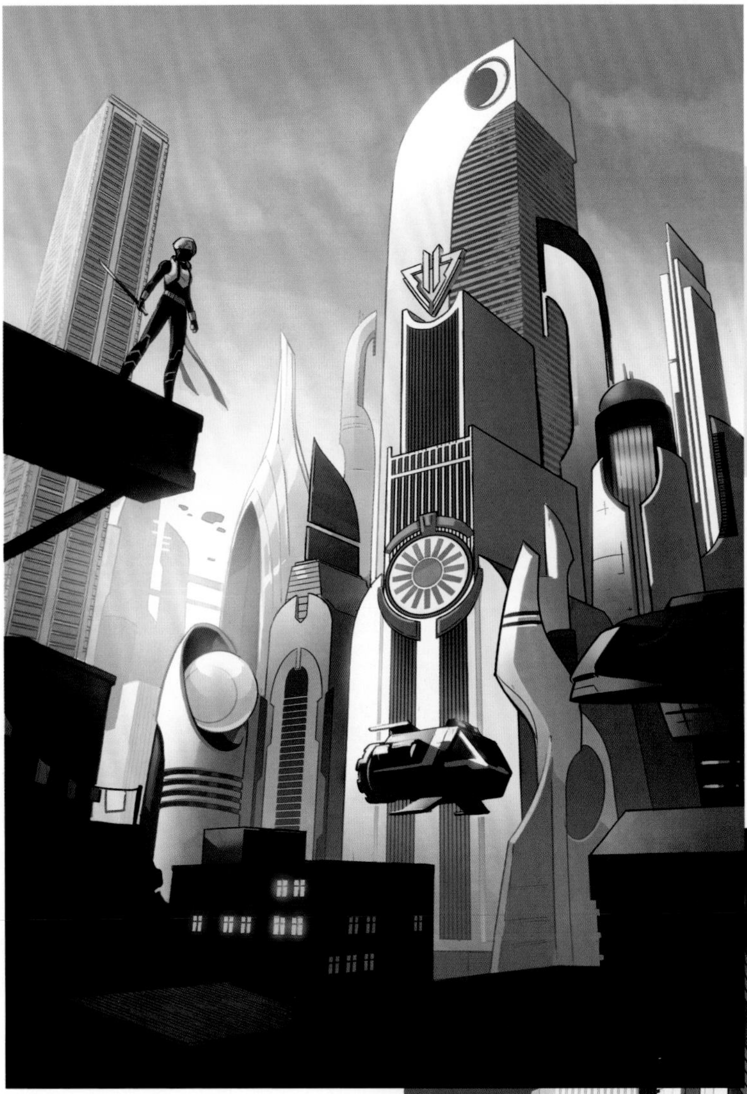

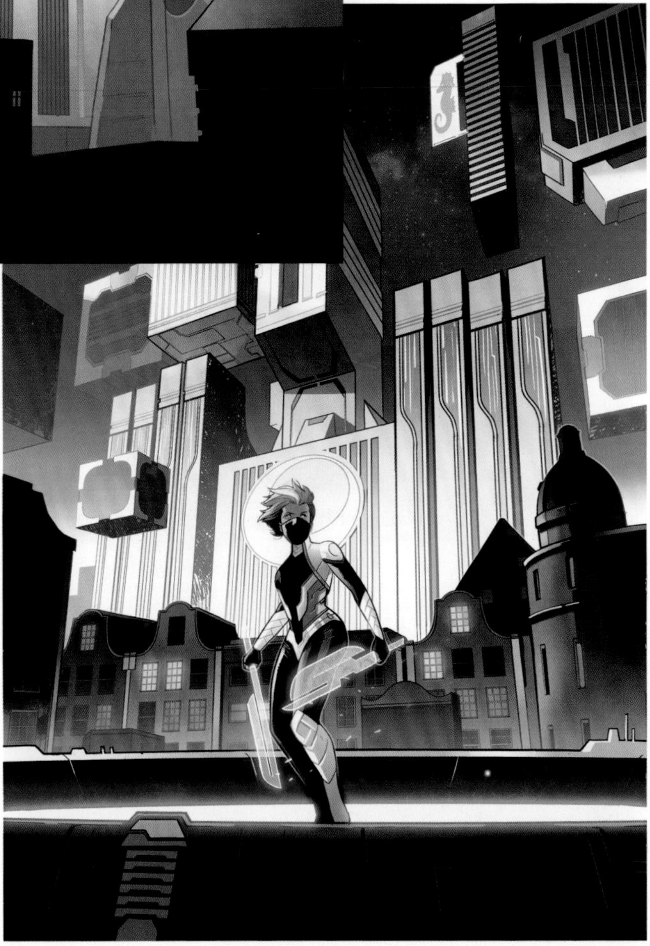

These were pieces of concept art for the overall look and feel of the book. I was trying to pull together costume design, tech concepts, color palettes, and environments to give a snapshot of what the world could look like.

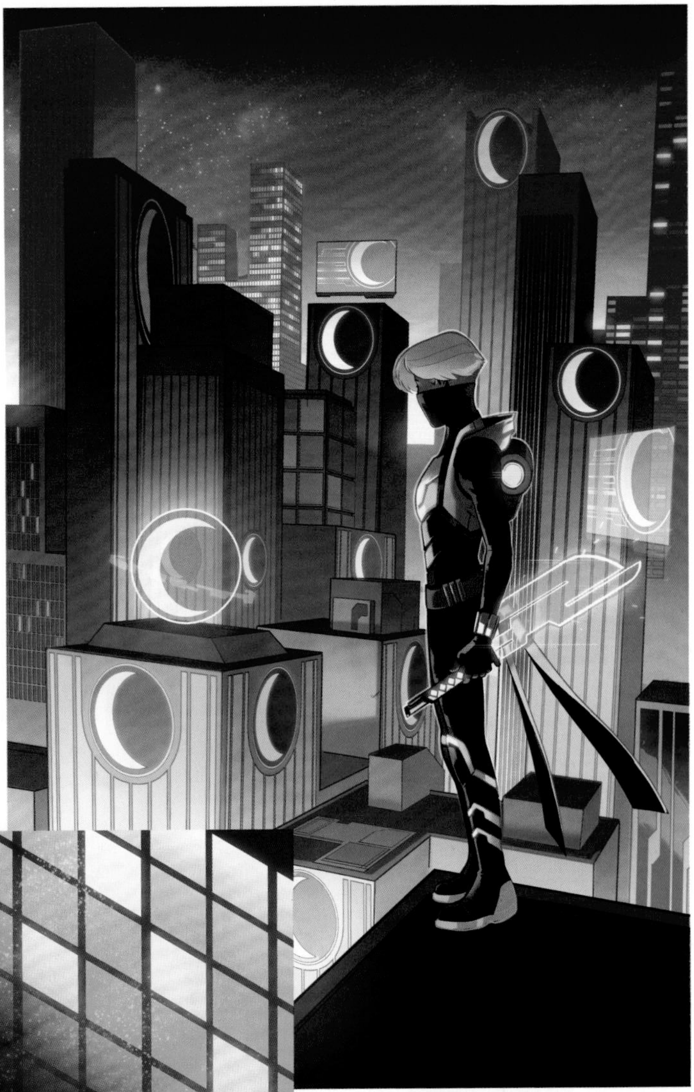

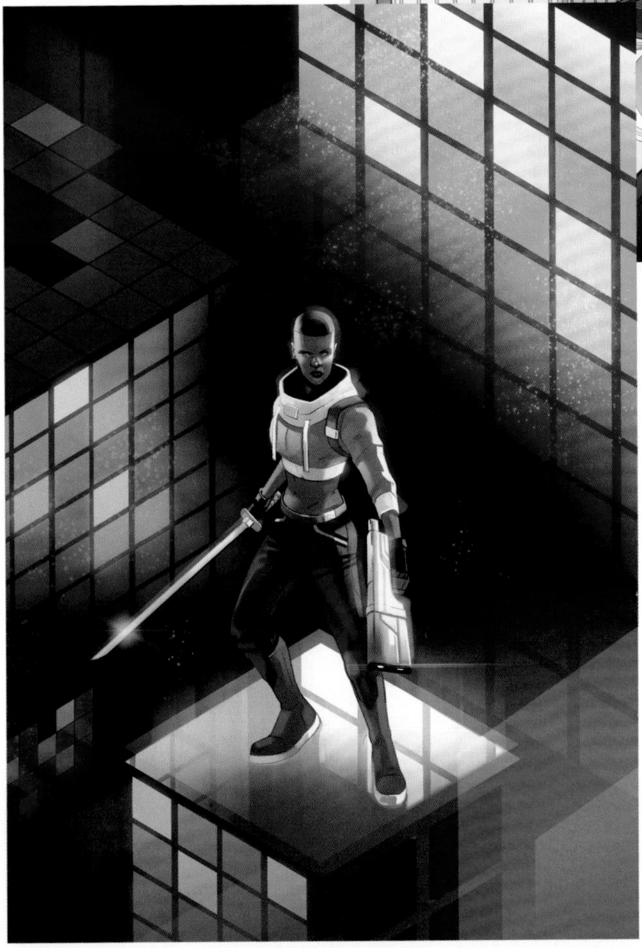

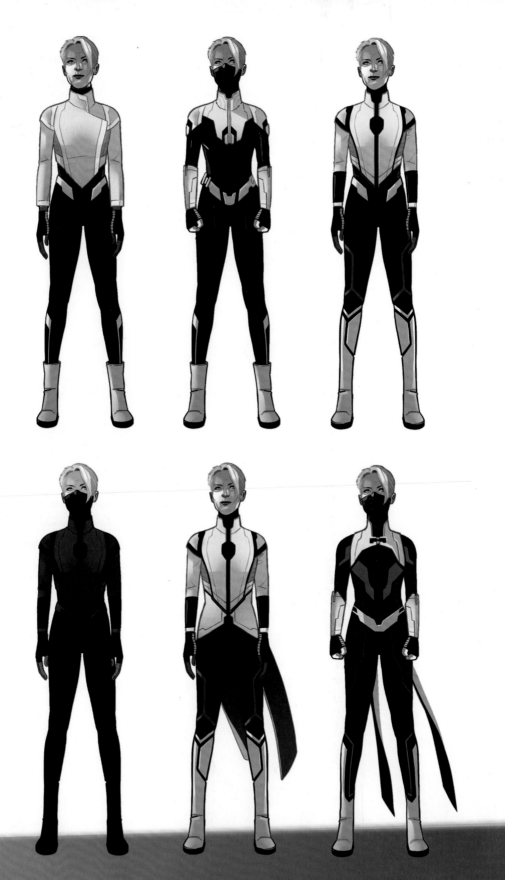

These designs for Joy were getting close to the final look. I had decided that I wanted to do a clean black-and-white modern-tech look, for both Joy herself and the Jonando Trust. I was trying to simplify and streamline the design choices.